LITERATURE INTO HISTORY

Also by A. D. Harvey

BRITAIN IN THE EARLY NINETEENTH CENTURY
ENGLISH POETRY IN A CHANGING SOCIETY, 1780–1825
ENGLISH LITERATURE AND THE GREAT WAR WITH
FRANCE (*editor*)

Literature into History

A. D. Harvey

St. Martin's Press   New York

First published in the United States of America in 1988

Printed in Hong Kong

ISBN 0–312–01598–4

Library of Congress Cataloging-in-Publication Data
Harvey, A. D. (Arnold D.)
Literature into history / by A. D. Harvey.
p. cm.
Bibliography: p.
Includes index.
ISBN 0–312–01598–4: $30.00 (est.)
1. Literature and history. I. Title.
PN50.H37 1988
809'.93358—dc19   87–27872
                                   CIP

Contents

Illustrations

Acknowledgements

Parts of Chapter 3 have previously appeared in *Études Anglaises*, *Essays in Criticism* and *Keats-Shelley Journal*.

The illustrations are reproduced by permission of the following: Nationalmuseum, Stockholm; Kunsthistorisches Museum, Vienna; Hamburg Kunsthalle; Nationalgalerie, Berlin; The Art Institute, Chicago; John Topham Picture Library; Musée de Louvre, Paris; Museo e Gallerie Nazionali di Capodimonte, Naples; Heidelberger Bibliothek.

I owe a special debt of gratitude to Ulrike Bolte, of the Ruprecht-Karls-Universität Heidelberg, who first encouraged my interest in art history.

A. D. HARVEY

Part I

1
Nations and Art Forms

*An ancient Mariner meeteth three gallants bidden to a wedding-feast,
and detaineth one.*

I

This book attempts to examine how, why, and to what extent
literature is shaped by the social and economic development of its
time.

This subject might seem large enough not to make it necessary to
hare off after French neo-classical painting and Fascist architecture
in Bloomsbury. It might also seem that windy generalisation and
untenable hypothesis might have been avoided by concentrating
on a single genre in a single culture. But this is what I did in an
earlier book *English Poetry in a Changing Society, 1780–1825* (London, 1980), in which I discussed the relationship between the
evolution of English Romantic poetry and the unique features of
English society in the late eighteenth and early nineteenth centuries. At the time, what I had written appeared to make sense. It
was only later, when I embarked on another project, on social and
economic mobilisation in Western Europe during the Napoleonic
Wars, that I began to suspect a fallacy – that although the striking
features of English society *c.*1800 were unique, the Romanticism of
the poetry wasn't. Romanticism was also the fashion in countries
with a completely different social and economic situation. If cultural developments are determined by social factors, therefore,
either what is called English Romanticism arose from social factors
other than the ones I thought relevant, or else it was in some
fundamental way different from what is called French or German
Romanticism. My feeling now is that, though most of what I said
in my earlier book was valid as far as it went, it did not go anything
like far enough: not only does it seem to have been a mistake to
concentrate on only one society, but poetry was too narrow a field,
and Romanticism too limiting a concept, to offer a generally useful
paradigm.

3

The particularity of a particular society can often be a useful point of reference. This is perhaps less a question of language than of the distinctive political and economic features of different communities. During the eighteenth century, for example, the Swiss cantons made an outstanding contribution to European culture, but the Swiss writers and artists like Rousseau, de Staël, Bridel, Bonstetten, Haller, Johann von Müller, Gessner, Bodmer, Lavater, and Füssli who made such an important contribution to pioneering this famous phenomenon of Romanticism, belonged both to German and French-speaking backgrounds: I am aware that Geneva only joined the Swiss confederation in 1815 and that in France it is pretended that Rousseau was a sort of Frenchman, but then the French are hardly noted for their sympathetic interest in German–Swiss culture, and can scarcely be expected to be sensitive to the parallels between *their* Rousseau and the Teutonic Gessner and Füssli, and the common features of their Swiss city-state background.

All the same, the lines drawn between different national cultures have as much reality as lines drawn on maps.

> Nationalism whummled on Border moor.
> Countries indistinguishable in Dark.

National boundaries have rarely hindered the migrations of sculptors, painters, architects, musical composers. With literature it is different, because books consist of words and have their effect only on those who understand the words of the language they are written in. But books can be translated, and even if they lose something in the process can be immensely influential in an alien guise. And many writers have direct personal knowledge of literatures other than that of their native country. During the last hundred years many writers have lived and worked in exile. A few even write in a language that is not their own. The Füssli mentioned above, living in exile in London under the name Henry Fuseli, became a formidable English letter-writer but can hardly be described as having a great literary reputation: and his contemporaries, the Englishman William Beckford who wrote *Vathek* in French, the Pole Jan Potocki who wrote *Manuscrit trouvé à Saragosse* in French, and the Dane Jens Baggesen who wrote his epic *Parthenäis* in German, may appear nowadays definitely minor; but in our own times second-language writers such as Vladimir Nabokov, Samuel Beckett and Elias Canetti have been recognised as authors of no small importance. It is interesting to note that the two most important novelists in the English language active c.1900, Henry James and Joseph Conrad, spoke French together when they met, and that twenty years later D. H. Lawrence, a writer linguistically rooted in idiomatic English if ever there was one, was translating the works of Giovanni Verga.[1] If our ultimate object is the understanding of a national artistic tradition in the context of a nation's social history, we will need to be very sensitive to the extent, and also the limits, of foreign influences.

In any case, national culture is not simply not a completely separate entity with regard to foreign cultures: it is not in itself a single unit, but an aggregation. It is an aggregation, first of all, of regions, often with different linguistic traditions. Regional differences cause us to think only very rarely of the United Kingdom as a single society; even within its component units, such as England, there are major variations, and a dialect literature, and such variations are often more marked in other European countries.[2] Secondly, a national culture is an aggregation of classes: not all artists create art for all their fellow citizens, because not all fellow citizens have similar cultural requirements and similar means of fulfilling them. As early as the 1580s we can identify different literary audiences in England, and different kinds of author trying to cater for them. The most élite literary audience in a country may share its language (more or less) with the least élite, but in other respects – type of education, sensibility, economic relationship with artists – may be much closer to the élite circles of another country.

The distinction between art forms is perhaps just as analytically counter-productive as the distinction between national cultures. Shelley wrote:

> all the inventive arts maintain, as it were, a sympathetic connection between each other, being no more than various expressions of one internal power, modified by different circumstances, either of an individual, or of society.[3]

Actually this 'sympathetic connection' is not always easy to trace. It may well be true what I once read on a lavatory wall in Aberystwyth, that Beethoven was so deaf that all his life he thought he was a great painter: but I might as well admit straight away that I have so far failed to come up with any useful ideas tying in developments in music with developments in literature and painting.[4] Between literature and painting themselves, what seems to me most useful is not the complete identity of development but the way in which the identity *fails* to be complete, so that one form provides information not offered by the other and alters, so to speak, our sense of scale and perspective. It may therefore, within the scope of an international cultural movement like Romanticism, be useful to compare a poet from one culture with a painter from another: this may be more helpful than comparing a painter and a poet simply because they had the same nationality.

It is now something of a commonplace to compare Wordsworth's poetry with the paintings of John Constable: this seems to me to typify the disadvantages and limitations of a single-nation perspective. The Wordsworth–Constable comparison seems legitimised by Constable's keen interest in English poetry, but though he met Wordsworth a couple of times and occasionally quoted some of his more banal lines, his favourite poets seem to have been Milton and Thomson. Of his own contemporaries Constable's chief admiration was Bloomfield, a late exponent of the tradition which Thomson had popularised in the 1720s and which, artistically, was virtually defunct by the time Constable started on the most characteristic phase of his career.[5] Constable's preference for poetry about the countryside belonging to (or at least imitative of) an earlier phase of English culture raises important questions about how far his vision of the countryside can be seen as an authentic critical response to contemporary socio-economic change: the point is not to attempt to separate Constable from his contemporaries but to see that his relevant contemporaries were an 1800s' version of Thomson's and that he was quintessentially the artist of a section of society which, though alert, intelligent and well informed, was determined not to notice social change: a section of society for whom the novelty of Wordsworth was only a distant bookish scandal.[6] A painter perhaps more comparable to Wordsworth is the German Caspar David Friedrich, the man of whom it was said, 'Voilà un homme qui a découvert la tragedie du paysage.' Perhaps both Constable and Wordsworth would have agreed with Friedrich that:

The artist should not only paint what he sees before him but also what he sees within him. If however he sees nothing within him then he should also omit to paint that which he sees before him.

Otherwise his pictures will resemble those folding screens behind which one expects to find only the sick or even the dead.[7]

Yet although one is aware of Constable's self-consciousness, he
seems much less successful in his struggle to come to terms with
his subjective state than either Friedrich or Wordsworth, less
deliberate in his use of nature as an idiom to express inner states
and in his selection of rural objects as ikons charged with spiritual
and emotional significance. Again, part of Constable's achievement is the presentation of the impersonality – or suprapersonality
– of nature, even in the man-made landscape of the Home Counties: with Friedrich, though in his best pictures he does not take
man as his focus of attention, nevertheless his enigmatic *dramatis
personae* facing away from the viewer insist on a human dimension,
just as the human dimension is always insisted upon in Wordsworth, though in both Wordsworth and Friedrich the landscape is
generally a primeval one in which man exists only as a tolerated
guest.

Another justification for international comparisons is that some
art grows out of experiences which are unmistakably international,
so that the identity of the experience underlines the peculiar
characteristics of the responses from within one national literary
tradition as compared to another. Take the First World War, for
example. The Arcadian and homoerotic traditions which coloured
so much of the most striking English war poetry seem to have had
no comparable influence in other countries. Richard Aldington's
Death of a Hero, in which the war is used to throw into relief the
values of pre-war and civilian society, is almost unique in English
literature, but has much in common with the presentation of the
war as part of an ongoing social process which is implicit in
Thomas Mann's *Der Zauberberg* and Robert Musil's *Der Mann ohne
Eigenschaften*, and which is paradigmatically and melodramatically
explicit in Arnold Zweig's fables of moral confrontation, *Der Streit
um den Sergeanten Grischa* and *Erziehung vor Verdun*. While in some
German writing about the First World War, there is a passionate
repudiation of the values of the defeated régimes, in some other
authors the war inspired the sort of self-destructive enthusiasm
which led to a second and greater catastrophe a generation later:

almost without any thought of mine, the idea of the Fatherland
had been distilled from all these afflictions in a clearer and

brighter essence. That was the final winnings in a game on which so often all had been staked; the nation was no longer for me an empty thought veiled in symbols; and how could it have been otherwise when I had seen so many die for its sake, and been schooled myself to stake my life for its credit every minute, day and night, without a thought?[8]

In much Italian writing about the war also, a tragic destiny was being prepared in the creation of images – the passive and resigned soldier peasant, the provincial lower middle-class subaltern involved for the first time in national as distinct from merely parochial responsibilities – which were to underpin the Fascist dictatorship which emerged in the post-war period. Again, Ernst Jünger's gruesome romanticisation of war in *In Stahlgewittern* seems perhaps just as typical of a certain strain in the German literary imagination as the mawkishness of Georges Duhamel's *Vie des Martyrs* or the dreary deflationism of Henri Barbusse's *Le Feu* seem distinctively French. It is only in an abstract sense that the 'blood, smell, lice, filth, shells, noise, weariness and death' were similar on each of the various fronts: the experience was everywhere different because nowhere was it experienced by minds that were purely *tabula rasa*.[9] And what is true of literature is equally true of the visual arts: it would be difficult to find an English First World War artist comparable to the German Otto Dix and George Grosz.

II

Of course, literature and painting are only two amongst innumerable cultural forms available to be studied. Since Raymond Williams urged, in *Culture and Society* (1958), that we should also look 'to the experience that is otherwise recorded: in institutions, manners, customs, family memories', it has even been fashionable to talk about studying things other than the literary and artistic canon.[10] The Birmingham Centre for Cultural Studies has done something, and elsewhere there have been studies of certain institutions which have developed internationally over a considerable period, notably the institution of museums.[11] But it may be that a certain degree of schizophrenia has developed: it has become legitimate to study football, or war memorials, or the manipulation of the press, as an alternative to Shakespeare, Milton and

Tennyson, but it is still frowned upon to write about third-rate poets like Bloomfield or Milman. And the rationale for studying, say, newspaper leaders rather than sonnets is partly negative, dependent on an assertion of the *élitism* and *irrelevancy* of the traditional canon; but if one abolishes the distinction between leading article and sonnet and argues that one deserves study as much as the other, one still needs to show why the choice should be limited to that between leading article and sonnet. There are an infinity of other written texts one might study: the advocate of deconstructing newspapers evidently has his ideological motives just as much as the defender of the canon, and it is not clear that the English Faculty is the best place to work out these ideological purposes, or a B.A. in Eng. Lit. the best technical training.

In any case, literature of a certain type, and a handful of other cultural forms differ from hair styles, football fandom and even *Times* leaders in involving a process of selection according to a certain category of conscious criteria: the process that we call *art*. These criteria come from somewhere and, more important, the conscious processes of the selection contain within them the key to explaining what, in social terms, is going on.

In suggesting that art can be defined in terms of self-consciousness, I do not mean that there is a line of demarcation between 'art' and 'inferior cultural forms' which may be discovered by weighing the various quantities of detectable self-consciousness. It is probably safe to say that each and every example of art differs in the precise quality and quantity of self-consciousness involved in producing it, if only because the producers, the artists, are not clones but individuals with individual personalities. Certainly, to set up a league-table of self-conciousness would involve an extravagant amount of insupportable conjecture and meaningless calculation and yield only confusion. Nor do I mean that 'art' is necessarily superior to 'sub-artistic products' either morally, politically, or aesthetically. There are many sonnets which compare badly with folk songs not simply in the moral and political implications of the sensibility they represent, but also, and even more strikingly, in what some people may wish to call the more purely aesthetic aspects of language and symbolism. Yet the self-consciousness of such sonnets, misdirected and misapplied so as to produce a very debased form of art, should enable the student to locate the poetry culturally much more easily than would be possible with a folk song, which would probably have been written originally by someone quite as sophisticated as the sonneteer, but regarding which little can be ascertained as to which parts were written or modified by whom, and under what circumstances, and why it has survived. Self-consciousness, where it is evident, provides an important type of information, and where available the cultural historian should use it: and the simple fact is that it is much more available at the high art end of the spectrum than at the popular culture end.

This view might suggest that high art rather than popular culture offers the best field of study for those who wish to ascertain the relation between culture and society; and to understand why the students of high art, and especially Literature with a big L, haven't come up with any very useful theories so far, we need to look at the way history – the systematic study of the past – is used in literary studies. This will be the subject of my next chapter.

2
Literature, Literary History, and History

The Mariner tells how the ship sailed southward with a good wind and fair weather, till it reached the line.

I

Every book written earlier than this morning is as much a portion and parcel of the dreadful past as anything else that happened before the present moment, and at least since the eighteenth century historical writing has been amongst the most widely read forms of literature and often the most influential in creating a society's image of itself. It is obvious, therefore, that what we call history and literature overlap. But if we leave history and literature with small initials and think instead of History and Literature as intellectual disciplines – I don't like this word discipline, it suggests an analytic rigour which may arguably be lacking in both instances – if we think of History and Literature as intellectual systems, or at least scholarly practices, we find the overlap less evident. There is some uncertainty at the moment as to what Literature (as in the title 'English Literature Faculty') is all about, and there has even been a tendency to pilfer from other so-called disciplines which, in a first-year student, would suggest personal problems. History seems more sure of itself, but subdivided into numerous specialisms, and it is to be noted that amongst all these specialisms there is none which concerns itself with literature. Historians are surely as entitled to interrogate texts as anyone else, and the novels and poems written, let's say, between 1790 and 1820 are as much a historical phenomenon as the political theories of Burke, the factory system, or the population increase as revealed by the first two national censuses. Yet these novels and poems are regarded as included in the commercial franchise of the English Faculty, which rejects most of them with disdain: loftily aspiring to protect the sacred name of critic from any stigma of pedantry or

11

trade, English Faculty members are often unfamiliar with even the names of once best-selling authors who influenced entire generations.

But Literature and History deal less with facts, simply as facts, than with understanding and interpretation, and a bringing together of Literature and History, if it ever happened, would involve not simply the exploitation of new territories of fact, but also of new modes of understanding. However, the problem of understanding which is at the centre of this overlap – which is also the problem that this book attempts to investigate, that is, how far literature reflects the features of the society which produces it, and the process by which society as an aggregate asserts its influence on the artistic work of the individual – raises issues that run counter to the whole tradition of English Literary Studies as they have developed in British and American universities during the last hundred years.

The probable connection between literature and society was first observed more than two hundred years ago. The assertion of Kenneth Clark, endorsed by Raymond Williams (of all people), that 'The idea of style as something organically connected with society, something which springs inevitably from a way of life, does not occur, as far as I know, in the eighteenth century' is not entirely just.[1] There cannot be a comparative theory of styles until it is perceived that there are different styles to compare, and this occurred in the Renaissance. Giorgio Vasari, in his 'Life of Cimabue,' thought that the Greek artists of the period before Cimabue 'were unambitious men and the work they executed in Florence was, as we can see today, carried out in the stiff contemporary style of that period, not in the fine antique style of Greece.'[2] The next step, the recognition of the possibility of choosing between different historical styles, seems to have been taken in England, at least in architecture, before 1750.[3] In the field of literary criticism, Richard Hurd, one of the earliest exponents of the revival of interest in older poetry, all but brought literary style and social conditions together in an equation in his *Letters on Chivalry and Romance* of 1762, in which he argued that,'the resemblance between the heroic and Gothic ages is very great . . . the parallel would hardly have held so long, and run so closely if the *civil* conditions of both had not been so much the same'.[4] What he was asserting was a parallel between manners and social conditions, without any specific reference to literary style, though he

did, in Letter III of his *Letters on Chivalry and Romance*, make a
vague connection between social conditions and artistic features as
distinct from the more inclusive term *manners*. Thomas Warton, in
his *History of English Poetry*, also came very close to seeing the
connection, but being an annalist rather than an analyst, failed to
get the two parts of the equation completely into focus:

> In an age advanced to the highest degree of refinement, that
> species of curiosity commences, which is busied in contemplat-
> ing the progress of social life, in displaying the gradations of
> science, and in tracing the transitions from barbarism to
> civility . . .
>
> On these principles, to develope the dawnings of genius, and
> to pursue the progress of our national poetry, from a rude origin
> and obscure beginnings, to its perfection in a polished aged,
> must prove an interesting and instructive investigation.[5]

In fact, peering into a distant and little understood past, Thomas
Warton never quite perceived the degree to which both the Middle
Ages he was studying and the eighteenth century he was living in
were involved in a remorseless process of change and flux, which
made each generation subtly but distinctively different from each
of its predecessors and successors.

It was not until the French Revolution that people began to
recognise the desperate pace at which their own world was changing. The upheavals of the period also stimulated a great deal of
theorising about society, and prominent amongst the theorists was
Louis-Gabriel-Ambroise de Bonald who, in August 1806, published
an article entitled 'Du style et de la littérature' which claimed that
'If style is the expression of man, literature is no less the expression
of society'.[6] Nevertheless, Bonald's discussion was in rather general terms: it required not merely an awareness of the process of
social change, but also a much more precise and specific sense of
particular artistic or literary traditions to perceive that in each
generation there were characteristic features which distinguished
it from other periods, and represented a common ground between
members of that generation. The earliest, and indeed classic formulation of this view is by Shelley:

> But there must be a resemblance, which does not depend upon
> their own will, between all the writers of any particular age.

They cannot escape from subjection to a common influence which arises out of an infinite combination of circumstances belonging to the times in which they live though each is in a degree the author of the very influence by which his being is thus pervaded . . . In this view of things, Ford can no more be called the imitator of Shakespeare than Shakespeare the imitator of Ford. There were perhaps few other points of resemblance between these two men than that which the universal and inevitable influence of their age produced. And this is an influence which neither the meanest scribbler nor the sublimest genius of any era can escape.

This is from Shelley's Preface to *Laon and Cythna* (1818). At this time Shelley was intimate with Thomas Love Peacock, and it is possible that the views expressed in the Preface developed out of the exchange of ideas between the two writers. Peacock seems so much less original a thinker that it might seem that he could have had little to contribute to the development of Shelley's ideas, but a few months later he wrote a somewhat different formulation of the same argument, extending its scope in a direction that suggests less the influence of Shelley than independent preoccupations of Peacock's own:

As every age has its own character, manners, and amusements, which are influenced even in their lightest forms by the fundamental features of the time, the moral and political character of the age or nation may be read by an attentive observer even in its lightest literature how remote soever *prima facie* from morals or politics. [7]

But Peacock's words were not even published in his lifetime, and since there was neither a systematic sociology nor a systematic study of English Literature for another sixty or seventy years, Shelley's insights were not merely not developed, they were rather buried under his posthumous reputation as an inspired lyricist.

G. M. Miller's *The Historical Point of View in English Literary Criticism from 1570–1770*, published in Heidelberg in 1913, asserted 'The necessity of the application of this [historical] method to literary study has been recognised by leading critics from the middle of the eighteenth century', [8] but this book (particularly the

Introduction) indicates the total conceptual vacuum at the centre of literary studies prior to 1914: Miller himself seemed unaware of the difference between a historical methodology and a vague general-ised awareness of the fact that writers write in some sort of historical context. The new German discipline of Intellectual His-tory might have contributed something in the way of method, but failed to. The great pioneer of Intellectual History, Wilhelm Dilthey, published in *Das Erlebnis und die Dichtung* (1905) studies of Lessing, Goethe, Novalis and Hölderlin as individual writers in relation to their times, providing by way of introduction a brief general history of European literature in its intellectual context: but in this general survey Dilthey did not go into details, and the whole book shows less tendency towards systematisation than much of his other work, thus if anything reinforcing the non-factual, non-theoretical tradition of literary studies. And events in Germany after 1914, taken together with the curious intellectual cross-currents pervading *Germanistik* studies during the Weimar and National Socialist periods, were hardly conducive to the devel-opment of a historical theory of literature: despite the considerable interest in recent years in the work of Walter Benjamin for exam-ple, all that he has left in this line hardly adds up to more than fragments of uneven quality.

Meanwhile, in Britain, Literature and History were both devel-oping away from their common ground. That this would happen was seen very early on by William Morris, who wrote, 'I say that to attempt to teach literature with one hand while it destroys history with the other, is a bewildering proceeding on the part of "culture".'[9] But the great Guardian Angel of academic English Literature was not Morris, but Matthew Arnold. Arnold was an important influ-ence on F. R. Leavis and T. S. Eliot, who between them dominated English academic criticism for forty years and did more than anyone else to establish what academic Eng. Lit. is.[10] But in his own right also Arnold remained a current critical voice at least till the 1940s, and he is still a name to be conjured with, or at least to be paraded as proof of one's own critical credentials when deni-grating the scholarly efforts of others, for instance:

As Dr. Harvey may unwittingly suggest, the gauntlet Words-worth seemingly threw down as a theory of poetic language was in effect a red herring which caused his critics to overlook or discount the revolution in feeling Arnold later noted as the poet's unique contribution to a revitalized conception of poetry as a criticism of life. [11]

Arnold and the conception of poetry as a criticism of life may rather have got in the way of other conceptions of poetry, and so his status as a critic deserves closer attention.

II

The clearest exposition of Arnold's views on literature is in his essay (originally an anthology introduction), 'The Study of Poetry' of 1880:

> But if he is a real classic, if his work belongs to the class of the very best (for this is the true and right meaning of the word *classic, classical*), then the great thing for us is to feel and enjoy his work as deeply as ever we can, and to appreciate the wide difference between it and all work which has not the same high character. This is what is salutary, this is what is formative; this is the great benefit to be got from the study of poetry. Everything which interferes with it, which hinders it, is injurious . . . To trace the labour, the attempts, the weaknesses, the failures of a genuine classic, to acquaint oneself with his time and his life and his historical relationships, is mere literary dilettantism unless it has that clear sense [of excellence] and deeper enjoyment for its end. [12]

In other words, any idea of using literature to understand the past, or of using historical criteria to assess the significance of great literature is WRONG. Not that Arnold eschewed historical analysis altogether:

> had Shakespeare and Milton lived in the atmosphere of modern feeling, had they had the multitude of new thoughts and feelings to deal with a modern has, I think it likely the style of each would have been far less *curious* and exquisite. For in a *man* style is the saying in the best way *what you have to say*. The *what* you have to say depends on your age. In the 17th century it was *a smaller harvest than now*, and sooner to be reaped: and therefore to its reaper was left time to stow it more finely and curiously. [13]

This presumably means that Shakespeare and Milton had less to say than, for example, the author of *The Scholar-Gipsey* for, as Arnold himself wrote, 'My poems represent, on the whole, the main movement of mind of the last quarter of a century', so the modern poet who was to be compared to Shakespeare and Milton was evidently himself.[14]

Arnold is, of course, still recognised not only as the founder of the correct mode of approach to Great Authors, but also as a major social critic. The profundity of his insight may be admired in his remark, not many years before the Franco-Prussian war:

> That the French will beat the Prussians all to pieces, even far more completely and rapidly than they are beating the Austrians, there cannot be a moment's doubt . . . [Lord Cowley] entirely shared my conviction as to the French always beating any number of Germans who came into the field against them.[15]

But it is as an interpreter of English rather than French or German society that Arnold is particularly valued. A member of one of those dynasties which from generation to generation maintain a dominance of the intellectual world, he did much to establish the Oxbridge High Table view of contemporary values: his work as a schools inspector placed him in a good position to know something of the England of his day, and made him an early example of the pontificating salaried expert, though one wonders if he enjoyed having to meet so many underbred Board School teachers. His style as a pioneer professional pundit may be gauged from such remarks as: 'The culture of this [highest] class is not what it used to be. Their value for high culture, their belief in its importance, is not what it used to be. One may see it in the public schools, one may see it in the universities.'[16] One wonders at his evident desire to overlook the achievement of his own father, Dr Thomas Arnold, whose headmastership at Rugby established the pattern for the classic nineteenth-century public school (still, it is good to know that Arnold would have been left appalled and incredulous by all those scholarly monographs on nineteenth-century public school and university reform[17]). Even more interesting are his views on the Victorian middle class, for on this subject he is still widely regarded (in English Faculties) as definitive:

it is the middle class which is the great reader; that immense
literature of the day which we see surging up all round us, –
literature the absolute value of which it is almost impossible to
rate too humbly, literature hardly a word of which will reach, or
deserve to reach, the future – it is the middle class which calls it
forth.[18]

The cads! One can almost imagine those famous Dundreary whis-
kers bristling with indignation at the thought of the readers
(mostly, one assumes, middle class) of the nearly 30,000 copies of
George Eliot's *Middlemarch* which were sold during the following
decade.[19] But *Middlemarch* was still in the future when Matthew
Arnold penned these words: the 'literature the absolute value of
which it is almost impossible to rate too humbly' refers presumably
to *Jane Eyre* and *Bleak House*, and ephemera of that kind.

Arnold seems in fact to have been interested hardly at all in the
contemporary novel. One might even think he lacked interest in
any kind of contemporary literature if it was not for his own poetry
(and not very much of that). Admittedly his inaugural lecture as
Professor of Poetry at Oxford, in 1857, was entitled 'On the Modern Element in Literature', but the word *modern* was used in a
rather specialised sense, so that Sir Walter Ralegh is presented as
less 'modern' than Thucydides, and the object of the lecture was to
'establish the absolute, the enduring interest of Greek literature'.[20]
The curious version of Greek, and more especially Roman history
in this lecture is also worth noting. Coming a little nearer his own
times, Arnold often had illuminating and acute things to say about
poets like Gray and Wordsworth, but one is occasionally brought
up short by remarks like: 'surely the one thing wanting to make
Wordsworth an even greater poet than he is, – his thought richer,
and his influence of wider applications, – was that he should have
read more books'.[21] Well, of course Wordsworth was a Cambridge
man, and Arnold did not have the assistance of the modern
scholarship which has placed the question of Wordsworth's literary culture, even as a young man, beyond doubt.[22] But it is
interesting that Arnold's own influential edition of Wordsworth
favoured the lyric poetry at the expense of the longer philosophical
works in which Wordsworth's intellectual range and sophisticated
literariness is most evident.

It may seem unkind, unfair, even (dare one say it?) unhistorical
to challenge Matthew Arnold's critical judgement in this way.

After all, the sociological views of Herbert Spencer, or the historical doctrines of E. A. Freeman and J. A. Froude have not worn
much better; but the point is that no one nowadays would dream
of citing Spencer or Freeman or Froude as a relevant authority and,
for all their contemporary reputation, their scholarly successors
soon emancipated themselves from their influence. This is precisely what did not happen in the case of Matthew Arnold.

III

At first glance, it might seem odd that in T. S. Eliot's and F. R.
Leavis's day, c.1920–50, Matthew Arnold's anti-historical approach
should have commended itself to scholars who were far from
uninterested in the past and who, in the pioneer days, had often
read History as part of their university degree. But, apart from the
exponents of Practical Criticism (and in America New Criticism)
who wished to separate literature from any kind of context, historical or otherwise, literary experts had very special uses for history.
Take T. S. Eliot:

> What really happened is that after Pope there was no one who
> thought and felt nearly enough like Pope to be able to use his
> language quite successfully; but a good many second-rate writers
> tried to write something like it, unaware of the fact that a change
> of sensibility demanded a change of idiom. Sensibility alters
> from generation to generation in everybody, whether we will or
> no; but expression is only altered by a man of genius. A great
> many second-rate poets, in fact, are second rate just for this
> reason, that they have not the sensitiveness and consciousness
> to perceive that they feel differently from the preceding gener-
> ation, and therefore must use words differently.[23]

It will be seen that Eliot's view of both language and sensibility is
completely idealist. Language changes and sensibility changes, but
they don't necessarily change together, and if their changing is
connected with anything else, Eliot doesn't mention it. His is the
history of events – largely linguistic events – without causes.[24]

F. R. Leavis was less concerned with language – except in his
constant endeavour to write as inelegantly as possible – but whereas
Eliot's rejection of the present seems to have grown on him
progressively, with Leavis repudiation of the present was always a

fundamental principle. There was, of course, nothing new either in condemning contemporary values nor in focusing, as Leavis did, on present day intellectual mediocrity: the remark: 'For a multitude of causes unknown to former times are now acting with a combined force to blunt the discriminating powers of the mind, and unfitting it for all voluntary exertion to reduce it to a state of almost savage torpor', is from Wordsworth's 1800 Preface. We have already seen that some decades later Matthew Arnold took a similar view and the rot seems to have continued thereafter because Leavis found himself obliged to compare his own benighted contemporaries to 'the educated public . . . that Arnold after all could count on as audience'.[25]

It was not Leavis himself but his wife, Q. D. Leavis, who produced the first major text revealing the urgency and alarmingness of the problem posed by 'the collapse of a widely held community of taste and judgement'. Queenie Leavis's *Fiction and the Reading Public* (1932) was a 'fully documented account of the development of popular reading habits during the hundred years or so in which fiction-reading had become largely responsible for spreading a lazy shoddiness of thought and feeling'.[26] There are those who believe Queenie was the dominant half of the partnership and F. R. Leavis certainly always used to look rather apprehensive whenever I saw him on the Backs at Cambridge, trotting homewards at mealtimes. Yet it was Leavis himself, in his supervisions and lectures, who did so much to establish that criticism as much as art was an expression of personality. With the strange compulsion of his messianic certainty and commonplace, laid-back manner, Leavis had something in common with Adolf Hitler. The Leavisites abhorred National Socialism, of course, and those of military age fought against it during the war in the Army Educational Corps, Guards Armoured Division and other appropriate formations. And yet like National Socialism Leavisism was a rejection of an outworn and effete civilisation, an attempt to create a new myth which, responding to the emergence of mass society, transcended economic realities and the inevitability of social change: a myth requiring an emotional rather than an intellectual adherence (Leavis wrote, for example, 'The standards proper to the field of literary study . . . can't be defined or demonstrated or produced').[27] The Leavisites' admiration of D. H. Lawrence underlines the parallel with the cloudier elements of National Socialist thought, as does the pervasive influence of the personal style of the two leaders within their respective movements.

The rejection of the present involved a glorification of the past, and it is curious how both Leavis and Eliot, with their very different objectives, agreed on preferring the seventeenth century to their own. Perhaps the most extensive Leavisite presentation of the early seventeenth century as a period of key relevance is L. C. Knights's *Drama and Society in the Age of Jonson* (1937), which still, after fifty years, holds its place as a seminal text and as a model for this kind of study by literary scholars.[28] Knights's handling of the problems of historical documentation, for example, has often been imitated. 'The facts used . . . are drawn almost entirely from the standard works on economic history' (p.x). It is not Knights's fault that these standard works nowadays seem very inadequate, and misled him, for instance, into a lengthy discussion of unemployment (pp. 130–9) without indicating that the main cause may have been rapid population increase. But even on the basis of what was known in 1936, the idea that villeins felt more relationship to their (frequently absentee) manorial lords than with villeins elsewhere (p. 18) seems odd (wasn't there a Peasants' Revolt in 1381?). But then, as one continues to turn the pages it becomes apparent that one isn't studying a work of scholarship at all. To begin with, the bland appeals to common sense, moderate opinion etc. suggest some sort of politician: 'the first necessity is to investigate the background of culture in a period when there is, by common consent, a healthy national culture to be studied. The late Elizabethan and early Stuart period was a natural choice' (p. ix). But soon moderation is left behind and the reader is called upon to commit himself to startling acts of faith, to believe, for example, that a handful of contemporary complaints prove that marriages arranged for financial reasons increased proportionately in the sixteenth century (p. 125), and that a study of books published in London shows us that 'National taste was remarkably homogenous' (p. 141). But Knights finds an ingenious way of sidestepping criticisms of his historical method: nothing less than an admission that the historical bits of his book are irrelevant anyway:

> I shall try to explain the nature of that 'criticism of society'. Obviously it does not consist in analysis at the level of economics. From the fifteenth century onwards, says Lipson, 'the

conflict of capital and labour was fought over three main grievances – low wages, payment in kind, and unemployment.' None
of these three main grievances has any prominence in the drama
of Jonson and his contemporaries. All of them attack usurers, but
they show no interest in the place of credit transactions in a
capitalist economy; they attack monopolists and patentees, but, as
one would expect, they show no sign of recognising the element
of monopoly in the older organisations, or the attempts to
regulate trade and industry by means of patents. (p. 175)

In the end, one simply doesn't see how Jonson's attacks on greed
belong specifically to the 1600s: they seem similar to Chaucer's
account of the Pardoner, and the 'Pardoner's Tale'. (Knights mentions Chaucer only twice, once on page 103 to say that Chaucer's
Man of Law, 'a great purchasour', became a more controversial
type in the sixteenth century and once on page 188 to admit
Jonson's knowledge of Chaucer.) The popularity of such themes is
interesting, of course: if we didn't know that Jonson and his fellow
Jacobeans were our touchstone of healthy, uncommercialised,
undegenerated authorship, one might possibly suspect them of
pandering in a vilely exploitative way, to an audience of shopkeep-
ers and apprentices.

Meanwhile – I am speaking of the period between 1920 and 1960
during which Knights floated nimbly up the ladder of academic
preferment and Leavis, equally inexplicably, remained immobile,
seething and fermenting, at Downing College – History proper,
History with a big H and lots of History professors, was developing into a congerie of specialisms, political history, diplomatic
history, economic history, ecclesiastical history, and so on. For the
same reason that a classic sociology never developed in Britain,
supposedly value-free technicalities being preferred to an all-
embracing and therefore politically supercharged general theory, a
truly synthetic overview tradition of history never emerged.[29]
Moreover, social history, the specialism that would have been of
most relevance to literary studies, developed in a somewhat unhelpful direction. There are actually two kinds of social history:
one that lies between political history and literary history and was
described by a leading exponent, G. M. Trevelyan, as the history of
a people with the politics left out; the other, a largely post-war
offshoot of economic history, that lies between sociology and social
statistics. Until comparatively recently only the first kind was much

developed, and since it was based mainly on literary sources, it posed no challenge to the favourite historical theories of literary scholars. The challenge of the second kind of social history is still only latent, as there are still enormous amounts of work to be done in most fields; but it is probable that the very irreducibility of statistically informed social history will go far to protect literary scholars from its implications.

The tendency of literary scholars to be interested in history only as a sort of intellectual moped that can be ridden anywhere can be illustrated by any number of examples. Here as a specimen is a statement by F. W. Bateson, founder of the journal *Essays in Criticism* and for many years the elder statesman of the Oxford English School:

> History is committed by its nature to the expositions of *differences* between one temporal event or period and another. A country in which no such differences can be distinguished is a country without a history . . . Literature, on the other hand, is necessarily 'esemplastic', to use Coleridge's term. The emphasis in it is on similarities rather than differences . . . Like oil and water, literature and history will not mix.[30]

Needless to say, no country without a history *could* exist, but by arguing from the premise of a totally imaginery and impossible non-history Bateson finds no difficulty in proving that literary history is a non-subject. Part of Bateson's problem of course is that at the beginning of his career many of his colleagues thought that English Literature was the non-subject *par excellence*: he illustrates the theory that a self-image of intellectual guardianship of a certain form of expertise psychologically inhibits engagement with other disciplines.[31]

New Literary History, the journal in which F. W. Bateson published the eye-opener quoted above, is the leading organ in the literary scholar's fight to avoid anything that a historian would recognise as a historical approach. A feature of *New Literary History* is special numbers on various methodological themes. There has never been one on 'History and Literary History' (or 'Literary History and Social History') and in its Literary and Art History special number (vol. III, no. 3, Spring 1972) none of the contributors referred to the social context of art: a philosophy professor from Australia was roped in to sum up the debate in order to keep things on an appropriately idealist plane. This special number particularly interested me as most of the contributors were decidedly cautious about the possibility of art-literature cross-referencing, which is precisely what I intend to attempt later in this book. Svetlana and Paul Alpers, for example, argue the impossibility of finding a painterly counterpart of *Hamlet* or *Paradise Lost* and say that cupolas cannot be compared to final couplets.[32] If they had tried just a little harder they could probably have found some paintings reminiscent of *scenes* or at least *characters* in *Hamlet* or *Paradise Lost*, but perhaps that's not good enough.

A less committedly ahistorical literary history is practised by Raymond Williams. Williams's work, representing the most sustained investigation to date of the issues tackled by this book, includes examples of both theory and practice. The theory – in *Marxism and Literature* (1977) and *Culture* (1981) – doesn't quite make the breakthrough to being an analytic theory, in the sense of a theory by which one can actually analyse anything.[33] Perhaps his formulations even get in the way of establishing such a theory (see Chapter 4 below). In any case, the example of his practice, in *Culture and Society, The Country and the City* etc. has been more influential. But in these latter books Raymond Williams doesn't try to explain, or even to measure, historical processes, but merely to pass judgement on them. He is less interested in what happened than in what certain individuals said had happened, and these individuals have been selected on the basis of having contributed to Raymond Williams's notion of what has happened. This is amazingly interesting, of course, but it is not History. History should at least be objective to the extent of giving fair attention to such facts as present themselves as relevant, but in Raymond Williams's work the curiously circular notion of relevance which is the hallmark of the Eng. Lit. mind means that only facts associated with Raymond Williams's chosen writers remain as facts: facts relating to any one outside the charmed circle will be ignored, though occasionally one of these outsiders will be singled out for the honour of being compared to an insider, being sometimes rather spectacularly misrepresented in the process.

But it would be unfair to concentrate on developments only in the English-speaking world: the situation is not much different in Germany or France. In Germany there is much interest in Reception Theory, of which Prof. Dr. Hans-Robert Jauss is the leading exponent:

History of literature is a process of aesthetic reception and production which takes place in realization of literary texts on the part of the receptive reader, the reflective critic and the author in his continued creativity. The continuously growing 'literary data' which appear in the conventional histories are merely left over from this process; they are only the collected and classified part and therefore not history at all, but pseudo-history.[34]

This seems much clearer in the original German. Jauss's point is that literary history is a chronological (or as really up to date people say, *diachronic*) procession of texts, readers, professors, and lastly authors – in that order – and evidently has nothing to do with cause and effect as such. Essentially in Reception Theory one tries to situate a text within the framework of cultural meanings in which it was produced, and then study the relation between this and the perspectives of successive readers, each equally carefully situated: in the end it is simply another strategy to evade the main point, which is that we know very little about cultural contexts and can't meaningfully locate anything in them until we have found a better way of studying them: just because simultaneous equations work in algebra doesn't mean they work in cultural studies.

In France, Roland Barthes's assertion, more than twenty years ago, that 'literary history is possible only if it becomes sociological, if it is concerned with activities and institutions, not with individuals', might have been a step towards an illuminating new methodology, but Barthes allowed himself to be side-tracked.[35] The side-tracking has continued with most of Barthes's successors in the French-intellectual-as-folk-hero rôle. The French-language critic who has made the most influential contribution in recent years to a historically orientated literary analysis has in fact been a Rumanian emigré, Lucien Goldmann: but under all Goldmann's theoretical jargon (*formes homologues* etc.) there is the same anti-historical Arnoldian bias towards a small number of outstanding texts that has dominated the English tradition: the distinction between '*grandes oeuvres culturelles* expressing the collective experience of privileged social groups whose consciousness and praxis are orientated towards a global ideal of man and nature, what I have called a *vision du Monde*' and works which 'lack functional coherence and as such are not an important and valuable work' militates against any reasonable attempt to assess either the society of a particular period, or the real shape of its culture.[36]

IV

But if academic literary studies are in a bit of a mess with regard to history, it would be an error to expect academic history to come to its rescue. In aligning literature and history, for example, a common assumption would be that history provides a solid foundation of hard and fast facts, upon which the more speculative structure of aesthetic perception and psychological insight may be built. Literary judgement hasn't altogether escaped from being a matter of personal preferences, while History more and more surrounds itself with the panoply of scientific method, or at least the ponderousness of data and the pretentiousness of statistical formulae. The way literary scholars pillage history books – generally undergraduate textbooks rather than research monographs – for usable facts indicates a belief that history books contain absolute and irrefutable fact: an assumption which Michel Foucault has condemned in the case of the Frankfurt School:

> It seemed to me that they did little history, that they referred to research done by others, to a history already written and evaluated and that they presented it as explanatory 'background' . . . they are 'users of history' as others have already fabricated it.[37]

The dangers of this sort of procedure were pointed out a century ago by the archaeological pioneer General A.H.L.F. Pitt-Rivers:

> Excavators, as a rule, record only those things which appear to them important at the time, but fresh problems in Archaeology and Anthropology are constantly arising, and it can hardly fail to have escaped the notice of anthropologists, especially those who, like myself, have been concerned with the morphology of art, that, on turning back to old accounts in search of evidence, the points which would have been most valuable have been passed over from being thought uninteresting at the time.[38]

Since Pitt-Rivers's day part of the function of the archaeologist is simply to record what he finds. But this has never been part of the function of a historian, and historians recognise that history books are not objective registers of fact, but merely interpretations of fact, illustrated by a *selection* of those facts which fit the author's argument; anything that tells the other way is downgraded as less significant, or suppressed. As E. H. Carr puts it:

> The facts are really not at all like fish on the fishmonger's slab. They are like fish swimming about in a vast and sometimes inaccessible ocean, and what the historians catches will depend, partly on chance, but mainly on what part of the ocean he chooses to fish in and what tackle he chooses to use – these factors being, of course, determined by the kind of fish he wants to catch.[39]

Many literary scholars don't even bother with the fishmonger's slab: they go to the fish and chip shop opposite where the fish are already cut up, covered in batter, and deep-fried. This doesn't mean that literary scholars avoid the historian's sin of only looking for pre-selected kinds of fact. Literary scholars are often exquisitely discriminating in their assessment of what is relevant to their field. 'I was quite a way into it,' writes one reviewer of my last book, 'before I felt confident that it would illuminate any circle of legitimate interest at all.'[40] If one has so many professorial commitments that one cannot spare much time for general reading, it is obviously vital to establish what are and what are not legitimate subjects for the books one is expected to review. But since the literary scholars, in their pursuit of the legitimate, will not be presenting the same arguments as the historians from whom they borrow their facts, and have not had the historian's opportunity to assess the value of the facts which seem, on balance and in their professional judgement, of minor relevance and safely to be omitted, literary scholars are trusting themselves to an unreliable guide whenever they take someone else's history book as a substitute for their own original research.

The problem is aggravated by the incredibly narrow focus most historians allow themselves. Like literary scholars, but with even less of a systematic rationale, historians tend to bunch together on certain topics and to neglect others that are less fashionable. Research on an unfamiliar topic is much less likely to be recognised, much less likely to be rewarded by academic preferment, than revisionist incourses into already overworked fields which derive their 'importance' from the number of scholars who have already established their reputations in that area: and, of course, the better known scholars also attract the best research students who therefore concentrate their attention on territory already largely marked out for them. When the resulting monographs are published, most people only bother to read the prefaces, to see which eminent patrons are being thanked: the text serves only as a kind of appendix, legitimising the grovelling compliments printed at the beginning of the volume.

My supervisor at Cambridge used to say that the university doesn't owe any particular historical period a living: but the result is that even at Cambridge, with a relatively large History Faculty, many of the lecture courses on important historical topics are given by people who have never done original research on them. And so, over vast tracts of the past political history, social history and economic history wend their lonely way in hermetically sealed rat-cages. No one would realise from reading E. P. Thompson's *The Making of the English Working Class* that most radical leaders in the 1800s were in the top income tax bracket, and that for every person who joined a radical reform association ten enlisted in local paramilitary organisations dedicated in part to resisting internal disorder.[41] Similarly, the fact that the fastest growing religious denomination in nineteenth-century Britain was Roman Catholicism, or that Britain's period of most rapid economic growth was the 1930s, simply won't fit in with political historians' established view of what was most significant about these periods. It is not really strange that work in one specialism using one lot of sources frequently poses an implicit contradiction to work in another specialism, but it does mean that, far from being a firm rock on which literary studies can build confidently, history turns out to be merely a rubble of fragments which don't even fit together.

Of course, works of literature often *seem* to contain indications of their precise historical context: but one needs some sort of historical judgement to assess the validity of these indications, as the next chapter will show.

3
Types of Information

The ship hath been suddenly becalmed.

I

All art contains information, although it is not always of the same kind. Each example of art yields information about the author or artist and his intended audience, but this may be difficult to decode and it is not always to be taken for granted that every individual author or artist is a subject worthy of a major expenditure of effort. All art that is not figurative or abstract yields incidental information about society – how people dress, how people speak – though there is no accompanying guarantee that this information is accurate: for example, Trollope's Palliser novels, which were recommended to me as an undergraduate as giving a wonderful insight into the mid-Victorian political world, are full of things no nineteenth-century politician would have said: the Duke of St Bungay suggesting blandly, 'I suppose you would wish that I should take the chair at the Council', exactly as if the Privy Council still met regularly with the President of the Council acting as chairman, and so on.[1] And all art, I believe, yields information about society as a whole: this proposition is merely the corollary of my basic argument, that all art can be shown to bear the impress of the society which created it.

The information about society as a whole is the information one should concentrate on; and not simply because it is the most relevant to the theme of this book. Though all works of art contain discrete facts illuminating society, it is not so easy to pick them out. There is the question of how significant, or even how true these facts are. Literature is not to be taken literally: if it is a reflection of reality we need to know something about the mirror. We might need to take into consideration not only thematic, stylistic and structural features, social preoccupations and relation to specific genre traditions, but also the nature of responses to particular works at the time of their appearance and, subsequently, the

29

organisation of the artistic or literary market, the relationship of the author's personal history to his work, and the modifying influence of the author or artist's personal social and ideological background.[2] All this sounds extremely time-consuming, and even more complicated than Terry Eagleton's mechanistic multiplying of meaningless analytic categories like 'Literary Mode of Production' and 'Aesthetic Ideology' in *Criticism and Ideology*, which is perhaps the best known attempt at a 'systematic' approach to literary studies.[3] And at the end of all these categories, all one has is a few fag-ends of supporting evidence. At best, one could compile only a very thin social history from artistic sources, and at worst one could go spectacularly astray. To use literature and art as a supplementary source of discrete items of information, integrated with economic and social statistics, official and private correspondence, memoirs, journalism, parliamentary speeches, and Joanna Southcott's box, would be a worthy ideal, but one should not exaggerate the benefits to be derived: historians, who so often manifest a stern philistinism towards art and literature, have enough difficulties already digesting their traditional source materials. In any case, literature and art would be much more useful as historical data if we think not in terms of points of detail but in terms of the overall themes, intentions and directions of a particular work, seen in the context of the kind of society which produced it, seen in fact precisely as a reflection of the society which produced it, but a reflection not merely of certain prominent features but of the whole entirety, albeit from a specific and unrepeatable angle.

The novel provides numerous cases where one can study the necessary distinction between detailed items of fact and underlying elements relating to the determining characteristics of society at a particular historical moment. In the following pages, I have selected various novels as illustrating different aspects of this distinction: the problem of knowing at what level to look for information and of avoiding the seduction of fictional scenarios that pretend to be authentic fact; the importance of not being taken in by traditions of interpretation that are without foundation either in the text or in the culture which produced it; the need to recognise the appropriate ideological context and to be sensitive to themes hidden and interwoven amongst a multitude of others.

II

Samuel Richardson's *Pamela* (1740) illustrates the question of the level at which a text contains its most valuable information. The genteel cockney tradesman Richardson really *isn't* the best guide to the conduct of country gentlemen when trying to seduce their village-born maid-servants; but it was Richardson who was the first to use sexual exploitation as a symbol for class exploitation, to show the squire's power to persecute his servant sexually as not merely a consequence or by-product but the mythic essence of the landowning oligarchy's power over the working classes. It is not the accuracy of the details, nor Richardson's undoubted success in bringing Pamela into focus as a character, but the shocking obviousness of the symbol which is important, and so shocking was it that Henry Fielding, in his attempts to burlesque *Pamela* in *Shamela* and *Joseph Andrews*, seems to have been unable to face up to the reality which Richardson depicted. Fielding detected how little the prissy Pamela resembled a real country lass, and indicated, in *Shamela*, how the poor were able to resort to trickery to subvert the objectives of the rich, but his insight extended little further. His chauvinistic portrayal of sexual predatoriness in Mrs Slipslop and Lady Booby in *Joseph Andrews* show just how seriously he took the sexual exploitation of women. In Fielding's view, the rich are rich and frequently overbearing and the poor are impoverished and frequently oppressed, but human nature is uniform so that both classes exhibit similar patterns of behaviour and the economic distinction can be romanticised away. The footman, Joseph Andrews, turns out to be the lost son of a gentleman, and the foundling, Tom Jones, brought up in a wealthy home but then cast off without a penny, finally comes into a fortune and marries the daughter of a neighbouring squire. If the world is hard and violent, that is apparently in the nature of things, and not the fault of a particular social system, and, for all his Englishness, Fielding attempts in *Tom Jones* to extend his terms of reference by suggesting the essential changelessness of human nature since the time of Ancient Greece. The hardness and violence have nothing to do with the conditions of a specific social structure and all Fielding can do is make a hearty joke of them and trust to last minute family revelations to put everything right. Fielding's comfortable, well-bred and well-fed high spirits are perhaps more attractive than Richardson's prolix, ungainly but always painful concern, but it is

Richardson, so much less colourful, so much less incisive and less zestful, so much thinner in detail, indeed so much narrower in his education and experience, who penetrates deeper into the eighteenth century.

The difference between the two writers is not simply a different understanding of society. There is also an illuminating difference in their treatment of sex. It would not be enough to say that Richardson sees sex through the eyes of women whereas Fielding sees women through the eyes of sex. *Pamela* is the announcement of a change of sensibility: the change of sensibility involved in presenting something as old as sexual exploitation as suddenly intensely interesting and shocking. Although class exploitation had obviously existed – and been recognised – much earlier, it was not possible till the eighteenth century to use sex to symbolise oppression in quite the way Richardson did. It is generally argued that Richardson's sexual morality derives from Puritanism, thus linking his attitudes with those of the previous century. Actually the Puritans condemned fornication by men at least as fiercely as fornication by women, and in so far as they were aware of the possibility of making a cult of virginity, they were hostile to it. At the same time, till the end of the seventeenth century at least it was generally held that women had stronger sexual appetites than men. The possibility of depicting the helpless inertness of an oppressed class in terms of the sexual passivity of women had to wait till the changing attitudes in the eighteenth century, when as part of a general and pervasive devaluation of the powers and independent volition of women, female sexuality became reduced to a question simply of virginity. The linguistic convention whereby it became standard to refer to a woman's virginity as a treasure or flower indicates the property element involved; and it was left to the genius of Richardson to bring out the implications of this readjustment of attitudes.[4]

III

It will be obvious that a certain amount of historical background will be required to make discriminations of this type. Another eighteenth-century novel about class oppression, William Godwin's *Caleb Williams* (1793), exemplifies the way in which the specific themes may be less illuminating than what lies beneath. *Caleb Williams* is the story of a poor youth who is taken up by the aristocratic recluse Falkland, and having stumbled on the secret of Falkland's criminal past, is not merely cast off but pursued by Falkland's malice till, unable to settle anywhere, universally re-jected, he finally succeeds in exposing Falkland's guilt. The nar-rative is occasionally dressed up with attempts at journalistic verisimilitude, but though Godwin was a major social theorist writing in a period of revolutionary ferment, the details of his story bear little factual relation to what actually went on in real life. But it is only possible to recognise this if the book is approached as a historical document rather than as a literary text.

Godwin indeed is one of those second-rate minds with a knack for getting things not quite right. Hawkins, who is later to be hanged for the murder committed by Falkland, is evicted by Underwood because he refuses to vote for Underwood's candidate in a parliamentary election. This may sound typically eighteenth century, and certainly such things used to happen in those borough constituencies where electors were entitled to vote by paying rates on property, or holding burgages or freeholds, that were actually the property of the borough patron. But Hawkins is evidently a voter in a country district where the franchise depended on the genuine ownership of a freehold, and though many freeholders were also tenants it was one of the conventions of the day that great landlords should not attempt to interfere with the indepen-dence of the county electorate by bringing pressure on the smaller freeholders. In several years of reading material dealing with elections, I never once came across an instance of an English county voter being positively ordered how to dispose of his vote – actually he had two votes – let alone of his being victimised for disobedience. Godwin has the advantage over me of having actu-ally lived in the eighteenth century but the only time he was in a county constituency during an election was when he was a 12-year schoolboy in Norwich during the Norfolk election of 1768. His account of the gang of robbers – deftly set off by convincing descriptions of the interior of gaols lifted from John Howard's *The State of Prisons in England and Wales* (1777–1780) – is not absolutely implausible, though rendered in ideal terms for obvious didactic reasons: but though coiners, smugglers, and a few years later, body-snatchers and people helping escaped French prisoners of war, all worked within extensive networks which might loosely by termed 'gangs', as far as I have been able to ascertain, there simply weren't any 'gangs of robbers' in rural England in Godwin's day.

Since the whole action of the novel is curiously detached from recognisable time and place, one begins to wonder what Godwin precisely intended by his original title, *Things as they Are*.[5]

Godwin himself claimed that his purpose was:

> to comprehend, as far as the progressive nature of a single story would allow, a general review of the modes of domestic and unrecorded despotism by which man becomes the destroyer of man . . . [and] to expose the evils which arise out of the present system of civilised society, and, having exposed them, to lead the enquiring reader to examine whether they are, or are not, as has commonly been supposed, irremediable.

This does not constitute a claim that the exposition of evils was guaranteed one hundred per cent factual: Disraeli's purpose was equally serious in his depiction of Wodgate in *Sybil*, fifty years later, but even though he took his details from a factory commissioners' report, he both selected and embroidered the facts to suit his theme. Godwin didn't have any blue books to crib from, and his interest in English local colour was much more incidental than Disraeli's: 'I was obviously led to place my scene, and draw my instances from the country with which I was best acquainted – England. Not that I thought the laws of England worse than the laws of most other countries.'[6] His concern was less with the particular details of a particular society than with the functioning of societies generally.

Caleb Williams then, is not a factual account of social justice, it is more of a visionary account of what was implicit in a society where some people had great wealth and power, and others only their ability to work. Caleb himself is the archetype of the man who has nothing but his manhood. The power which Falkland mobilises against him is not merely economic and political: he has an almost superhuman capacity to establish his own view of social values, so that he is able to make Caleb an outcast from society. 'Everyone, as far as my story has been known, has refused to assist me in my distress, and has execrated my name' (vol. 1, chap. 1). The virtuous Laura casts him off without staying to hear his explanation. Even the 'amiable, incomparable' Mr Collins shrinks from him. Caleb feels this bitterly:

> The greatest aggravation of my present lot was, that I was cut off from the friendship of mankind. I can safely affirm that poverty

and hunger, that endless wanderings, that a blasted character and the curses that clung to my name, were all of them slight misfortunes compared to this. I endeavoured to sustain myself by the sense of my integrity, but the voice of no man upon earth echoed to the voice of my conscience. 'I called aloud, but there was none to answer; there was none that regarded.' (vol. 3, chap. 4)

But since Caleb's crime has been merely to stand up to a man richer and more respected than himself, his total ostracism by society seems rather extreme, and the closer one looks at the novel the more it seems to be about social ostracism than about the real mechanisms of social injustice.

The particular use of first person narrative, and the way the plot manages to involve the reader in Caleb's tribulations, marks the novel as one of the pioneers of existentialist fiction. A comparison with Godwin's previous book, the theoretical treatise *An Enquiry concerning Political Justice* (1793) suggests only the contradictions and inconsistencies of Godwin's own career: *Caleb Williams* seems less a fictional gloss on the rationalism of *Political Justice* than a repudiation of it.[7] The novel has the awkward sincerity, not of inchoate political discourse, but of momentarily revealed personal trauma. The self-destructively symbiotic relationship of Caleb and Falkland, the nightmarish way in which actions provoke the opposite consequences from those intended, the novel's strong sense of inevitability and fatality, all suggest the human psyche hopelessly cast adrift in a world that has ceased to be comprehensible.

Caleb Williams, of course, is one of the first explorations of the theme of the individual isolated and outside society, a theme which was to become characteristic of the next thirty years: one thinks of *The Rime of the Ancient Mariner*, *Alastor*, *Frankenstein*, *The Siege of Corinth*, *Manfred*, *Melmoth the Wanderer*, and Godwin's own later novels *St Leon* and *Fleetwood*. To emphasise *Caleb Williams's* ostensible theme of social injustice seems to detract from the novel's relationship with other fictional portrayals of isolation: but equally, its emphasis on societal pressures suggests possible reasons why the theme of isolation became so peculiarly central to this period. Charles Maturin's *Melmoth the Wanderer* (1820), with its aristocratic protagonist condemned to walk the earth in perpetuity, cannot really be depicted as a study of the psychic stress arising from social mobility and the increasing atomisation of society, but there is more than a hint of these themes in *Caleb Williams*. What is just about discernible in one text may be concealed, but still important, in another, and to take the first text simply at face value may be to miss the whole point about it.

IV

Another novel requiring circumspection from the student is *Frankenstein* by Godwin's daughter Mary, the second wife of Percy Bysshe Shelley. *Frankenstein* is too often set up as the first ever science fiction novel, or at least the first fictional response to the new issues of moral responsibility created by industrialisation.[8] But Mary Shelley herself thought it proper to assert that *Frankenstein* was the product of a period of reading 'German stories of ghosts', which shows that she conceived of it as a Gothic Horror novel rather than anything else: the name of the protagonist and the continental setting also suggest the Gothic tradition. Although Victor Frankenstein is made to say that he outgrew his early fascination with Cornelius Agrippa, Albertus Magnus and Paracelsus (chap. 2) he remains a magician rather than a chemist, taking his materials from the charnel house and the abattoir in the best necromantic tradition (chap. 4). His laboratory is simply 'a solitary chamber, or rather cell' (chap. 4) and singularly ill-equipped even by Industrial Revolution standards: 'my candle was nearly burnt out, when by the glimmer of the half-extinguished light, I saw . . .' (chap. 5). And Frankenstein's grisly experiment leads to a strictly *private* retribution. If he had indeed unleashed the forces of science, they might have been expected to affect his whole society, but instead he is singled out as a special victim. His brother, his friend, his wife, who are all murdered by his creature, never know the connection between Frankenstein and their killer. It is Frankenstein alone who understands the full horror of what he has done. What he has unleashed is not a new scientific reality but a private nightmare.

Mary Shelley does not even set her action in the present, but in the past. Walton, whose letters begin and end the novel and who comes on the scene subsequent to the greater part of the action, dates his first letter 'Dec. 11th 17–'. We may take it that Mary Shelley conceived of the action having taken place before the time of her own birth, in 1797.[9] The object of this displacement in time is surely not sociological accuracy but simply a desire to create a kind of romantic distance (this is rather a convention in the earlier nineteenth century: we see the same thing later in *Wuthering Heights* by Emily Brontë (born 1818) where all the events are prior to 1802: at the end of chapter 7 there is a pretty specific date, 'the summer of 1778, that is, nearly twenty-three years ago').

Scholarly emphasis on *Frankenstein* as a prophetic representation of the new scientific era tends to distract attention from the novel's resemblance to *Caleb Williams*. Mary Shelley dedicated *Frankenstein* to her father as 'Author of Political Justice, Caleb Williams, &c' and her debt to Godwin as far as philosophical theme has long been recognised.[10] But *Frankenstein* also borrows *Caleb Williams's* plot. Both are novels of pursuit in which the pursuer and the pursued have a crucial pseudo-familial realtionship with each other. In *Caleb Williams*, Caleb admires Falkland and seems to regard him as a substitute father, and is overcome with remorse when he finally brings him to justice. In *Frankenstein*, the monster acknowledges Frankenstein as his creator and on Frankenstein's death plans to cremate himself. Both father figures seem similar in character and in both novels their rejection of their pseudo-sons plays a crucial part. In both novels the roles of pursuer and pursued are shown to be interchangeable. Falkland persecutes Caleb, till Caleb turns on him and exposes him; the creature hounds Frankenstein until at last Frankenstein turns and chases the creature to the Arctic. In both cases, the process of pursuit is set in train by the 'father's' rejection of the 'son' but actually has its origin in an antecedent act, Caleb's discovery of Falkland's secret, Frankenstein's creation of the monster, and in both cases the motivation of the act is the thirst for knowledge ('My offence had merely been a mistaken thirst for knowledge' (*Caleb Williams*, vol. 2 chap. 2).

In some ways *Frankenstein* is a symbolic rewriting of *Caleb Williams* from Falkland's point of view, but there is a crucial difference. Caleb's relationship with Falkland is seen in the context of society as a whole, whereas Frankenstein's relationship with his creature is private, secret, existing apart from the rest of human experience. Caleb is the victim of social prejudices, whereas Frankenstein is the victim only of himself, a man hunted down not by social forces but by a bogey of his own creation. Caleb's worst fate is his exclusion from 'the friendship of mankind', whereas Frankenstein, so long as he has family, friends and fiancée, deliberately isolates himself from them: 'the same feelings that made me neglect the scenes around me caused me also to forget those friends who were so many miles absent' (*Frankenstein*, chap. 4).

The product of solitary researches, the creature merely acts to extend Frankenstein's isolation and it is only when he is totally separated from society that he begins to be obsessed by the loved ones he has inadvertently caused to die (chap. 24.) If the theme of *Caleb Williams* is the individual's isolation in society, *Frankenstein* is a parable about self-destruction through solitary endeavour. As such it is an important text as regards the theme of the solitary: but it has nothing to do with industrialisation.

V

The belief that *Frankenstein* was a response to the Industrial Revolution is based on the well-known theory that a great event cannot occur without being noticed, so that all contemporary comment apparently referring to that event cannot in logic be supposed to refer to anything else. This theory proves, for example, that Romanticism in English poetry in the 1790s was a response to the French Revolution, which was the big event of those times. Why the French Revolution failed to have the same immediate effect on French poetry I have never entirely understood: perhaps they were so busy being French Revolutionary they could only spare the energy for a feeble neo-Grecianism.[11] The theory also proves that writers, being serious *engagé* persons of the type who nowadays read *The Guardian*, must have said something about the Industrial Revolution. Blake's

> And did the Countenance Divine
> Shine forth upon our clouded hills?
> And was Jerusalem builded here
> Among these dark Satanic Mills?
> (Verses from *Milton*)

is usually mentioned at this point. As we all know Blake was a visionary and therefore able to describe Lancashire textile factories as 'dark Satanic Mills' without needing to have ever been to Lancashire. The theory just cited shows that, despite Blake's strong views on organised religion and the capitalist exploitation of human vice, he would not have wasted such a powerful phrase on churches with walls blackened by smoke from domestic chimneys (like the blackening Churches appalled by the Chimney Sweeper's cry in 'London'), or on the great breweries which were the largest industrial buildings in the London of his day. The Mills later on in the same poem:

O Satan my youngest born, art thou not Prince of the Starry Hosts
And of the Wheels of Heaven to turn the Mills day and night?
Art thou not Newton's Pantocrator weaving the Woof of Locke?

are clearly not churches. And churches and breweries weren't
new, whereas textile factories were, and in a poem about Satan
and Milton Blake was obviously writing about contemporary
events. The argument goes something like that: I apologise if I
have inadvertently pruned it of its complete subtlety and depth by
excessive abbreviation.

I don't mean to suggest, however, that there was no such thing
as an Industrial Revolution, or at least, a period of rapid industrialisation. Nor do I mean that people not directly involved were
unaware of what was going on. While factory developments drove
some people away, the wars with France between 1793 and 1802
and between 1803 and 1814, by rendering Grand Tours on the
Continent impractible, made it quite fashionable to visit industrial
areas. Tourists even made a point of visiting the insides of factories.[12] And while many regarded factories as eyesores, others found
them picturesque. It became one of the clichés of the day to
compare industrial sites with their excess of smoke and flame and
already gigantic scale, to Dante's Inferno.[13] Health conditions
inside factories became a matter of some controversy and are
discussed even in Thomas Love Peacock's *Headlong Hall* (1815).
Accidents in coal mines, which during the second half of the
eighteenth century had been barely reported in local papers at the
request of the mine owners, became so spectacular in scale that
they obtained wide publicity: there was even a play written on
the subject (*Kendrew, or The Coal Mine*, by the Revd J. Plumptre,
1809).

And yet none of these developments was a sudden dramatic
event. It was not even an event or a process in itself, but only one
part of a process. The value of incomes from commercial and
industrial sources assessed for property tax in 1812 clearly shows
the relative unimportance of the industrial areas:

England	£32,069,808
Lancashire	£1,583,781
Yorkshire	£1,762,535
London and Middlesex	£13,348,769[14]

I should guess that in both Lancashire and Yorkshire the assessed incomes add up to a slight predominance of the commercial over the industrial. Contemporaries generally referred to the 'new commercial system' and often seemed more aware of the spread of urbanisation rather than the spread of machines.[15] The important thing about this period was that the country was becoming immensely wealthy: industrialisation contributed to this but it was by no means the whole of the process. Accordingly, what interested Wordsworth, for instance, was not factories as such but the way the country was changing psychologically as a result of the new sources of wealth. Book 8 of his *The Excursion*, with its famous description of a textile mill, urges that industrial strength be harnessed to 'the moral law' and expatiates on the misery and ignorance of beggars and agricultural labourers: long-established evils remain unchanged, new opportunities are being lost for the same old reasons: factories are only a part of the complex fabric of a society which Wordsworth understood perhaps better than his interpreters. His views ought to be seen in the context of the period's criticism of the demoralisation of urban society, which addressed itself mainly to the phenomenon of the city: those who wrote on the moral corruption of factories showed a relatively restricted perspective.[16] Typically, the classic description of industrial England in Robert Southey's *Letters from England; by Don Manuel Alvarez Espriella* (1807), which brings together nearly all the themes which were later to be the standard critique of industrialisation, amounts to only twenty-five pages of a thousand page, three volume work.

Another point: there are a handful of English paintings of this period depicting industrial scenes, of which Loutherbourg's 'Coalbrookdale by Night' is perhaps the most striking, but there is no English equivalent of the corpus of 125 paintings of mines and metal foundries in Sweden by Pehr Hilleström. Born at Väddö in Uppland in 1732, Hilleström was trained from childhood in Stockholm's academy schools, not as a painter but as a tapestry weaver. In his mid-twenties, however, he went to Paris and studied under the leading exponent of frothily elegant rococo painting, François Boucher. Back in Stockholm, Hilleström became a court painter: his industrial canvases, including several large format royal commissions, date from the 1780s. Despite his incongruous association with Boucher, Hilleström seems to represent what has come to be a characteristic Swedish tradition of sympathetic response to the technical and the practical. But his paintings are sufficiently accurate and detailed to enable one to see that the technology depicted is already out of date by the standards of Dowlais and Cyfartha. Even as a primary producer, let alone as a manufacturing economy, Hilleström's Sweden was falling behind compared to Britain. His paintings illustrate not an Industrial Revolution but the absence of one. Hilleström's 125 paintings, and the absence of an English Hilleström provide an interesting commentary on the theory of direct linkage between event and artistic response.[17]

VI

Nevertheless some artistic work presents itself as a contemporary statement almost as crudely and obtrusively as a parliamentary speech or faction pamphlet: one thinks of Benjamin Disraeli's *Coningsby* and *Sybil* as examples. So let us look a little closer at Disraeli: he is a good instance of the need to understand specific contexts.

The historical disquisitions in the Young England novels are usually seen as an agreeably eccentric attempt to rewrite the history of the Tory party so as to assist Disraeli's own struggle to the top of the greasy pole. But in reality he neither invented the doctrines he expressed, nor found them already domiciled when he joined the Tory ranks. This sounds, surely, very much like Disraeli describing the Whigs:

> dull and pompous Aristocrats, who, assuming a popular title for private purposes, despise equally popular feelings and popular sentiments; who, bolstered up with heaps of wealth, and stiffened into one compact mass by family alliance, with cold selfishness turn their backs at once on the Monarch and the nation.

It was in fact written in 1815 by Thomas Barnes, later editor of *The Times*.[18] The idea that the aristocracy, and most notably the *Whig* aristocracy, was the enemy of both Crown and people was not only a cliché in Disraeli's childhood, it was a cliché especially favoured by extreme radicals, whether lower class like Thomas Evans, spokesman of the Spencean Philanthropists:

Both king and people now find themselves paralized and sub-
jected to one of the most unfeeling powers that can exist, namely
an oligarchy, that degrades the crown by granting or witholding
at their pleasure, and questioning, calling upon, and compelling
its agents to account for every shilling in its expenditure; while
they engross, possess and enjoy the country, uncontrolled and
unlimited in their acquisitions, destroying the people by their
exactions to gratify their lust of power, corruption and oppression, wallowing in wealth, and grasping at the command
and plunder of the world:[19]

or upper class, like Lord Cochrane, later Earl of Dundonald:

Our liberties in these days are not in danger from violent and
open exercise of regal authority; such acts, because free from the
deception practised by the mock representatives of the people,
would not be tolerated for an instant. No, Gentlemen, it is by the
House of Commons alone that the Constitution in subverted,
the prerogatives of the Crown usurped, the rights of the people
trampled upon.[20]

It will be recollected that when, as a young man, Disraeli tried to
enter politics as a radical, he attacked the Whigs in much the same
vein. He certainly remembered Lord Cochrane because the Stock
Exchange fraud which virtually ended Cochrane's parliamentary
career was one of the most talked about incidents of his childhood,
and perhaps the more appealing to him because his own early
politics were the politics of outrageousness. Nevertheless, he
scarcely changed his tune when he joined the Tory party: 'the
Conservative party is the really democratic party in the country,
which surrounds the people with the powers of the Throne to
shield them from the undue power of the aristocracy'.[21] Still, it
wouldn't be really true to say that Disraeli managed to graft radical
populism on to the Tory tradition, since the notion of the Whigs
being out to exploit both King and people turns out anyway to
have been originally a Tory doctrine, dating from the time when
the Tory party was reconstituting itself during its struggle against
the Grenville–Foxite coalition government of 1806–7: though this
particular line of attack was soon given up, for a period it was the
policy of Tory supporters to describe the Grenville–Foxite alliance
as 'An Ambitious Aristocracy engrossing both the power of the

Crown, and of the People' and to denounce their conduct as 'an attempt on the part of the Aristocracy to acquire such a permanent interest and influence, as to enable it to influence both King and THE PEOPLE'.[22]

But the influence of a previous tradition of political polemic is not confined in Disraeli's novels simply to the overtly political passages. For example, the somewhat dubious distinction between Saxons and Normans which is frequently alluded to in *Coningsby*, and which provides much of the dramatic machinery of *Sybil*, had been a commonplace of radical ideology since Disraeli was a child, and indeed for many years previously, though perhaps it owes its wider currency to Scott's *Ivanhoe*: it is even glanced at in the first chapter of *Martin Chuzzlewit*.[23] Even the idea of using the novel as a vehicle of political propaganda belonged to fairly recent history. In the 1790s, there had been a minor spate of anti-reform novels, and though none of them resembles Disraeli's work, dealing with theoretical doctrines rather than the minutiae of political gossip, Disraeli can hardly have been unaware of their existence since one of them was written by his own father.[24]

The essential point however is that the politics in Disraeli's political novels is not something that is hung on to fictions which, without these extraneous elements, could safely be entrusted to the transcendent insight of literary critics: the politics are central to the political novels not because they are generically political novels as opposed to any other kind of novel, but because politics happens to be the mode of human interaction which they are about. Disraeli himself explained, in his Preface to the 1849 edition of *Coningsby*:

It was not originally the intention of the writer to adopt the form of fiction as the instrument to scatter his suggestions, but, after reflection, he resolved to avail himself of a method which, in the temper of the times, offered the best chance of influencing opinion.

His discussion of political principle (e.g. *Coningsby*, book 2, chapters 4 and 5; book 5, chapter 2; book 6, chapter 3; book 8, chapter 3) turns out to be mainly negative, and it may in part have been Disraeli's inability to specify any Tory principles or to argue their practical outcome which forced on him the fictional approach.

Of course, in both *Coningsby* and *Sybil* the paint is too thin. We see the drooping Levantine features and curled hair peeping through the Englishness, and amongst the hastily sketched in trees of the Midlands countryside we catch an incongruous glimpse of a fantastically embroidered waistcoat. And when he aspires nearest to epic, he sinks lowest into hollow rhetoric:

> Will it be her proud destiny at length to bear relief to suffering millions, and with that soft hand which might inspire trouba-dours and guerdon knights, break the last links in the chain of Saxon thraldom? (*Sybil*, book 1, chap. 6)

Yet these strainings are not merely political for they evidently aim at a new dramatic, even epic view of politics. Disraeli's political novels are not merely fictions about politics: even the politics has a new imaginative dimension. The public to which Disraeli was addressing himself was the first generation for whom mass interest in politics was actively encouraged by professional politicians like himself. It was not enough to offer them the old brand of politics. Later the problem of an unleashed mass-electorate was confronted by Mussolini with Roman circuses and strutting, by Hitler with talk of the *Volk*: Disraeli's myth had less inherent appeal, and he needed to persuade his colleagues as much as his voters, so he dressed it up with literature. He once said, 'The greatest stretch of intellect in the world is to write a first rate work of fiction', and perhaps his own best talents were for salon repartee and the posturings of politics; but if the thinness of his epic vision is the fault of the thinness of his talent, nevertheless, no one could deny the clarity of his perception of the need for myth in politics, especially the new politics of mass participation.[25]

VII

The example of Disraeli suggests that we should not look at literature and politics as alternative or opposites but as separate – not necessarily completely separate – elements in a social dis-course; and certainly a number of novelists of Disraeli's period included material in their fictions of a type now usually found in learned journals. In part this is simply a concern for context. Since Scott at least novelists had been very aware of the precise time and place of their action; as George Eliot later wrote, 'there is no private life which has not been determined by a wider public life' (*Felix*

Holt, chap. 3). But there is more to it than that. Tiresome as they possibly are, Tolstoy's chapters on the philosophy of history in *War and Peace* could only be omitted to the detriment of his serious intentions as a novelist: in spite of his ostentatious dislike for Napoleon he is, after all, only tackling from a different, if uncongenial, angle the question of man's relationship with his times which, as can be seen most clearly in his Epilogue, is central to his study of Pierre and Nicholas. And *Silas Marner* without the sociology of its opening pages would be not merely less convincing in its handling of the scenes it evokes, but would lose that part of its force as a moral fable which depends on its truth to reality. Nor would anyone wish to edit out the following, from chapter 20 of *Middlemarch*:

> The weight of unintelligible Rome might lie easily on bright nymphs to whom it formed a background for the brilliant picnic of Anglo-foreign society; but Dorothea had no such defence against deep impressions. Ruins and basilicas, palaces and colossi, set in the midst of a sordid present, where all that was living and warm-blooded seemed sunk in the deep degeneracy of a superstition divorced from reverence; the dimmer but yet eager Titanic life gazing and struggling on walls and ceilings; the long vistas of white forms whose marble eyes seemed to hold the monotonous light of an alien world: all this vast wreck of ambitious ideals, sensuous and spiritual, mixed confusedly with the signs of breathing forgetfulness and degradation, at first jarred on her as with an electric shock, and then urged themselves on her with that ache belonging to a glut of confused ideas which check the flow of emotion.

In such a passage the quality of critical thought and intellectual judgements transferred into a series of images not only show us George Eliot's poetic power and enable us to see something of the relationship between the Westminster intellectual and the hot-blooded country girl she had once been, but also provide one of the key sections of the novel in that, more strikingly here than elsewhere, the intellectual sensitivity of Dorothea, indeed the whole orientation of her personality, is actually depicted rather than merely stated. If twentieth-century novels are less likely to have these digressions into politics, history, sociology and philosophy, it is not because we understand better how to write novels; it is because our idea of what a novel is, and what it should consist of, has changed: and a society's notion of its own art, and the purposes of its own art, is surely one of the elements involved in the process whereby art reflects society.

Of course, *War and Peace* and *Silas Marner* and *Middlemarch* and Disraeli's political novels actively invite attention to their historical moment, even when the dramatic scenario is displaced some years in time: but what about *A Christmas Carol*? The ghost of Marley (who had died only a few years earlier) appears in a costume – 'in his pigtail, usual waistcoat, tights and boots', – placing the story's action at least three or four decades previous to its publication in 1843, but *A Christmas Carol* belongs as much to its period as *Sybil*. After all, it sold 16,000 copies on the day of publication: testimony to a rather powerful topicality, *of some sort*. We may even without difficulty read into *A Christmas Carol* a distinction between the capitalist rich and the capitalist poor that is as striking as the two nations distinction spelt out in *Sybil*. The story's setting in the past is in keeping with the emphasis on the traditional in the Victorian period's progressive commercialisation of Christmas, but the displacement in time also serves both to exorcise the bitterness of the theme and to hint a critique of the present in which latter-day Scrooges flourish unrepentent. Whereas *Sybil* offers a complex myth of the good old days, or at least a counter-present, to serve the purposes of the complex, artificial system of politics, *A Christmas Carol* sets down a much simpler myth of dissatisfaction and reconciliation at the heart of the social system on which the world of *Sybil* is built. Still, *A Christmas Carol* isn't quite so *obviously* related to its historical context as *Sybil*. But this doesn't mean it is any less historical, any less of a historical document. After all, we are trying to get away from the *obvious*.

VIII

A Christmas Carol, as it happens, is only one of Dickens's minor texts. Dickens poses as many problems of interpretation as half a dozen other writers. It is as difficult to analyse his real value as an artistic reflection of society as it is to do justice to his real stature as a novelist, and indeed the two issues are and must be closely connected. He provides an outstanding instance of the need for caution in picking up themes. The vast extent of his popularity and readership gives an idea of the intelligence and open-mindedness of very considerable sections of middle-class and lower middle-class England that one might not have had otherwise. In part Dickens's popularity was so great because, in literary terms, he was outstandingly proficient in perhaps a wider range of genres than any other novelist: crime thriller, social satire, love romance, domestic farce, social criticism, gothic horror, social *reportage*. He was also more successful than any other writer in dealing with a wider range of social types: if his characterisations are not as convincing as George Eliot's rural bourgeois portraits, it would nevertheless be difficult to find another writer who handled as successfully any *two* of the numerous social groups tackled by Dickens. Then, of course, he was the creator of images of almost surrealistic force. Perhaps too long familiarity with Dickensian 'characters' has robbed his Bumbles and Barkises and Podsnaps of their original impact, but his descriptions of townscape remain amongst the most highly charged evocations of the Victorian scene; and some of his more complex effects, such as Miss Havisham sitting year after year in her decaying bridal finery amongst the cobwebs of her life, surrounded by clocks stopped precisely at twenty to nine, are both cruelly ludicrous and yet totally controlled in their presentation of the face of human tragedy.

But like some other outstanding writers, Dickens frequently undersold himself from the sheer facility with which good things came to him. It is the sheer exuberant variety of his eclecticism which undercuts, in my opinion, the Leavis attempt to suggest that his seriousness as a novelist is comparable to that of Tolstoy.[26] The notorious difference between the vitality of Dickens's comic characters and the woodenness of his main protagonists – something Dickens seems to have taken over from the drama of Morton and Reynolds which had dominated the London stage at the beginning of the nineteenth century – shows an attitude towards literature *vis-à-vis* a committedly observed reality which is very different from Tolstoy's. Because Dickens never had to work for his effects they rarely seem to have as much point as they might do, though this is part of their charm: and some of his best effects have no particular point at all:

There was early coffee to be got about Covent-garden Market, and that was more company – warm company, too, which was better. Toast of a very substantial quality, was likewise procurable: though the towzled-headed man who made it, in an inner chamber within the coffee-room, hadn't got his coat on yet, and was so heavy with sleep that in every interval of toast and coffee he went off anew behind the partition into complicated cross-roads of choke and snore, and lost his way directly. Into one of these establishments (amongst the earliest) near Bow-street, there came one morning as I sat over my houseless cup, pondering where to go next, a man in a high and long snuff-coloured coat, and shoes, and to the best of my belief, nothing else but a hat, who took out of his hat a large cold meat pudding; a meat pudding so large that it was a very tight fit, and brought the lining of the hat out with it. This mysterious man was known by his pudding for on his entering, the man of sleep brought him a pint of hot tea, a small loaf, and a large knife and fork and plate. Left to himself in his box, he stood the pudding on the bare table, and, instead of cutting it, stabbed it, overhand with the knife, like a mortal enemy; then took the knife out, wiped it on his sleeve, tore the pudding asunder with his fingers and ate it all up. The remembrance of this man with the pudding remains with me as the remembrance of the most spectral person my houselessness encountered. Twice only was I in that establish-ment, and twice I saw him stalk in (as I should say, just out of bed, and presently going back to bed) take out his pudding, stab his pudding, wipe the dagger, and eat his pudding all up. He was a man whose figure promised cadaverousness, but who had an excessively red face, though shaped like a horse's. On the second occasion of my seeing him, he said huskily to the man of sleep. 'Am I red tonight?' 'You are,' he uncompromisingly answered 'My mother,' said the spectre, 'was a red-faced woman that liked drink, and I looked at her hard when she laid in her coffin, and I took the complexion.' Somehow, the pud-ding seemed an unwholesome pudding after that, and I put myself in its way no more. ('Night Walks', from *The Uncommer-cial Traveller*)

But Dickens, the elaborator of symbols, has more to him than this. His most celebrated specific symbol is the fog, denoting the Court of Chancery, or the English legal system generally, at the beginning of *Bleak House*, and his most formally extended and complex is the presentation of Coketown and its Gradgrind-dominated culture in *Hard Times*. I find neither novel amongst Dickens's most impressive. *Bleak House*'s fog symbol, which has been held up to public admiration at least since G. K. Chesterton's introduction to the 1907 Everyman edition, is irrelevant and otiose, as John Carey has shown.[27] It seems to me that the real drift of *Bleak House* is the corrupting effect of depending too much on expectations of inheritance, a theme tackled earlier in *Martin Chuzzlewit* and again later in *Great Expectations* – features such as the emphasis on the spoilt character of the male protagonist, and, in *Martin Chuzzlewit* and *Great Expectations*, the awful relatives hanging on for their share of the hand-out, suggest a process of reworking and refining which extended ultimately over eighteen years. The Court of Chancery in *Bleak House* presents itself as a symptom rather than a cause of the process of corruption; or perhaps, like the Circumlocution Office in *Little Dorrit*, it is simply a piece of not entirely irrelevant political satire blown up a little too large for its original framework.

Such questions of balance and proportion are handled somewhat better in *Hard Times*. The whole Coketown scenario is not only the most coherently organised symbolic exposition in Dickens's *oeuvre*, it is the most penetrating single study available of Victorian capitalist culture: perhaps we would not have such a deeply incised vision of the mid-nineteenth-century mill town and its implications if this novel had never been written. And yet in comparison with Dickens's other novels it seems virtually lifeless. Like such different writers as George Eliot or James Joyce, Dickens's strongest sense of reality was for what he had experienced as an adolescent: he could inject vitality into his pictures of London and small-town southern England, but the north was too distant from him; he could describe it eloquently but he could not make it real to us. As Raymond Williams says, '*Hard Times* is an analysis of Industrialization, rather than an experience of it.' It has been argued, of course – some people will argue anything – that the colourlessness of characterisation is deliberate, a strategy to evoke the cultural impoverishment of Coketown, but this view could only seem convincing if one ignores Dickens's mode of approach in his other novels.[28] *Hard Times* is contrived and second-hand, and in the end it may seem more worthwhile to go behind it to the sources from which Dickens derived his picture, Southey and Carlyle and Mrs Gaskell.

With Dickens as with other novelists I have discussed, the most illuminating material is not in the obvious, would-be authentic parts but buried some way below the surface. Take for example his repeated tackling of the rags-to-riches theme. This is not a new theme – important themes never are completely – but originally it belonged to a tradition of rôle inversion which celebrated the underlying inevitability of inherited social position, and which found expression in the age-old rituals of Carnival. If, as has been argued, it was the anonymous *Fatherless Fanny* of 1819 which gave a revived currency to the theme, nevertheless it was important to Dickens in a painful, private, personal way as the social conditions of Coketown could never be. The experiences of his adolescence provided Dickens with more than just his townscapes: all through his life he seemed to have been grappling with the trauma of his sudden descent as a teenager from modest gentility to wage-slavery in the Blacking Factory. In his various depictions of oppressive and exploitative parents, Dickens was writing for a public which was in the process of developing the ideology of family love, at a time when children were still terribly vulnerable: but he was writing from out of the bitterness of his own experience, and the picture he gives of economic insecurity is distinctively Victorian. Richardson had portrayed one class directly and personally misusing another: Dickens shows us an atomised, impersonal society where the poor are not harassed by richer neighbours but by economic forces, where tyranny is to be expected not from hereditary masters but from those who exploit the crude power of the market: Scrooge, Dombey, Gradgrind, and, even more typically, that long line of Dickensian creditors, Ralph Nickleby, Quilp, Casby, Smallweed, and so on. And it was the particular stage in the development of the market economy which Victorian England was passing through that helps explain Dickens's preoccupation with inheritance. In Richardson's day, the propertied class was relatively small and cohesive and inherited money moved mainly in predictable directions; indeed the system of entail fixed the descent of most landed property generations ahead. Within fifty years of Dickens's death, changes in tax and salary structures reduced the overall social importance of inherited wealth as compared to earned income. But in Dickens's lifetime, economic expansion and increasing social mobility, together with the survival of huge inequalities of income, established the unexpected inheritance as an element in folklore.[29] And inseparable from Dickens's handling of the rags-to-riches theme is his portrayal of the corrupting influence of wealth, which, again, is something more than a rehash of traditional wisdom because of his closely observed depiction of the processes and symptoms of this corrupting influence. It is undoubtedly part of the cause of Dickens's commercial success as a writer that he addressed himself to these aspects of the economic structure of his day, and it is also part of his importance as a novelist and as a historical source.

IX

In this brief survey of novelists from Richardson to Dickens, I have been dealing (except for Mary Shelley) with authors who took their subjects ostensibly from their own society and at least approximately from their own day. This had become the convention in literature, and modern authors who do not write about their own time and place are recognised as indulging various fictive strategies. But it was not always the convention. Even writers as involved in the events of their own day as Dante or Milton did not choose contemporary subjects for their major works. Shakespeare understood the relationship between the individual and his historical context as well as anyone:

> There is a history in all men's lives,
> Figuring the natures of the times deceas'd
> (*Henry IV:Part 2*, Act 1, Scene 1, lines 80–1)

It would have been fascinating if he had written about Elizabethan England: but he didn't. Yet his subjects are just as vitally related to his period and culture as are those of Dickens to his: it is simply that the relationship is different.

Of course, some of Shakespeare's isolated passages or characterisations are cited as something like *reportage*: Justice Shallow and Justice Silence, for example, in *Henry VI: Part 2*. But if one remembers that Shakespeare was writing for a satirically minded and relatively affluent metropolitan audience at a time when country JPs were extremely busy with keeping the rural poor in order during successive years of crop failure, while executing the oppressive laws against the still numerous Roman Catholic population and assisting in the collection of the money and manpower needed to maintain English armies simultaneously in Ireland, France and the Netherlands, one might have a clearer idea of the probable relationship between Shakespeare's cackling senile gossipy JPs and the energetic, closely supervised county magistracy of late Elizabethan reality. To 'tell it like it is' is less often the function of literature than to tell it like it isn't.

In terms of indirect information, it is a familiar view that Shakespeare's history plays were an expression of a belief (clearly demonstrated by Shakespeare and apparently shared by his audience) that strong stable government was a desirable thing. This seems very probable though I am not clear what other approach a late Elizabethan might have reasonably selected, and it is not certain that the subjects from English History 1390–1485 were entirely Shakespeare's own independent choice. As propaganda documents the history plays have some interesting features; thus the characters of Fluellen, Jamy and MacMorris, the Welshman, the Scot and the Irishman, in *Henry V* show how even before 1600 some people were beginning to identify the whole British Isles as an extension of England. Simply as relatively early examples of popular history being used as national propaganda, the history plays are striking. But as literature they can hardly be said to have commanded the same degree of critical approval as the other parts of Shakespeare's *oeuvre*.

The other plays are not simply *not* English in their setting, they are usually vastly remote from contemporary English preoccupations. Take *Julius Caesar*. The relationship between personality and ideology, between private character and public action, between personality defect and political pose, between individual achievement and mythic reputation, is worked out in a way that seems directly relevant to the experience of the twentieth century: yet nothing could have been further from the English mental universe of 1600 when rulers were hereditary and by Grace of God and when even to talk of a change of government was not merely prosecutable but something like theological sin. Except that it is always difficult to detach Shakespeare's characters from the language they speak, *Julius Caesar* seems to me by and large convincing as a study of Rome at the end of the Republic, and indeed intensely Roman despite Cassius's attempt to give a general application to his tyrannicide:

> How many ages hence
> Shall this our lofty scene be acted over
> In states unborn and accents yet unknown!
> (Act III, Scene 1, lines 110–12)

The Roman-ness of the play is a major imaginative feat, and presupposes something similar on the part of the audience, though I wonder if the clock striking and the doublet which Cassius opens to the storm are less the result of haste and carelessness (let alone ignorance or taste for anachronism) than of a desire to hint a similarity between Rome and London that underpins the obvious differences which Shakespeare was depicting. It is instructive to compare Shakespeare's Roman plays with Ben Jonson's *Sejanus* of 1603 (which Shakespeare acted in). Jonson's tragedy is at once much more conceptually confined to the subject it depicts, more outwardly 'foreign' and yet more crudely 'topical' in its depiction of treachery in high places and fawning Elizabethan-type courtiers: the author was in fact summoned before the Privy Court to be interrogated with regard to treasonable elements in the play.

Or take *King Lear*, with its exploration of the theme of social and natural order presented as a study of rôles. Rôle-playing is a recurrent *motif* in Shakespeare: Richard III and Hamlet, Angelo and the Duke in *Measure for Measure*, Julia in *The Two Gentlemen of Verona*, Rosalind in *As You Like It*, Viola in *Twelfth Night* and so on, but in *King Lear* almost everybody consciously adopts rôles, changes roles, or, like the Fool, has rôles forced upon them, in an almost paradigmatic exploration of the implications of rôles in society. Perhaps the only important exception is Cordelia, who is central to the play precisely because of her refusal to put on a performance as Lear's loving daughter, and her insistence on being only what she genuinely and essentially *is*. The theme of the relationship between a man's personal identity, his inner essence as an individual, and his social identity as fulfilling a rôle in society, is one which the twentieth century finds deeply intriguing, but if it had not been for Shakespeare we might have thought that the distinction between social rôle and residual essence (as opposed to the more obvious distinction between false and true identity) was totally divorced from sixteenth-century ways of looking at people. The only recent precedent for *King Lear* that Shakespeare could have known about, Charles V's abdication and division of the Hapsburg Empire between his sons Ferdinand and Philip in 1554, merely emphasises the originality of King Lear, for when Charles gave up his political rôle he also as far as possible gave up his personal identity, retiring into a monastery to end his days in prayer and contemplation. Admittedly involuntary deposition, as in *Richard II*, raises some of the same issues of personal identity and codes of expectation but in *Richard II*, Act IV, Scene 1, the situation is merely presented and the emphasis seems to be on the bitterness of stripping off, not on what is left behind:

> Now mark me how I will undo myself: –
> I give this heavy weight from off my head,
> And this unwieldy sceptre from my hand . . . etc.

Part of the modernity of *King Lear* is the way in which the theme is painstakingly explored in all its ramifications, and applied not simply to one character but, in different ways and through the medium of different types of relationship and codes of expectation, to practically the whole cast.[30]

Shakespeare's plays demonstrate the range and depth and originality with which it was possible to think of social and moral issues in Renaissance England. The lack of a specifically English politics and any real exploration of contemporary religious issues, suggests less a desire to avoid embroilment with the Privy Council than a lack of willingness to waste time on issues of such limited and local interest. It thus becomes difficult to know what to make of Shakespeare's relationship with society if we conceive the seventeenth century in terms of the Revolution of the 1640s, as essentially an age of ideological engagement: but perhaps after all Shakespeare helps us understand both people's openness to new ideas during the revolutionary years, and the sophisticated pragmatism of those who contrived to flourish during the transition from Commonwealth to Protectorate and from Protectorate to Stuart Restoration: is it so far-fetched to see a temperamental resemblance between Shakespeare and Pepys?

In any case, the difficulty of answering questions about Shakespeare's relationship to his period is far from invalidating them. For an understanding either of Shakespeare as an individual artist or of his society, such questions are obviously more useful than forced attempts to dig up apparently contemporary references in the plays: the truly historical approach must be, to look less for nuggets taken out of context, than for the questions which literature raises about its context. But we shall come back to Shakespeare later. In the meantime, there are some general analytic issues to tackle.

4

Towards a Social Theory of Artistic Change

The ancient Mariner beholdeth a sign in the element afar off.

I

The obvious alternative to blundering around after random bits of history in random texts would be an approach based on a systematic *theory* of the relationship of literature, and any example thereof, to its social context, and this chapter attempts to outline such a theory. People who don't like theory should skip the next few pages and resume reading at page 75: part of the object of the discussion which immediately follows is to argue that an overall theory must be too hugely complex to serve as the basis for a viable analytic programme, and from page 75 onward I deal much more with specifics, though those who read this chapter will see how the later chapters fit in with the ideas put forward here.

As people who read the top and bottom of the page simultaneously will see, I am taking Marxist theory as my starting point. In doing so I am not making a profession of political faith: it is merely that Marxism provides the only developed body of theory capable of dealing with both literature *and* society. Even L. C. Knights started with Marx in *Drama and Society in the Age of Jonson* (pp. 1–4). It is true that Marxist literary history tends either to soar metaphysically far beyond such mundane phenomena as specific texts and specific historical situations, or else, if condescending to go into details, become crudely reductionist, in melancholy contrast to the sensitivity and flexibility of Marx's own approach to literature; and no Marxist critic has so far established an analytic paradigm that has been applied faithfully by another critic to another historical context: but that is hardly Marx's fault.[1] The Marxist critic currently most widely respected, Walter Benjamin, is notable for his selective and unsympathetic use of Marxist theory and the assimilation of incompatible elements such as surrealism

and Goethe's notion of *Urphänomen*.[2] His Weimar Republic quality
has an irresistible appeal in our own Weimar Republic society; we
can be sure Marx would have loathed him for just that reason.

II

One of Marx's own most promising theoretical formulations, the
base-superstructure dichotomy, was used by Walter Benjamin
merely as one of the casual metaphors in which he expressed
himself, and nowadays seems to have been given up by Marxist
scholars. Marx wrote of 'the economic structure of society, the real
foundation, on which rises a legal and political superstructure and
to which correspond definite forms of social consciousness'.[3] But
to utilise the base-superstructure division, as generally understood, it is first necessary to enquire where economic base ends
and superstructure begins; and the consensus of recent western
Marxist writing on culture is that this enquiry is not worth pursuing. Raymond Williams has pointed out that the political order,
which might otherwise appear superstructural, comprises material
productions such as 'prisons and workhouses and schools' and
that even music is involved in material relations and cannot be
excluded from the sphere of the economic. And Nicos Poulantzas,
in perhaps the most influential formulation of recent years, has so
to speak outflanked the base-superstructure dichotomy with his
redefinition of mode of production to include, amongst other
things, politics:

> By *mode of production* we shall designate not what is generally
> marked out as the economic (i.e. relations of production in the
> strict sense), but a specific combination of various structures and
> practices which, in combination, appear as so many instances or
> levels, i.e. as so many regional structures of this mode.

Gregor McLennan has shown how this extended concept of mode
of production works against the base-superstructure division; in
fact it embraces and unites the two halves of the equation.[4]

One of Poulantzas's most important achievements is that he has
reintroduced a commitment to historical specificity into Marxist
cultural analysis, as had been called for by Louis Althusser. An
analytic programme in which mode of production refers only to
feudalism or capitalism, where the 'substitution of *epochal* for con-

nected historical analysis is especially characteristic', where terms such as hegemony can refer to 'only a fundamental class (that is to say one which occupies one of the two poles in the relations of production)' isn't going to tell us very much about Wordsworth. But although Poulantzas has provided us with the analytic tools to describe the specificity of a society at a given historical moment, he hasn't actually shown us how to identify this specificity: it is virtually impossible to apply his theory to actual historical form-ations.[5]

In any case, it seems presumptuous of Marxists to give up an analytic approach suggested by Marx himself. Expressed in crude terms of a base-superstructure dichotomy, his formulation seems indeed open to the objection that superstructural forms partake of base economic elements. But what Marx actually said was that there was an economic foundation 'on which rises a legal and political superstructure and to which correspond definite forms of social consciousness'. He did not say that the legal and political superstructure and the definite forms of social consciousness were the same thing, nor that they have the same relationships to the economic foundation. Elsewhere he referred to 'an entire super-structure of distinct and peculiarly formed sentiments, illusions, modes of thought and views of life' but he bases this superstruc-ture 'upon the social conditions of existence', of which the econ-omic foundation, presumably, is only a part. Earlier he had written: 'Assume particular stages of development in production, com-merce and consumption and you will have a corresponding . . . civil society. Assume a particular civil society and you will get particular political conditions.'[6] Instead of a crude twofold division Marx was evidently thinking here of a number of distinct, analys-able levels of correspondence. But, presumably because he never found the opportunity to address himself to the details of this particular problem, he tended to telescope the different levels together and include them either with the economic (which after all was the area of his most intensive studies) or with the spiritual.

This assimilation of different levels, almost as a form of private shorthand, is evident in the distinction Marx made between ma-terial production and spiritual production:

> in order to examine the connection between spiritual production and material production, it is above all necessary to grasp the latter itself not as a general category but in *definite historical*

form . . . If material production itself is not conceived in its *specific historical* form, it is impossible to understand what is specific in the spiritual production corresponding to it and the reciprocal influence of one on the other.[7]

In general terms, the material production-spiritual production distinction corresponds to the base-superstructure dichotomy as generally understood: in fact Raymond Williams uses the term 'material production' in his critique of the base-superstructure model.[8] But the material production-spiritual production dichotomy is not open to the same objection as the base-superstructure division, the objection that it is impossible to demarcate the beginning and end of the two halves of the equation. There is no possibility of supposing that an elegantly bound volume of poetry, a copy of a Hellenistic statue, the Old Bailey and Pentonville Gaol are to be seen as examples of spiritual production; spiritual production is clearly only the poetry in the volume, the laws and prejudices enforced in the law courts, and so on. In one sense, these spiritual products have no objective existence outside their material and materially produced manifestation, but the argument that Marx's distinction is difficult to translate into objective reality misses the point that he was attempting not to label self-evidently distinct objects but to indicate a conceptual division within a vast and complex process. And it is evident that Marx saw some utility in looking at spiritual product as something analytically distinct from its material presentation and the material constraints on its production. In his Paris Notebooks he wrote about culture as something much more than the epiphenomena of material relations:

> Only through the objectively unfolded richness of man's essential being is the richness of subjective *human* sensibility (a musical ear, an eye for beauty of form – in short *senses* capable of human gratifications, senses confirming themselves as essential powers of *man*) either cultivated or brought into being.

And in his 1859 Preface to *A Contribution to the Critique of Political Economy*, he wrote:

> a distinction should always be made between the material transformation of the economic conditions of production, which can

be determined with the precision of natural science, and the legal, political, religious, aesthetic or philosophical – in short, ideological forms in which men become conscious of this conflict and fight it out.[9]

In his own very numerous pronouncements on literary topics, Marx tends to discuss specific texts without reference to the material aspect of their production. Literature was one of the consuming passions of his life: it was too important to him to be stuffed brusquely into a theoretical pigeon-hole. Only occasionally did he even begin to explore literature's theoretical implications. One of the subheadings in the *Grundrisse* is 'The uneven development of material production relative to e.g. artistic development' but he was soon side-tracked by the question of legal relations. A little later he made another attempt at the same theme –

> In the case of the arts, it is well known that certain periods of their flowering are out of all proportion to the general development of society, hence also to the material foundation, the skeletal structure, as it were, of its organization

– but this raised so many fascinating lines of enquiry for Marx that in the end he passed over what is surely the central problem and went on to reflect on what is perhaps only a side issue:

> But the difficulty lies not in understanding that the Greek arts and epics are bound up with certain forms of social development. The difficulty is that they still afford us artistic pleasure and that in a certain respect they count as a norm and as an unattainable model.[10]

And he never really returned to this problem.

Though Marx believed literature could provide evidence concerning the society which produced it, what is most striking about his literary references is his sensitivity to the specificity of texts. Above all it is evident that he adhered to what was essentially an idealistic concept of literary value and literary talent. This should not simply be dismissed as backsliding into recidivistic Hegelianism – especially as the question of literary value is precisely where modern Marxist critics tend to be at their weakest – but as relating to the distance Marx evidently perceived between the realm of material production on which he concentrated his researches, and the realm of spiritual production to which he turned for refreshment.[11]

III

In some senses, therefore, Marx's own writings leave literature, art, spiritual production both literally and theoretically up in the air, above the material world and not too evidently connected. The material and the spiritual may perhaps be reintegrated by means of Gramsci's concept of *hegemony*, the process whereby a ruling class governs less by a physical monopoly of the institutions of government than by the maintenance of a pervasive ideology which determines how every member of society perceives his rôle within the community: *hegemony* refers, therefore, to the determining aspect of the ideological relationship that both underlies and penetrates all material relationships. The use of the concept of hegemony has already been suggested by Raymond Williams as an *alternative* to the dualist base-superstructure approach and its derivatives.[12] If, however, we think not in terms of the base-superstructure division but in terms of material production-spiritual production the concept of hegemony has most value as mediating between the two halves of the equation.

But since the dualist or multiple-layer approach is incompatible with Poulantzas's dynamic, complex but essentially holistic *mode of production*, we need an alternative means of treating specific historical formations. Actually specific historical formations do not exist in a void but in relation to one another; they are moments in a continuing process of change; the concept of 'specific historical formation' suggests something like trying to take a cross-section of a river. In any case, the specific historic formation at AD 1750 will look different if examined in the light of AD 1850, and different again in the light of AD 2050, not simply because each generation has a different understanding of the principle developments of the past, but because developments which in one age may seem objectively insignificant, may turn out in retrospect to have been the beginnings of future-defining trends.

It may be more useful to take the general concept of *epochs* – e.g. feudal epoch, capitalist epoch – periods of long duration and problematic delimitation. Within these epochs the economic situation is not to be seen as stable and uniform but necessarily subject to the changes and developments which will lead eventually to the emergence of another economic epoch; as Marx wrote, 'new, higher relations of production never appear before the material conditions of their existence have matured in the womb of the old society itself'. Étienne Balibar describes such changes simply as the development of contradictions, and a little later as 'periods of transition . . . characterized by the *coexistence* of several modes of production'.[13] I find neither of Balibar's formulations helpful; we need a concept that avoids focusing either on imminence of collapse or appearance of stability. I would prefer to call these changes and developments *sub-epochal*, not as relating to sub-epochs – we are talking about continuums, overlapping processes, not divisions into periods – but simply as relating to developments *within* epochs.

The sub-epochal development to which Marx devoted most attention was the crisis of overproduction, 'the most striking form in which advice is given [to capitalism] to be gone and to give room to a higher state of social production'. It is to be noted that capitalism is forced into crisis, and other developments of this order, 'not by relations external to it, but rather as a condition of its self-preservation', in other words, the crisis is organically part of the capitalist system.[14] The classic discussion of a sub-epochal change is, of course, Lenin's *Imperialism*, which should serve to remind us that sub-epochal changes are not simply economic phenomena as such but also their cultural and political expression. Imperialism, for example, covers a variety of economic forms: its basic identity is at the political level. Similarly the emergence of individualism, the creation of a leisured bourgeoisie, and the consequent subordination of women are crucial sub-epochal changes that cannot be reduced to economic terms.[15]

Other sub-epochal changes would include the emergence of nation states (partly determined by the creation of national markets), the consequent growth of central government and its expenses, the consequent social struggle for the control of central government, the build-up of armed forces, and the increased scale of wars relating to the extension of foreign markets: all of which, taken individually, can be related to economic causations only by reasonings that would appear somewhat reductive, but which, taken together, are the inevitable concomitant of the constantly developing economic order. It will be noted that sub-epochal changes can be simultaneous, because having different rôles in the economic process, e.g. the rise of literacy, the increased industrial employment of women. A specific historical formation will in fact be a specific combination of simultaneous sub-epochal processes.

Although these sub-epochal changes are accompanied by a consciousness that will seek to explain, justify, or even to oppose or deny them, their determination is to be seen as essentially economic, for as Marx wrote:

> Just as our opinion of an individual is not based on what he thinks of himself, so can we not judge of such a period of transformation by its own consciousness; on the contrary, this consciousness must be explained rather from the contradictions of material life.[16]

The economic determinants of sub-epochal change will normally be complex and may involve geopolitical realities underlying economic formations. The emergence of France, and the failure to emerge of Germany, as a unified state between 1200 and 1500, the separation of Sweden from Denmark in the 1520s and Denmark's retention of Norway till 1814, the establishment of independence in the northern Netherlands, and the strengthening of Spanish rule in the southern Netherlands in the later sixteenth century cannot be explained in terms of spiritual factors but only by adducing a complex interreaction of essentially material factors.

Such changes, however, necessarily privilege different sectors of society. The growth of a royal court will be to the benefit of a section of the aristocracy, just as the pacification of a military frontier will be to the disadvantage of another section. The opening up of new trade routes, or the exploitation of new industrial processes, will benefit one lot of bourgeois investors at the expense of another. The growth of central administration will create a new class of bureaucrats but will perhaps damage the interests of *rentiers* by increasing their taxes. Groups disadvantaged by new developments will only partially be able to arrange a transfer, and establish themselves within the emergent interest; on the other hand, they will not disappear overnight, and may survive to stage some sort of counter-revolution. These changing relationships between different social groups or class-fractions involve developments which we may call *fractional*, i.e. relating to the social and ideological and subjective experience of fractions within major classes.

Although these fractional developments are provoked by sub-epochal changes which are economically determined, the form which these fractional responses take is not itself economically determined in any visible sense, but derived from a reformulation of the consciousness that had come into existence in concert with material developments up to this point. The distinction between sub-epochal and fractional is, in Marx's words, the distinction

> between the material transformations of the economic conditions of production, which can be determined with the precision of natural science, and the legal, political, religious, aesthetic or philosophic – in short, ideological forms in which men become conscious of this conflict and fight it out.[17]

Ideological forms relate to material forms in two ways. First, ideological forms have material forms as their subject – but they are material forms subjectively perceived, not objective material circumstances. Objective reality has to be subjectively perceived before it can be responded to, and both the process of perception and that of response are ideologically conditioned. Of course, the ideology may sometimes bear an apparently faithful imprint of the economic conditions which shaped it, but it is still an ideology. Men may riot for want of bread: economic conditions may be the *occasion* for their rioting, but we cannot say that economic conditions are the objective cause, for perhaps men even hungrier in another time or place refrain from rioting. The hunger and the riot are connected by an intervening layer of opinions concerning hunger, riots, social justice, the past, the future, the weakness of the police – in short, ideology. Secondly, ideology does not consist only of ideas. It is given shape, as churches, universities, armies, the physical destruction of war. Even the ideas of our rioters relate to a social structure which consists principally of elements that have been given material form.

It is perfectly correct, therefore, to argue that 'pure' ideological production cannot exist in any visibly demonstrable sense. Yet however great the material involvement, the spiritual never becomes reducible to the same laws as the strictly economic, and cannot be 'determined with the precision of natural science' by the analytic tools proper to the investigation of the economic realm. This is the essential point of Marx's distinction between material transformations and ideological forms.

To adopt the jargon of Althusser, of *determination in the last instance*, is to refuse to accept the utility of Marx's distinction, which necessarily predicates that the mode of determination of the economic and the mode of determination of the spiritual will be of different types anyway. What we call spiritual is derived from responses to the material, and is expressed in material forms, and, more crucially, operates within a specific historical formation which owes its fundamental characteristics to the determination of economic processes – I would rather say, participates in a general historic process which is determined by economic processes. It is only in this obvious and general sense, remote from the possibility of analysis, that the economic can be seen as in itself determinant of the spiritual.

The distinction between the economically determined and the spiritual – between the sub-epochal and the fractional – can be illustrated by reference to the history of the twentieth century. It has been inevitable that there should have been a power struggle for economic mastery of Europe, inevitable that such a struggle should sooner or later involve the United States and Russia, and inevitable that the technological advances in the means of waging war should outstrip the managerial skills needed to direct them. It was, however, not inevitable in any meaningful economic terms that the wars should break out precisely in 1914 and in 1939, that, to date, the USA and Russia should have been involved in armed conflict only on the same side, or that in the course of the general process scarce resources should have been diverted to the production-line liquidation of 6,000,000 Jews.

The processes of connection between the economic and ideological are difficult but not perhaps ultimately impossible to trace, but we must be wary of short cuts. Poulantzas's argument that 'a social formation . . . presents a particular combination, a specific over-lapping of several "pure" modes of production' suggests a kind of vertical bonding between the 'different economic, political, ideological and theoretical levels or instances' of each of the modes of production found in combination.[18] But it may be doubted if there ever could be such a thing as a 'pure' mode of production coexisting with other 'pure' modes of production, for surely one such mode would be transformed by and adapted to its coexistence with the other modes. It may also be doubted if there will ever be found a one to one relationship between economic components and the corresponding political and ideological components of the same mode of production, or that a political and ideological *status quo*

will ever simply consist of an aggregate of the political and ideological components of coexisting 'pure' modes of production. Poulantzas's use of the adjective 'overlapping' does not remove this
objection but merely shows that he has recognised the problems
posed by his own categories.

It is true that material production is always accompanied by
spiritual production, because so long as man exists ideology exists,
but similar material formations – or the material formations of the
same society at different periods when there has been no intervening material transformation – may be accompanied by different
ideological forms, even by different institutional mechanisms.
Modern capitalism, for example, can exist both with a *laissez-faire*
system in which the social position of the individual is fixed by the
market, and with a *dirigiste* system committed to engineered social
justice. Most capitalist societies have attempted to put both ideologies, and also various combinations of the two, into practice at
different times. This doesn't affect the underlying economic realities, of course, but it certainly makes some difference to the
subjective experience of practically everyone involved. Even great
public events at the fractional level have no real effect on underlying economic realities. In the eighteenth century, Sweden's social and economic development during the Time of Freedom,
under parliamentary government, was not so different from that of
Denmark under royal absolutism: the defeat of Germany in 1918
created social and economic conditions comparable to those
brought about by victory in Italy, and so on. The mass triumphs
and traumas of human consciousness usually determine remarkably little in the long term.

IV

The ideological, or fractional, is connected with the economic or
sub-epochal by a complex historical process, and to understand
this we need to examine where the fractions come from, and why
their rôle is essentially ideological. At any given historical moment
a specific material formation will involve groups – fractions of the
major economic classes – who are particularly involved with the
peculiarities of that material formation, and these groups will have
a consciousness by which they explain to themselves their particular rôle. But since these fractions neither emerge nor vanish overnight, any society existing in the real world will consist of an

accretion of layer upon layer of such fractions, layer upon layer of such fragmented consciousnesses: some emergent, some residual, but all imbued with potential political energy. It is the sheer number and variety of these groups, which together form an amalgam that can never be exactly reproduced either in a different geographical space or in a different chronological time, which determines the uniqueness of a particular society at a particular historical moment. And these different fractions, with their different consciousnesses – which we may also call largely inchoate ideologies – will be constantly jockeying for position. At times their struggle will present itself in clear economic terms; occasionally it will appear as conflict between major classes, as for example in the English Civil War, which is so often held up by reductionist Marxists as a classic example of conflict between a feudal régime and an emergent bourgeoisie; but most of the time it will simply be an unremitting guerilla war of ideas and prejudices and fashions, of vested interests and pressure groups and little shits on the make.

The competition between the different fractions is not a free-for-all between equals. Marx wrote, in 'The Eighteenth Brumaire of Louis Napoleon': 'Men make their own history, but they do not make it just as they please, they do not make it under circumstances chosen by themselves but under circumstances directly found, given and transmitted from the past.'[19] Accordingly, some fractions have inherited a superior position, and these dominate the rest. Poulantzas's formulation of the *power-bloc* is useful here. He derives it from 'the "plurality" of dominant classes (and fractions)' and defines it as 'a contradictory unity of politically dominant classes and fractions *under the protection of the hegemonic fraction*'.[20] The individual ideologies of the differing fractions will have much in common, deriving as they must from a shared history, and are subsumed in a common ideology which in its entirety is the property of only one fraction, but which is accepted, if only temporarily, by the other dominant fractions, and is maintained by them in concert at the expense of the dominated classes.

The concept of hegemony is now widely understood and used, but is generally applied only to the form of relationship between ruling classes (and fractions) and the ruled. This relationship is, of course, an ideological form in that it consists not of material constraints and material pressures so much as values and concepts and epistemologies. So far no term has been coined to describe, as a conceptual entity, the ideological content of a specific hegemonic system at a specific historical moment. By and large it would be misleading to reduce hegemony, or a specific instance of hegemonic control, to distinct components such as ideological content, or institutional agencies, because the institutional agencies do not simply represent or embody an ideology, they *are* in part the ideology, and the ideology is not an abstraction but in part an arrangement of social, even material, relationships: in hegemony the medium *is* the message, and vice versa. But the point here is not to explain hegemony, but to analyse ideology, or forms of it such as literature and art, and in order to do so we will have to make the analytic distinction indicated by Marx and point to the ideological content of specific hegemonic systems at specific historical moments; and this ideological content, which will be much more, and much more pervasive, than a conscious ideology, I shall call the *hegemonic coding*.

Just as hegemony itself, and within a system of hegemony the dominance of a hegemonic fraction, derive from the normally bloodless but incessant competition of differing fractions, so the hegemonic coding derives from the conflict and assimilation of the overlapping ideologies of the different fractions. The hegemonic coding in fact will be a kind of compost of ideas, often including latent elements that are irreconcilable, but temporarily marshalled into an appearance of psychological coherence. It will be the common property of most people in society, and particularly of virtually everyone within the dominant fractions, since the whole point about hegemony is that it depends on the inability of different classes and fractions to distinguish their own interests from those of a society conceived as an organic unity.

If a society were genuinely stable the same fractions would remain forever in the same relationship, and there would be no occasion for the hegemonic coding to change. But the remorseless workings of economic forces are constantly throwing into disequilibrium the balance of power amongst the fractions making up society, while at the same time altering the general perception of the problems facing the society as a whole. The very complexity of the society, and thus of the ideological ingredients compacted together in the hegemonic coding, will cause objectively minor changes at the sub-epochal or economic level to be translated into major stresses and breakdowns of cohesion at the fractional or ideological level. And though the whole system of hegemony depends on the dominated (and even the dominating) classes being unable to recognise, even for a moment, the practical possibility of an alternative system, these crises will inevitably lead to readjustments within the power-bloc and ultimately to readjustments within the hegemonic coding.

In talking about the hegemonic coding, I don't mean to suggest that it is necessary to say that a particular hegemonic coding consists of x, y, and z, and excludes p, q and r: the concept will probably be more useful as indicating the conceptual link between a hegemonic system and individual examples of its art, rather than as constituting in itself an accessible topic of research. It will be in the nature of a hegemonic coding to be ambiguous and self-contradictory: even at times when the hegemonic coding seems unusually consistent this consistency will conceal a mass of unassimilable elements. It would be best never to lose sight of the fact that the hegemonic coding is only a function of a particular, historically evolved set of socio-economic circumstances. Thus, in the early nineteenth century Neo-classicism and Romanticism may be seen as components of single hegemonic coding, different facets of the same complex cultural aggregate. It could perhaps be argued further that Neo-classicism and Romanticism correspond each with different fractions within the power-bloc – I find, for example, in the case of churches built in the 1820s the preference for the Gothic Revival style in English provincial cities, as compared to the preference for Greek Revival in London, rather suggestive – and even that Neo-classicism related to a consensus which was in the process of being superseded by elements more involved with Romanticism. But to my mind the emergence and mobilisation of new fractions in this period would be more profitable as an area of primary study than the question of the balance of power between Neo-classicism and Romanticism considered as ideological abstractions: in any case, they together constituted only a *part* of the hegemonic coding. At the same time, without some overall picture of a society, both economically and culturally, it will be impossible to identify more than a few of the operative fractions: in this field there is necessarily a big gap between theoretical explanation and detailed analysis.

V

The principle reason why the hegemonic coding of a given society at a given historical moment is so difficult to study is that it is expressed and incorporated in so many different forms. Parliamentary speeches, legislation, case law, are manifestations which may be quite closely related to the then current balance of fractional ideologies subsumed within the hegemonic coding, though in every case detailed analysis would be needed to establish even the most apparently banal public utterance in its precise location within hegemonic coding as such. Parliamentary speeches or legislation, of course, have an apparently practical function in civil society: in reality their function is even more symbolic, but nevertheless they present themselves as the normal means by which a society tells itself what its rules are. Philosophy or scientific theory, on the other hand, will presumably be relatively remote from the day-to-day needs of the hegemonic system, though it is is significant that twentieth-century totalitarian dictatorships, especially Stalin's, felt constrained to attempt a take-over even in these fields. Probably even the most abstruse metaphysics will infect, or be infected by, the requirements of even the most pluralistic-seeming hegemonic coding, but it is the hegemonic coding which determines the relative prestige of different disciplines and allocates their differing ideological functions. In fact the hegemonic coding determines not simply what is expressed in a specific expressive form, but also who the expresser is, and who is audience, and the relationship between the two. There will also be a material relationship between the writer and his readers – i.e. how much he earns, how much they pay – but this will hardly be the dominant element in their interrelation and in any case will be perceived largely in ideological terms.

With regard to literature, the hegemonic coding determines why people read books, why people write them, even why people publish them. But it will not always be obvious how far the hegemonic coding determines what is *in* a book. One literary work might come close to a political statement in its apparent relevance to contemporary affairs, though the obviousness of its contextualisation will, as in any other political statement, conceal a complexity of ideological origins: another literary production may appear utterly remote from mundane affairs, but by its very remoteness contributes to some identifiable though probably unconscious strategy in the maintenance or overthrow of a specific hegemonic order.

It has happened only once – *so far* – that there has been a political revolution in Britain involving the expulsion of nearly the whole of the original power-bloc and, in consequence, a violent discontinuity in the hegemonic coding: and it so happens that the greatest writer of the period was intimately involved in these events. John Milton is the unique example in English Literature of a major writer who had a leading rôle in one régime and survived as an object of condemnation and suspicion to its successor. We can see in his earlier works the continuation of the English Renaissance traditions, perhaps even see in *On the Morning of Christ's Nativity* a kind of parallel with Rubens. There is little in *Comus* which prefigures the later apologist of the regicide republic and pioneer advocate of divorce. The years of the Civil War and Interregnum, in which he became the most trusted assistant of those deciding England's foreign policy, left him little time for literature. After the Restoration, in embittered retirement, he began to compose poetry again. *Samson Agonistes* and *Paradise Lost*, in their defiant note of individual struggle, of individual testimony against fate, indicate a repudiation of the Restoration, though there is a hollowness in those vast echoing structures erected on the gantries and scaffolding of his verse which suggests a lack also at the centre of the republic Milton had helped administer before 1660. But there is also an important element of rebuilding, reassembling a shattered culture, of struggling to incorporate a profound and European classicism into a contemporary English idiom, an attempt to revitalise a common intellectual inheritance that suggests a parallel with Racine, himself the greatest writer of a France recently recovered from civil strife.

As the example of Milton shows, artists and writers are not always in line with the dominant ideology of their time but they represent tendencies implicit in it, and in their emphases pinpoint areas and show directions for necessary growth: hence in fostering a consciousness that will be ready for the next phase of change, they take on a prophetic rôle such as Shelley described, becoming 'the mirrors of the gigantic shadows which futurity casts upon the present'.[21]

But the sheer variety of literature militates against any conclusive statement of the range of possible connections between literature and the general hegemonic codings: in any case theoretical typologies are much less use than the analysis of specific problems and areas. It may be useful, however, to write a history of the changing hegemonic codings embodied within a relatively enclosed and insulated system of literary discourse: academic literary criticism would provide an ideal laboratory control for studies of this kind.

Taking the literature of a period as a whole, it will be seen that the different levels of literature – what used to be called high-brow, middle-brow and low-brow – relate to the way in which, in contemporary western culture, different social groups manufacture different images of culture which serve to underpin the separation of one social group from another, and particularly the separation between dominating and dominated factions and classes. Seen in terms of the necessarily interlocking social relationships, the ideological content of a high-brow novel will not be incompatible with that of a contemporary low-brow novel, despite the differences in presentation: both novels will derive from the hegemonic coding but will be intended for different audiences within the hegemonic system.

Another point: each hegemonic coding can do no more than *pretend* to absorb or to abolish its predecessors under previous dispensations. A particular novel, therefore, will owe much to the previous tradition of the novel, and at least as much to the individual situation of an author in a specific stage of personal development, though it is in its relationship to the general hegemonic coding that these debts will be manifested.

VII

The formulation of an analytic progression from epoch to sub-epochal change to fractional development to hegemonic coding to specific work of art, with each stage fraught with complex problems of identification and discrimination, is not exactly simple: it may even suggest a Heath-Robinson type contraption of levers and cogs. It is none the less a formulation elaborated to deal with a specific issue, the problem of Neo-classicism and Romanticism to be discussed in chapter 8. The first two versions of this chapter were actually written between the first and second drafts of my discussion of Neo-classicism and Romanticism. But it will be seen from what I have already written that theory, in itself, cannot provide an immediate means of analysing either individual texts or groups of texts. There is not only the problem of the vast cumbersomeness of factual circumstances and unknown imponderables: there is the problem of the texts themselves. We can't quantify the entire context of literature because we lack the data, and we can't quantify the texts themselves because such a quantification would be meaningless. Though it may readily be agreed, for example, that Max Beerbohm is not so great a novelist as Thomas Hardy, it

will not be so readily agreed how and why he is not so great, or to
what measurable extent and in what qualities: and, of course, as a
comic novelist Beerbohm is not inferior to Hardy at all: and so on.

What we need is an approach to texts that derives from characteristics of texts themselves, and since any attempt at analysis
involves a process of aggregation, this becomes a question of
relating texts to one another. In the next three chapters I shall
attempt to give a historical dimension to the question of how texts
differ from one to another in terms of their value as art and in
terms of their relationship to their audience, and then go on to
discuss ways in which texts can be grouped together for purposes
of comparison.

Part II

5

Second-rateness

No twilight within the courts of the Sun.

I

It has been observed that György Lukácz, in *The Historical Novel*, refers to Balzac forty-two times, Mérimée six times, de Vigny four times, and Dumas, the most successful and influential historical novelist of that or any other period, not once.[1] The refusal to think about certain authors because they are allegedly worthless as literature is almost a house-rule in literary studies. For example, H. T. Swedenberg's *The Theory of Epic in England 1650–1800* (1944), B. Wilkie's *Romantic Poets and the Epic Tradition* (1965), and the two articles on romantic epic by D. M. Foerster in *PMLA* 1954 and 1955 do not even mention the dozens of epic poems published in the period covered. It will be remembered that William of Occam, the medieval academic who established the principle of cutting through the tiresomely irrelevant parts of a subject in order to get to the central issue, was an Englishman. Nowadays he probably would have been a Professor of English Literature with strong views on legitimate and illegitimate fields of interest.

This peculiarly selective methodology is justified by a concentration on only first-rate literature. 'Can that which is most essential and significant in an era truly be represented by "third-raters?"' the friends of first-rateness bleat, though in practice, habit being what it is, the same approach is applied to the second-rate too.[2] But this mode of pursuing excellence means that 'Literature and society become abstractions, phantoms. How, upon these theoretical notions, can one base a concrete sociology?'[3] The answer is, of course, that one can't, and has simply to face the sad fact that a study such as this must oppose itself to the conventions of literary criticism. It was F. W. Bateson who wrote, 'The more closely great Literature is examined, the remoter its connections turn out to be with any sort of history.'[4] Obviously we will have to avoid Bateson's way of looking closely at great Literature.

This does not mean that questions of quality are irrelevant to our purpose but we must be aware, first of all, how even our perception of the first-rate has been distorted. The chimaera of literary excellence and literary significance has led to the later Elizabethan–Jacobean period being studied in an anomalous way, for example. As with other periods, only a part of the literature enjoys much reputation today, and perhaps only a few desperate graduate students read Humfrey Gifford's *A Posie of Gilloflowers* or Michael Drayton's *The Barrons Wars*. Where the later Elizabethan–Jacobean period is unusual is that the literature most intensively studied belongs mostly to the same format: drama. This means not only that special emphasis is given to the centrality of a particular genre, but also that relatively minor practitioners are studied alongside the major. The situation in, say, the Romantic period is very different: there enormously varied types of poetry need to be considered alongside the work of novelists as diverse as Walter Scott, Jane Austen, Thomas Love Peacock, Mary Shelley and John Galt, so that the impression given is of a number of very different types of text written by very different types of author for very different types of audience. The fact that all these major authors were originally working in the same field as numerous minor authors (and usually knew it) tends to be pushed out of view: and the decision as to which authors are major and which minor is left in effect to a committee of professors that never actually meets.

The relative significance of major writers and minor writers would be much less of a problem (and much less interesting) if all major writers were major in exactly the same way: but they are not. Part of the greatness of a great work is that it is great in its own manner. It is not simply that, as Sir Francis Bacon says, there is 'no excellent beauty that hath not some strangeness in the proportion'; we also associate greatness with the kind of genius Wordsworth defined as 'the application of powers to objects on which they have not before been exercised, or the employment of them in such a manner as to produce effects hitherto unknown'.[5] In so far as all examples of art are different from one another, not identical, not alike, then we might suppose all examples of art to be original and novel, but actually we can often find equivalents in different authors' handling of themes, problems, scenarios: originality is the property of not possessing significant equivalents. The areas in which originality may be encountered cannot be defined, because if defined they offer no scope for originality. Characters, *types* of character, setting, dialogue, symbolism: these can only be original in an as yet undefined way, and in relation to something which can only be apprehended at the moment of recognising originality: this, quite simply, is why originality frequently is not recognised.

Because originality involves the expressing of what has never been expressed before, it is always in some sense at the boundary of expression: the boundary between what was previously known and communicable, and what had not been previously recoverable from the psychological dimensions lying beyond. Schelling, in the early nineteenth century, saw the hitherto inexpressible as somehow contributing by its own initiative to the creation of great art:

> not everything in art is the outcome of consciousness . . . an unconscious force must be linked with conscious activity and . . . it is the perfect unanimity and mutual interpenetration of the two which produces the highest art. Works which lack this seal of unconscious science are recognizable by the palpable absence of a life which is autonomous and independent of their creator.[6]

The 'life which is autonomous and independent of their creator' is only an illusion perhaps, but it is the process itself of going beyond the previously expressible which creates the feeling of life, life as a sensation of constantly fresh experience, and this is easily to be distinguished from a merely second-hand report of it.

It is not lack of originality and novelty in any obvious sense which defines the second-rate. Evgenii Zamyatin's novel *We* and Cyril Connolly's short story 'Year Nine' subtract from George Orwell's *1984* some of its traditional status as one of the great defining mythic works of our era, but do not demote it from major league to minor. It was always minor. Tragedy doesn't consist in what the State sets up in the way of clocks striking thirteen and anti-sex movements but in what it does to people, and the sense of people is weaker in *1984* than it is in Orwell's pre-war novels, though even there the attempt always seems to be to blame a third-rate culture for third-rate individualities.[7] Rex Warner's *The Aerodrome* of 1941, is a much more original and subtle dystopia, with its strange eponymous symbol and its evocation of the drab oppressive atmosphere of a nation taken over by military organisations which seem less concerned with fighting a remote enemy than with regimenting an uncertain population in preparation for an even more remote future. But its originality doesn't make it automatically a better novel than *1984*: somehow the myth isn't large enough and the characters aren't alive enough, so it doesn't matter what happens to them: it's a novel about an *us* that we no longer believe is *us*. In the end, both *1984* and *The Aerodrome* suggest that one can succeed in being only minor in as many different ways as one might succeed in being major.

II

I have already cited T. S. Eliot's view of the difference between first- and second-rate writers, with its implied distinction between form and sensibility: 'A great many second-rate poets, in fact, are second-rate just for this reason, that they have not the sensitiveness and consciousness to perceive that they feel differently from the preceding generation, and therefore must use words differently.' This certainly seems applicable to late nineteenth-century artistic movements like Symbolism, Art Nouveau and Jugendstil, which were what the younger generation were revolting against about the time T. S. Eliot came to Europe from America. Art Nouveau and Jugendstil clearly demonstrate a dissatisfaction with earlier artistic forms, combined with an inability to break away from them, while Symbolism, with its sham spirituality and hollow portentousness, combines a worn-out iconography with a worn-out religious tradition.[8] The then fashionable idea of art for art's sake, which implied making a religion of art itself, for want of another, denied the social functions of art, almost as if artists no longer felt capable of performing them. Occasionally, as with Edward Burne-Jones's paintings of long-limbed Girton undergraduates, caught in the trancelike tragic motions of myth, the art of the Symbolist-Art Nouveau-Jugendstil period seems to have distilled some unique statement from the repertoire of superannuated gestures: but perhaps Burne-Jones's strength was in how little of ostensible import he desired to communicate. The complex of movements seems summed up by Arthur Machen's *The Hill of Dreams* (1907) where the obsessed writer writes himself to death in a garret, leaving a pile of manuscripts which, since Machen had nothing for him to say, necessarily turns out to consist of 'illegible hopeless scribblings'. Actually the weakness of Symbolism, Art Nouveau, Jugendstil seems not so much one *either* of form *or* of sensibility, but a connected inability to break through on either front. The fevered reprocessing of outmoded themes gave this period more than a passing resemblance to an earlier transitional phase, Mannerism. Much of the work of Lelio Orsi, 1511–87, could pass as symbolist: his 'San Giorgio' at Capodimonte, Naples, could be the work of Gustave Moreau, and his 'Sacrificio della Messa', with every spare inch of the picture piled with mass-produced-looking crosses, suggests a surrealist-symbolist contemporary of Dali.

The First World War swept away much of the ideological, intellectual cobwebbing: as we now see in retrospect the artistic and iconographic impasse was already dissolving before 1914. Eliot's views, as we may deduce from his career, had a special reference to the English Georgian poets of the pre-1914 generation, who represented the literary counterpart of Art Nouveau. It does not appear that his theory of second-rateness can be applied very generally to other periods, or to other art forms, such as the novel.

Perhaps a better way to approach the question of defining the greatness of great literature would be to ask questions about personal experience and the use made of it. All art is expression, and the thing expressed is personal experience, either external or internal: the congruence between the experience and the expression is also an issue. Henry James refers to this in his Preface to *The Portrait of a Lady* when he discusses the artist's sensibility:

> There is, I think, no more nutritive or suggestive truth in this connexion than that of the perfect dependence of the 'moral' sense of a work of art on the amount of felt life concerned in producing it. The question comes back thus, obviously, to the kind and degree of the artist's prime sensibility. The quality and capacity of that soil, its ability to 'grow' with due freshness and straightness any vision of life, represents, strongly or weakly, the projected morality. That element is but another name for the more or less close connexion of the subject with some mark made on the intelligence, some sincere experience.

That experience may not be transcribed literally in the art, but that's not the point: even in a transposed form it will be recognisable as some sort of authentic human experience, some sort of directly obtained 'vision of life'. And as it would impossible for one human to experience something totally alien to all other sensibilities, it is not simply the recognisability but the level at which the expression of it touches the reader that is important. Though it would be both undemonstrable and irrelevant to say that artists experience things more deeply than other people, it is both demonstrable and, as James argues, relevant that some artists, because of the 'quality and capacity' of their sensibility, experience things more freshly, more creatively than other artists.

And having experienced them, the artist has to express them. He may or may not see it as necessary to give great attention to a suitable form of expression: he may even be like Dylan Thomas who claimed:

'When I experience anything, I experience it as a thing and a word at the same time, both equally amazing'. He told me once that writing the 'Ballad of the Long Legged Bait' had been like carrying a huge armful of words to a table he thought was upstairs, and wondering if he could reach it in time, or if it would still be there.[9]

Or it might not even be altogether clear what these experiences are till the only appropriate mode of expression has been worked out. An attempt at a psychological map, showing all the possible routes linking experience to expression, would only confuse the issue at this stage: every artist who has attempted to discuss the creative process has provided a different account. The relevant point is that while our artist is experiencing and expressing, he is living in a world where other people experience and express. He cannot help but be influenced by these others: even if they are not specifically his subject or proxy subject, they are part of his real life. These influences from spouse, friends, colleagues, the journalists who write his Sunday paper, might be beneficial, assisting him to a greater clarity and focus in his working out of experiences and the problems of expression: or they might provide too many easy answers, too may short-cuts and cop-outs, too many glib phrases and stock attitudes.

It will appear then, that one work of art may be an original expression of the impressions of an original sensibility, another merely an immaculate reworking of experiences, perceived certainly, and recognised by the artist himself, but essentially filtered and predigested for him by those around him or by the other artists whose material he has reworked. Research has been done – e.g. John Livingston Lowes's *The Road to Xanadu* of 1927 – to show

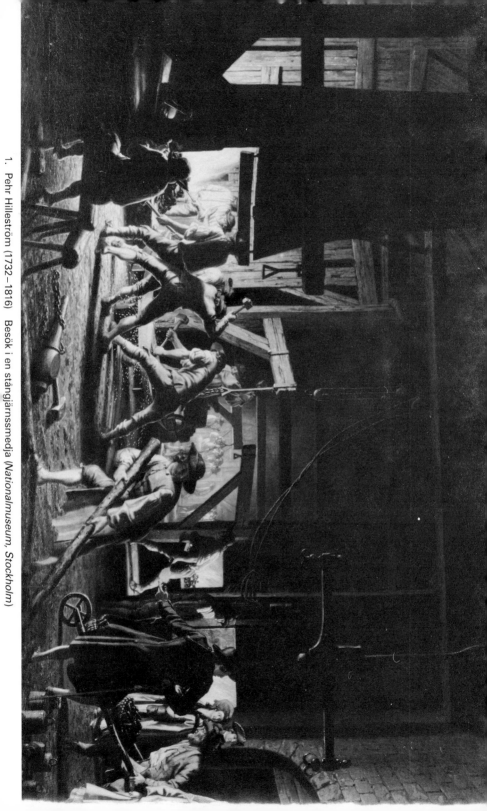

1. Pehr Hilleström (1732—1816) Besök i en stångjärnssmedja (*Nationalmuseum, Stockholm*)

2. Caspar David Friedrich (1774–1840)   Aus der Sächsischen Schweiz bei Dresden
(*Kunsthistorisches Museum, Vienna*)

3. Caspar David Friedrich   Der Wanderer über dem Nebelmeer (*Hamburg Kunsthalle*)

4. Karl Friedrich Schinkel (1781–1841)   Das Felsentor (*Nationalgalerie, Berlin*)

5. Grant Wood (1892–1942)   American Gothic (*Friends of America Collection, courtesy The Art Institute, Chicago*)

6. Charles Holden (1875–1960)   University of London Senate House (*John Topham Picture Libra*
Edenbridge)

7a. Louis David (1743–1825)   Le Serment des Horaces (*Musée de Louvre, Paris*)

7b. Vincenzo Camuccini (1771–1844)   La Morte di Giulio Cesare (*Museo e Gallerie Nazionali di Capodimonte, Naples*)

how a truly creative mind like Coleridge's transmutes other people's prose into poetry: at least as common must be the reverse process whereby fresh, first-hand, shockingly poignant insights are transmuted into tamer, second-hand, more generally palatable conventionalities. To suggest then that all literature should be studied according to completely standard criteria and procedures – 'If one admits that a literary fact is a social fact it is not possible to have degrees of literariness'[10] – would be to overlook differences in actual relationship of social fact to social reality.

Originality in art is, to adopt the language of the last chapter, a category of relationship with the existing hegemony: second-rateness is a kind of parasitic dependence on the first-rate and original. But in seeking to understand society through the reflection of its art, the derivative might be as significant as the original, especially as the writer of original sensibility who manages to express what he genuinely feels will probably have a smaller audience than the man who merely expresses what he has persuaded himself he ought to feel. The derivative might be as significant as the original: but only because they have different types of significance. A book with few readers might provide a shockingly original symbolic understanding of society; a book with many readers which copies the symbolism and spoils it in the copying might also be worth studying because its success shows how many people there are who at least are ready for the symbol in its diluted and more palatable version. Precisely what is first- or second-rate about two such books – the particular breakthrough or breakdown – is precisely what, in each respective case, one should be looking for.

III

In retrospect the second-handers and second-raters are ridiculously easy to detect. Byron is now taken nothing like as seriously as he was a hundred years ago: on the one hundred and fiftieth anniversary of his death, I suggested to the then chairman of the English Faculty at Cambridge that his old university might like to commemorate him with a lecture, and was answered, 'I don't think anyone is much interested in Byron these days.' Nobody even knows what the initials L.E.L. stand for and Mrs Hemans is remembered only for 'The boy stood on the burning deck', which always elicits ironic smiles. Thomas Moore and Sir Henry Taylor are all but forgotten. We read contemporaries' fulsome praise of George Meredith and George Moore with the same bored incredulity as those accounts of brilliant common-room conversations in the reminiscences of Oxbridge dons. The reputation between the wars of hacks like Warwick Deeping and Hugh Walpole now seems barely credible.

And yet perhaps even today the situation is essentially the same as when Henry James wrote, 'There's a hatred of art, there's a hatred of literature – I mean of the genuine kinds. Oh, the shams – *those* they'll swallow by the bucket.'[11] In our day many of the supposedly responsible organs of criticism are involved in the imposture, frequently as criminal accessories, and the faking has become more elaborate, more sophisticated, almost to the point of becoming a type of High Art in itself. And the consensus, so much better educated and more numerous than ever before, has obtained a frightening authority. Even members of English Literature faculties tend to say things like, 'Of course, I don't get a lot of time to read contemporary fiction, though I do try to have a look at the novels that receive favourable full-length reviews in the Sunday papers.' It is regarded as eccentric to say that there is little of lasting value in Saul Bellow and Doris Lessing and even less in Umberto Eco and Anthony Burgess. Afterwards it will be easy enough to say what were the important things that are happening to us – not that I think the post-mortem experts always get this right either – but at the moment we are as unable as any previous generation to comprehend our present and to recognise which authors really speak to and for our times.

We seem to be living in a great hiatus, between the horrors of the World Wars and the horrors that possibly lie ahead, reading in our newspapers of distant massacres and waiting unheroically for the war that will end the world, or for the final lurch towards a livable future. In the meantime, we need to be amused. The great success of Saul Bellow, Doris Lessing, Umberto Eco, and Anthony Burgess certainly doesn't seem due to their being 'the hierophants of an unapprehended inspiration; the mirrors of the gigantic shadows which futurity casts upon the present'.[12] Their great success comes surely from giving us the images we are ready for, and gives the clue to their artistic failure.

One needs to be intensely aware of authors' relationship to their time: it is not simply a question of rectilinear development, a quasi-mechanical intermeshing of influences, but also of lower and higher levels of self-realisation, of selling out, and facing up to issues. All authors start with a passionate love-affair with their talent which sooner or later settles down into a boring middle-class marriage: but there are differences in the original quality of the talent. The achievement of second-rate success is perhaps less a whole biography of secret compromises, a simultaneous progress towards spiritual death and the Nobel Prize, than the result of a kind of innate and unreflecting mediocrity which might have been detectable from the beginning. And the irresistible appeal which mediocrity has for its contemporaries explains why it is the exception rather than the rule to be a success both with one's contemporaries and with posterity.

In English Literature, Shakespeare and Dickens are the two outstanding instances of a success that has endured uninterruptedly since their own day: and all they prove is that contemporary success does not in itself necessarily exclude the possibility of first-rate talent. Both Shakespeare and Dickens were unusually fortunate in being able to write for an audience that was developing and maturing very rapidly during their careers; both developed with, and helped shape their audience; both established their reputations with work that modern critics regard as far from their best: the history plays and early comedies in the case of Shakespeare, *Sketches by Boz* and *Pickwick Papers* in the case of Dickens. That they commanded an audience for their best work was at least partly because they had already established their audience and helped educate it.

The period does not create the genius of the brilliant writer, for all that it does affect the way the genius is expressed, but it *does* create the possibility of fortuitous meetings between a particular kind of audience and a particular stamp of creative mind. There are plenty of instances of authors who have been less lucky than Shakespeare and Dickens: authors like William Blake, John Keats, and Gerard Manley Hopkins who achieved reputation posthumously, or like William Wordsworth and Thomas Hardy late in life, or had a modest reputation which then declined dramatically, like John Ford or Philip Massinger or John Donne, or even, in extreme cases, slipped entirely out of view for centuries, like William Langland and the author of *Gawain and the Green Knight* or, more recently, Thomas Traherne.

This uncertain process of submersion and resurfacing – we could call it Cambridge Roulette – is not likely to serve the present age very well. The involvement of academe with publishing, professional authorship and reviewing is now so close, and the same people who tut-tut at Keats's neglect by his contemporaries and sneer at the prejudices that condemned *Jude the Obscure*, hail novels like *The History Man* and *Stepping Westward* with such enthusiasm that it is not at all obvious that the really serious literature of our time will receive any notice. Whatever happened to writers of former times, in the present busy and overmobilised century there is undoubtedly great truth in Somerset Maugham's claim that

> posterity makes its choice not from among the unknown writers of a period, but from among the known. It may be that some great masterpiece which deserves immortality has fallen stillborn from the press, but posterity will never hear of it; it may be that posterity will scrap all the best-sellers of our own day, but it is among them that it must choose. (*Cakes and Ale*, chap. 11)

Success, then, is not the same as enduring significance, though it might be a source of confusion as to what is truly and enduringly significant. Enduring significance, of course, is irrelevant to the historian of culture: he is looking merely for significance relative to the period being studied, and even those texts which allegedly transcend their period belong to their own time and only coincidentally to posterity. So, in the end, the historian of culture has to make his own choices with his own criteria, though he will to some extent be assisted by the consensus of academic criticism in distinguishing mere commercial successes from the works which embody an original and creative view of their times.

But this whole issue of the relationship between commercial and artistic success raises the question of the literary audience: and it is to this subject that we will now turn.

6

The Audience and the Artist

By the light of the Moon he beholdeth God's creatures of the great calm.

I

In the last chapter I was talking about books mainly as things written: but no less important is the question of books as things read. Literature, if shaped and determined by the pressure of society, does not, when formed, soar off into the empyrean and thereafter cease to belong to society. It remains part of its world, part of the mechanism of shaping and determination, and the way in which we are able to perceive this mechanism is itself shaped and determined by the life that books have once they come out of the private world of the author and become part of the shared experience of his audience. Indeed the distinction between the private world of the author and the shared experience of his audience may sometimes be an unhelpful one because of the intimacy of the relationship which links author and audience together.

Another way of putting it would be to say that the author's relationship to his audience is a part of the even larger and more pervasive issue of the author's position within the prevailing hegemony: but even if it is one of the parts of the larger problem which we can more easily focus on, that does not mean that a clear picture can readily be arrived at. Nothing shows up the retardedness of Literary History so much as the state of knowledge, or ignorance, about literary audiences. The topic is of central interest to sociologists of literature but the same theoretical generalisations have been rehashed to the point of cliché. Nevertheless, some interesting work has been done on the Continent on specific aspects of the problem of literature in its different economic relationships.[1] For England, on the other hand, there is almost nothing: the standard work on the nineteenth century is still R. D. Altick's

The English Common Reader of 1957, which is based unduly on
unreliable published sources and which, despite chapters on education, Mechanics' Institutes, 'The Self-Made Reader' and so on,
makes no pretence of trying to establish a systematic typology of
the nineteenth-century reading public, or even the lower echelons
of it.

II

There are several problematics but the importance of the audience
may be examined from two angles. First, there is the artist-within-
his-audience. A writer does not assimilate the objective conditions
of his time directly, but through a distorting medium which consists partly of the ideas he lives amongst and the books he has
himself read, partly of his own notion of his relationship to the
people around him from amongst whom he might expect to find
his readers. I have already mentioned the real world the author
lives in as a potential influence on the genuineness and originality
of his work, but apart from questions of quality, the author's
general cultural environment necessarily determines much of the
linguistic and personal detail within his work. Included in this
general cultural environment are the author's own literary antecedents, but though authors influence one another in their writing
and though one author's relationship to the external world may
help us understand that of another, we should beware of conflat-
ing the two processes. For example, Q. D. Leavis says in connection with Dickens:

> George Eliot, writing *Middlemarch* a generation after, was able to
> profit by Dickens's achievement in ultimately knitting together a
> large reading public at least willing if not eager to tackle a long
> novel demanding serious and sustained attention; without his
> work she could not have made a fortune by writing novels to
> please herself only.[2]

Yet surely Charlotte Brontë and Bulwer Lytton and Thackeray, and
before them Walter Scott, had laboured just as hard, if not as
nobly, to nurture the same reading public, and Anthony Trollope
and George Meredith seem to have inherited it alongside George
Eliot. Great writers do not hand torches to one another on a person
to person basis like competitors in a relay race: George Eliot

belonged to a moment impregnated with a mass of ideas and traditions which are impossible to particularise and which cannot simply be reduced to the influence of the author of *Oliver Twist*.

Yet through all the babble of multitudinous voices, writing is a kind of dialogue. The author addresses himself directly to his audience, like a prophet speaking to his people. The people answer, and if encouraged the prophet speaks again. If he is a certain type of prophet he may even respond to what he had heard. But of course this talk of dialogue is only a metaphor: author and audience are not two people in a room together. The actual intercourse of author and audience may vary from direct physical confrontation to something as remote and dislocated as a spiritualist communication from beyond the grave.

The particularly striking thing about Shakespeare and the other playwrights of his time is, not simply that they had an extremely demanding and variegated audience, but that they were in almost direct contact with the whole of it. Writing for a single audience and a single acting company, with little hope of being staged anywhere else, they actually observed in the theatre how their entire audience responded to their work, and doubtless their personal impressions were supplemented by the comments of the actors who interpreted their scripts and with whom they also had much closer and more equal relationships than later playwrights – for later actor-playwrights were actor-managers whose relationship to the other actors was that of employer. Nothing like this degree of intimate exposure to what was effectively a mass audience was achieved again until the rock stars of the 1950s onwards.

At the other extreme there have been authors living in retirement, perhaps professing disillusion and disgust at the superficiality of their contemporaries. Some such have had an uncanny knack for hitting their contemporaries' taste; like Thomas Gray with his *Elegy Written in a Country Churchyard*, and W. N. P. Barbellion whose *Journal of a Disappointed Man* had a certain vogue on its publication in 1919 (though it went through fewer editions than his best-selling study of the bed-bug). But the retirement usually turns out on examination to have been exaggerated, and it is very doubtful if anyone's work has ever genuinely benefited from cutting oneself off in this way. It is noteworthy how many of the very greatest writers resist artistic isolation, reach out towards the world of their day with a passionate commitment, and unsatisfied by artistic success also set themselves up as social theorists, social commentators: Dante established the pattern; in England, there were Milton, Wordsworth, Shelley, Dickens, D. H. Lawrence; the outstanding exceptions were Shakespeare, who evidently got as close to his public as he wanted, and Goethe, who found in his career as the Duke of Saxe-Weimar's court genius either a practical substitute for social conviction or an incentive to avoid it.

The artist face to face with his audience, and the artist in retirement are the two extremes: in between there is the whole range of degrees of involvement, engagement, sympathy, connected not simply with what the writer actually does in life when not writing, but with his upbringing, his education, his tastes, even his health. And it is not enough to distinguish the degree to which the author has his audience before him: there are different audiences, there is the writer's own personal perception of his particular audience, his attitude to his audience, even the fact that some writers, even perhaps Shakespeare, have been prepared to write to different audiences.[3] All these colour the author's approaches to his subjects and when we try to equate literature and society we will need to have a pretty specific sense of the writer's particular position.

We also need a pretty specific sense of the audience. It may be that it is the audience side of the artist–audience symbiosis which explains why some countries in some centuries seem to produce geniuses by the score, and at other times none at all. If one believes that great artists and writers are born, not made, their uneven distribution over time and place may be explained by sunspots, or the Divine Plan, or statistical randomness, but I believe that, while talent is an accident of birth and upbringing, a quite private miracle, the realisation of talent, its fulfilment in works of original achievement, is a social phenomenon, explicable in terms of the features of society. Italy, after a fourteenth-century peak, maintained a high literary level till the time of Tasso, but there followed three hundred years of really not very much.[4] (Similarly, in painting and drawing, after Piranesi there were at least a hundred years in which Italy was an artistic Nowhere. The importance of the Italian contribution to physics, physiology etc. in the same period makes this literary and artistic slump all the more striking.) It seems that for up to three hundred years, Italian writers simply lacked a motive to burst out of traditional or (with Foscolo and Manzoni) borrowed forms. It surely cannot be a coincidence that Italy during the same period was a society with a middle class in profound stagnation, consistently lacking a rôle beyond that of consumption. Then, after the Risorgimento, we find a new liberation of energy, first, very very crudely, d'Annunzio inflating a meagre talent till it burst, then Pirandello, Futurism (*and* Fascism), Montale, the cinema of Visconti and Pasolini and Fellini: we may see in the august figure of Benedetto Croce, on the other hand, the vast prestige still available to a philosopher of second-rate philosophy, a creator after the old style of nothing. Something similar seems to have happened in Spain after the era of Cervantes, Calderon and Lope. This is obviously an immensely complex phenomenon: I only mean to suggest here that probably the decadence of an audience mediates between the decadence of a society and the decadence of its literature.

III

The study of the artist-within-his-audience focuses ultimately on artists as individuals or groups of individuals; to really understand audiences we must attempt to study literature as a social activity involving readers rather than writers. In other words, we must study the audience-in-itself. The importance of the audience-in-itself is that literature reflects not the objective realities of the past but its subjective realities, and in order to reconstruct the subjective reality of an epoch we need to reconstruct its entire mental world. One of the larger components of this world, and a component where the subjective appears as the objective, is the literary audience, or one should rather say, literary audiences.

The audience-in-itself is not merely one of the more crucial indexes of the subjective reality of past periods, it provides a kind of laboratory control with which to check information about other types of social activity, like politics or religion. Literary taste is much more responsive to new developments than religious belief or political doctrine, both of which, even in our democratic era, present themselves behind a bodyguard of professional vested interests organised over the years and committed to maintaining continuity of attitudes. It is difficult to believe, for example, that the market forces of supply and demand operate freely and with pristine immediacy in politics when it is so difficult to launch a new political party with any real prospect of achieving power. In any case, it is only comparatively recently that political participation has been on as wide a basis as book-reading or play-going: in

Shakespeare's day politics, in a recognisable sense, was confined
to a minority and had only a limited influence on public policy
which, itself, dealt with a rather narrower range of public affairs
than is the case now. Moreover, the literary audience is simply
different from other human aggregates within a society. The aggregates overlap, of course, and it may be illuminating to see that the
population which re-elected Eisenhower was soon afterwards
avidly reading *Peyton Place*, that the population which elected
Thatcher was queueing up for *The Country Diary of an Edwardian
Lady*. Just as we need more than one eye to judge distance, we
need to study more than one social aggregate in order to understand the complex mechanisms of human community.

The reconstruction of the literary audience obviously requires
different data and involves different problems from the reconstruction of other social aggregates. With regard to the problems,
twentieth-century experience, as so often, is rather misleading.
Financially and educationally almost the entire European population of today has equal access to books: the financial and educational divisions which are relevant to the analysis of the literary
audiences of the past no longer operate: yet the audience has not
become more uniform but is mixed and anomalous as never before. At the same time, the social statistics for typological analysis
of the components of society in their various social rôles – Tory
voter – wife-beater – heroin addict – holiday-maker in Benidorm –
Oxbridge undergraduate – engine-driver – are much more detailed
than for previous periods. There is even, in terms of bulk, more
information known about modern audiences because some publishers conduct market research, though the results often remain
confidential and pertain only to certain categories of popular literature: it remains true therefore that today the reading public is more
difficult to study than other social aggregates. But the situation
reverses itself as soon as one reaches back to the nineteenth
century; progressing backward decade by decade the social statistics become less and less available, till we reach the 1801 census
prior to which there are virtually none at all; so that it is easier to
study readership in the past than almost any other kind of social
activity.

The most important source for the study of readership is books.
Not just a random selection of texts favoured by English Faculties,
not just a couple of novels or a play which *somehow* seem to give an
especially cogent account of the intellectual milieu they describe,

but *all* the books read at a certain period. This is why we have an unusually comprehensive picture of the Elizabethan audience: English Faculties have been prepared to take *all* the books of the period as worthy of at least *some* attention.

Not that it will be necessary to give all books the same amount of attention. There is the question of quality which I have discussed in the previous chapter. There is also the question of quantity. The number of copies sold indicates the number of readers: even if we don't know how many readers read each book, we can probably assume that a book which sells a thousand copies has proportionately more readers than one which sells a hundred. But there is often only patchy and uncertain data available on the number of copies sold of individual titles in the nineteenth century: the destruction of several publishers' offices during the London Blitz means that certain lacunae will never be filled. For the period prior to 1800 it is difficult to find any overall numbers at all. One alternative would be to count the number of editions, but editions *c.*1800 might vary from 500 to 6,000 copies, though 1,000 was usual: to object, as some critics do, that variations in the size of editions totally invalidates the exercise of counting them, even though one does not have a better solution, suggests a desire not to know that wretched poetasters frequently had larger audiences than those we call major poets.[5] To find the number of editions of English books, the British Library Catalogue and the National Union Catalog may be used, but even for the 1800s they lack numerous titles. The first autobiography to describe working-class conditions during the Industrial Revolution, *Truths No.1, or The Memoirs of Charles Whetstone, or an exposition of the Oppression and Cruelty Exercised in the Trades and Manufactures of Great Britain* (Derby 1807), survives in a unique copy in Derby Public Library. It is rather dull, apart from some stock diatribes against Methodism, and not very informative: were all the other copies read to pieces or simply thrown away in disgust? Even more intriguing is Sophia Sutton Cooke's *Memoirs*, published in four volumes in 1829, which is actually a novel about being married to one of the professional gamblers who proliferated during the gaming epidemic of the 1800s. It is a harrowing account of an unhappy marriage that should be a key text in the history of feminist consciousness: volumes one and two may be inspected in the William Salt Library, a charming institution in Stafford: volumes three and four seem to have sunk without trace, along with all the other copies and all the women who originally purchased them. If we go further back the gaps in the holdings of the great research libraries become progressively more frequent: the British Library, for example, is estimated to hold only 30 per cent of titles published in Britain in the eighteenth century, and it is quite possible that books once outstandingly popular *c.*1600 may have totally disappeared, or survive only as unique examples in little-known collections.[6]

In any case mere numbers and copies provide only a basic framework of reference. The information in the books requires decoding. It cannot usually be assumed, to begin with, that the readers of the book will belong to the same social group as the characters in it. Hospital novels written by doctors are not intended to be read by doctors (unlike university novels by academics which are favourite reading *particularly* amongst academics). There is indeed a tradition of Romantic fiction that has endured at least three hundred years in which the sentimental affairs of the rich, gifted and glamorous are presented as a form of escapism for readers evidently neither gifted nor glamorous, and marketed at a price accessible to the far-from-rich. As this example itself suggests, the key to interpreting readers by their books is the value systems embodied in the books: not so much what is said or how it is said, but more why anyone should be interested in what is said. The bawdiness of Restoration comedy indicates, not simply a widespread reaction against the repressive Puritanism of the Commonwealth, but the hysteria of a newly reassembled *beau monde*, reestablishing fashionable society after more than a decade of exile or rustication: the adolescent smuttiness is not the human libido's revenging itself on years of sexual repression but much more precisely one lot of human libidos revenging themselves on another lot of human beings: the courtiers' revenge for the sober citizens' support of the anti-Royalist cause during the Civil War and Commonwealth. The tradition of pastoral, which appeared in the sixteenth century and flourished again in the eighteenth, indicates not simply the enduring appeal of country life, but a mainly urban-oriented social élite fantasising that their lives would be somehow more authentic and intense if they were penniless and unable to go to town for the winter season. And so on, through a whole gamut of day-dreams indulged, fears exorcised and prejudices worked off.

It is only in the last hundred years or so, with the vast improvement of living standards and expectations in western society, that there has developed a mass readership which is essentially interested in *itself*, more or less as it really is, as a subject. One can trace the development from Dickens, with his characters taken from a particularly wide range of social levels and his protagonists often having an extremely anomalous class status: the poor miraculously become rich, the genteel become destitute, – almost none of them not assimilable, in the course of either upward or downward mobility, to the social class of the average reader. By the time one arrives at H. G. Wells's *Ann Veronica* and *Kipps*, the protagonists are solidly, even complacently, placed in the suburban background they share with their creator and their audience. This was also very strikingly the case with the successful novelists of the 1950s, Kingsley Amis, John Wain, John Braine. Successive (ephemeral) nostalgia revivals in the 1970s and 1980s focused on earlier periods of suburban culture, neatly combining a restrained escapism into a recognisable, familiar but nevertheless lost past, with a reaffirmation of the *average* way of life of the average citizen-reader. It may not be totally without significance that one of the early classics of this brand of nostalgia, *Coming Up For Air*, is by George Orwell, who had to work so awfully hard not to appear an old Etonian ex-officer.[7]

If, in our attempts to discover readers in the texts, we ask ourselves what kind of person would have wanted to read such and such a book when it first appeared, we may come up with some unexpected answers. A very great deal of the most popular early nineteenth-century verse was liberal-progressive in political complexion. Thomas Campbell's *The Pleasures of Hope*:

> Hope, for a season, bade the world farewell
> And freedom shriek'd – as Kosciusko fell!

came out in 1799, at a time when there were still political reformers held without trial in English gaols and many public houses displayed notices declaring *No Jacobins Here*. The son of a Virginia merchant, brought up in a rather Whiggish climate in Glasgow, Campbell had elder brothers who had emigrated to the United States. During his visit to Germany, in 1800, he associated with United Irish exiles in Hamburg (hence his once well-known poem *The Exile of Erin*) and wrote admiringly of the French army as 'the conquerors of Lodi and Marengo'. His associates were perhaps more radical than his verse. In *The Pleasures of Hope* he attacked, in paroxysms of breathless stodge, the partitioners of Poland (they were the ones who felled Kosciusko), slavery, and the British in India; but even the last was a fairly safe subject, and much of his rhetoric seems rather general:

> Departed spirits of the mightly dead!
> Ye that at Marathon and Leuctra bled!
> Friends of the world! restore your swords to man,
> Fight in his sacred cause, and lead the van!
> Yet for Sarmatia's tears of blood atone,
> And make her arm puissant as your own!
> Oh! once again to Freedom's cause return
> The patriot Tell – the Bruce of Bannockburn!

Still, there couldn't have been much doubt as to where his sympathies lay. The same liberal political line was evident in the poetry of Thomas Moore – a United Irish suspect in 1798 – and of Lord Byron. These two, though not the sentimentally prudish Campbell, also produced lyric poetry of a distinctly titillating nature:

> Why that little wanton blushing
> Glancing eye, and bosom flushing?
> Flushing warm and wildly glancing,
> All is lovely, all entrancing.
>   (Moore, *Sweet Seducer*)

Yet despite the working-class unrest which finally climaxed with Peterloo in 1819, and in spite of fashionable sympathy with the victims of oppression in distant countries, and even in Ireland, the Britain of Byron and Moore's heyday was a staunchly conservative society, with an increasingly solidly entrenched Tory government and a parliamentary opposition that was almost as reactionary. And, despite sexual scandals in high places, it was also the period of the Evangelical Movement's efforts to raise the moral tone of society, the period of expurgated Shakespeares, of criticisms of the sexual explicitness of Fielding and Hogarth, of Coleridge's immortal remark:

Let me ask, who now will venture to read a number of the *Spectator*, or of the *Tatler*, to his wife and daughters, without first examining it to make sure that it contains no word which might,

in our day, offend the delicacy of female ears, and shock femi-
nine susceptibility?[8]

It seems strange that, in such a moral climate, Thomas Moore
should have become rich by teaching 'all the boarding-school girls
and other misses of the present day to screech indecency as well as
political reformation'.[9]

The explanation is, I think, that Moore's readers, and Campbell's and Byron's, came from a different section of society from
those who determined the overall political complexion of society:
the sexual titillation, the commonplace libertarian politics, the
enthusiasm and escapism are all indicative of a poetry that was
mainly read by *young* people. Indeed, it is arguable that most
people do most of the reading they ever do in their lives during
their tens and twenties. These young readers of the 1800s would
doubtless have included many of the 'sickly tradesmen and en-
amoured apprentices' sneered at by the *Edinburgh Review*: first- or
second-generation migrants to Britain's growing cities, still dis-
orientated by the stimulus and trauma of living in unfamiliar
environments: but I think the main point is that they were simply a
younger generation partly in revolt against their elders.[10] A little
earlier some of them would have joined reform societies: many of
the leaders of the London Corresponding Society had been in
their mid-twenties, and William Hone had joined when he was 16:
somewhat later these youngsters resurface in the pages of Dickens,
as dissatisfied lawyers' clerks like Dick Swiveller or William Guppy,
or frustrated primary school teachers like Bradley Headstone, or
simply the commercial gentlemen of Todgers's in *Martin Chuzzlewit*.
It is surely no accident that Chatterton, who killed himself at 18,
posthumously achieved almost mythic status and that some of the
great reputations of the day were poets who had died exception-
ally young – Thomas Dermody, Henry Kirke White – a little later
John Keats was to steal this niche – or, even more to the point,
poets who gave up writing verse while still young in order to
concentrate on more adult pursuits: Bryan Waller Procter, Thomas
Dale, Henry Hart Milman, George Croly, Leigh Hunt: even perhaps Coleridge.[11]

If one likes one can see this as an example of an emergent
element within the pattern of hegemony, though it would perhaps
be too crude and reductive to argue too specifically in terms of a
new fraction and a new fractional consciousness. Even though it is

surely more than a coincidence that the teenagers who were enraptured by Byron *c.*1814 were responsible citizens in mid-career during the reforming 1830s, the only firm point I wish to make here is that the early nineteenth-century audience for poetry shows up in especially clear relief only because of a discrepancy with what appears to have been the dominant tone of the times. We cannot always rely on such discrepancies being evident. In any case, the audience for particular kinds of poetry is only part of the total sum of audiences in a period, and even if one proposes to understand an audience through its reading, it will obviously not be easy to use reading material to *define* an audience.

IV

Evidently there is a number and variety of different audiences. One could perhaps distinguish between metropolitan social élite – metropolitan bourgeois – provincial bourgeois – metropolitan proletariat – metropolitan intellectual – sectarian – rural popular, and so on: but some periods seem to demand more categories than these, and some fewer. And as a society changes over time its components change qualitatively as well as quantitatively. The metropolitan bourgeois of 1600 was just as bourgeois as that of 1900 – that is, its relationship, in certain fundamental terms, to the means of production and to other socio-economic groups was essentially the same – but it was much smaller, differently educated, and hardly as metropolitan in the sense in which the term might have been understood in 1900. In the same way, the phrases *the economy in 1600* and *the economy in 1900* use the word economy in exactly the same lexical sense but refer to very different entities. We need to give our categories some sort of historical dimension: after all we are talking about comparing art produced over a period of centuries with a society changing over a period of centuries.

The best paradigm of the changing *social* position and relationships of an audience over time is provided by popular culture. It is difficult to say what popular culture *is* – that is part of the process of change in question – but easy to say what it *was*. Seven hundred years ago the vast majority of people in England (and everywhere else) lived in very similar conditions and were engaged in similar work – agriculture. They had their local varieties of music and their local legends and their local customs which, being largely unrecorded, can now scarcely be studied in any comprehensive way.

The music and customs and legends obviously had an origin in the past, but these origins had been lost to memory, or subsumed in legend. The traditions were entirely oral, and regional variations were mainly the result of geography or of long-forgotten history. That was what popular culture was a long time ago. But from the fifteenth century onwards this vast majority of the population which lived by the sweat of its brow began to lose its uniformity: new types of employment flourished, towns ceased to be mere coagulations of the countryside or the back quarters of palaces, and the invention of printing and the spread of literacy meant that a larger part of popular culture came to comprise elements that have been preserved to us. Then, in the later nineteenth century and, much more, in the twentieth century, the working classes became mobile, subdivided, self-assertive and, above all, affluent to a degree hitherto inconceivable. With their new spending power, their appetite for entertainment became the target for massive commercial exploitation, while the technological changes which had made possible their affluence also, after 1900, brought into being new forms of entertainment. Even seven hundred years ago local legends and rituals probably consisted largely of the infinitely decayed remnants of the customs and artistic traditions of once tightly organised colonial communities, petty aristocratic courts, locally established religious cults, and so on. At any rate, as far back as there is available material to reconstruct specific components of folk-culture, these components turn out to have been dependent on the structure of political domination. Miracle plays, for instance, were composed by educated persons, priests or schoolmasters, and organised by guilds or by the town authorities. The idea that ballads were somehow written corporately by *das Volk* established itself in the early nineteenth century as a result of the influence of the brothers Grimm and belongs to the Romantic tradition of *völkisch*-ness. This idea of their popular origin was strengthened by the fact that they were in many cases *recovered* from an oral tradition. But the surviving ones seem to date from the fifteenth century or later, and were mostly disseminated in printed broadsides as soon as they were composed, i.e. their wide currency relates not to centuries of diffusion but to the power of the commercial press. Thus in both cases, miracle plays and ballads, the literature shows the influence of social and economic structuring just as much as élite literary genres. Another characteristic development was the taking of obsolete elements of the

culture of the dominating classes and reworking them into simpli-
fied forms such as the chapbook narratives of Guy of Warwick and
Bevis of Hampton. The dependent relationship with the dominant
culture was underlined by the fact that before children's books
became common in the eighteenth century, children of the dominant classes read a great deal of material intended for the lower
classes: Coleridge, for example, read Tom Hickathrift, Jack the
Giant Killer, etc. in his aunt's '*every-thing*' shop at Crediton as a
child.[12] Thus dominant culture could be said to *include* lower class
culture.

Only very occasionally did members of the lowest classes man-
age to reassemble this reach-me-down culture into something
distinctively new and their own. *Pilgrim's Progress* is perhaps the
outstanding instance, and its historic moment is of great importance in explaining why it was possible. The book was written by a
member of an oppressed, dominated class which, for several years
during the English Revolution, saw the system of oppression
collapsing overhead. *Pilgrim's Progress* is the expression of a subordinate class which has suddenly become vocal and self-confident:
it is an eschatological Christian counterpart of the Levellers' arguments in the Putney Debates, but from an even lower social
standpoint. The Bible taught men like Bunyan how to speak and
write, but it was the Civil War and particularly the endless dis-
cussions by campfires and in bivouacs amongst the young men
drawn from plough and work-bench to fight for Parliament, which
first gave men like Bunyan the opportunity to express themselves.[13] After the Restoration the system of repression was re-
erected – Bunyan himself spent twelve years in Bedford gaol – and
when, late in the eighteenth century, men of Bunyan's class began
to speak out again they were usually much less accustomed to
open debate with their social equals, but much more familiar with
a vastly wider range of books than the Bible-bound Bunyan, so that
they were either unable to find an audience to address themselves
to, like William Blake, or else mimicked the style of their social
superiors, like Alexander Richmond, whose *Narrative of the Conditions of the Manufacturing Population* (1825) begins by referring to
Adam Smith and ends with a quotation from Oliver Goldsmith.[14]

At a time when the working classes were poor, and communications were slow and expensive, those who made a career of
catering for working-class entertainment needs were necessarily
poor themselves, and were therefore recruited from the same

economic level as their customers, and suffered from the same limitations of intellectual opportunity. Religion – especially Evangelicalism after 1790 – gave the richer and more privileged an incentive to provide the plebs with cultural nourishment in the form of tracts (such as those disseminated by Hannah More), inculcating obedience to squires and hatred of foreign ideas, and sentimental novelettes such as the Revd Legh Richmond's *The Diaryman's Daughter*, of which 2 million copies were printed between 1810 and 1829.[15] These were not simply crude alien impositions gratefully accepted by the forelock-tugging poor for use as draught blocks and chair stuffing; it is evident that they appealed to many working-class readers and reinforced the dependent and traditional tendency of working-class culture. George Eliot's village pundits in *Silas Marner* are surely true to life, but their conversation often sounds as if it was written by Hannah More.

But as the nineteenth century progressed, the amounts of money to be made from catering for working-class tastes increased, and the do-gooders began to be shouldered out by increasingly sophisticated professional operators. George W. M. Reynolds, a leading practitioner of new sales techniques such as publication of longer works for the working-class market in cheap serial parts, and author of various rip-offs of *Pickwick Papers* and later of *The Mysteries of London* (1846–8), had been at Sandhurst, had left the army on inheriting a smallish fortune, and had begun his career as an author writing for his own class. James Rymer, author of the best-selling cheap format trash-novels *Ada the Betrayed* (1845) and *Varney the Vampire* (1846), had originally been a civil engineer and technical draughtsman, and had tried to cater for a bourgeois market by founding the unsuccessful *The Queen's Magazine*.[16]

Today, the sums of money to be earnt from the mass market make it problematical whether working-class entertainers are themselves working class or merely *nouveau riche*. And with the commercialisation of culture it is now unclear how far the market creates the goods or the goods, judiciously publicised, create the market. Films, pop records, even books, often establish themselves successfully without exceptional publicity whereas especially elaborate publicity campaigns occasionally flop. Perhaps in the end advertising merely endorses existing tastes.[17] In any case, distinctions in terms of economic class are now much less crucial in establishing a market than cultural and educational differences: *Coronation Street* is no more watched exclusively by the wives of

manual workers than are Open University broadcasts exclusively
by the wives of academics and librarians. Popular culture has
become less homogeneous. Or, to put it another way, popular
culture was once essentially proletarian culture and only incidentally
non-élite culture, whereas now it is essentially non-élite culture and
only incidentally, and intermittently, proletarian culture.

One may if one wishes distinguish between a folk culture in the
past and a mass culture in the twentieth century. But just as the
term folk culture is used by those who wish to deny the pervasive-
ness of economic and political power structures in the good old
days, so the term mass culture is employed by those who wish to
present as a uniform aggregate what is in reality a vast diversity of
elements. And while some of these elements are derivative and
mindlessly traditional – Mills & Boon novels might be instanced –
others are not.[18] Perhaps all the components of popular culture
which belong to traditional genres and embody an explicit or
implicit loyalty to traditional values tend to be inferior imitations of
something that was original and vital a long time ago. But not all
popular culture is aridly formulaic, and with the democratisation
of society in the present century it may be that it is in the area of
popular culture that we may expect to find the truly creative and
responsive art which will be the present period's most important
cultural bequest to the future. Dynamic forms which have thrived
on mass-marketing and freedom from the deadening influence of
academically respectable artistic tradition include rock music and
science fiction. Not that I mean to suggest that *all* rock music and
all science fiction represent significant artistic achievement: the
sheer multiplicity of examples makes one think much more of a
cultural mass movement than of individual practitioners and individual works, and it seems difficult, perhaps unprofitable, to try to
pick out masterpieces. But I shall return to rock music and science
fiction later.

V

Popular culture was once the culture of the economically subordinated majority: now it is definable as the culture of those unap-
preciative of *real* culture, the culture of so-called cultured people.
Either way popular culture is defined in terms of its inferiority to
some other level of culture. If cultures and audiences coexist, they
do not coexist as equals.

It will be obvious that some audiences will be composed of people who employ or govern the members of other audiences (though this is perhaps less true now than it used to be); and a political dominance may be observable, obscurely but inescapably, in some sort of cultural dominance. This is precisely the phenomenon which Gramsci began to analyse by means of his concept of hegemony (see Chapter 4). But though *hegemony* helps us to describe the relationship of the subordinate sectors of society to the ruling class, it does not help us to identify the ruling class. Since the demise of feudalism (an event which refuses to be located more precisely than somewhere between the outbreak of the Black Death in 1348 and the execution of Charles I three centuries later), it has actually been rather difficult to show which economic class in Britain has been the dominant political class: thus while it has been asserted that nineteenth-century society was a period of bourgeois hegemony, the available tax statistics show that in the early years of the century only about 28 per cent of income in the over £2,000 per annum tax bracket was enjoyed by businessmen. Moreover, a reading of Disraeli or Trollope suggests irresistibly that professional politicians and post office officials believed that the country was still dominated politically by an active and energetic landed aristocracy. Even Richard Cobden, tribune of the emergent middle classes, thought the same, writing in 1858: 'During my experience the higher classes never stood so high in relative social and political rank compared with the other classes as at present. The middle classes have been content with the very crumbs from their table.'[19] That these higher classes had somehow managed to be taught to think bourgeois seems unlikely in view of all anti-bourgeois thinking being published from Coleridge and Carlyle onwards.

Poulantzas's concept of the power-blocs (see Chapter 4) seems much more plausible than the notion of the hegemony of a single, essentially uniform class. But if we think in terms of a pyramid-like arrangement of various audiences, arranged according to their relationship, in hegemonic terms, to a number of dominant fractions in the power-bloc at the apex, we will encumber ourselves with a model of extreme complexity, incorporating far too many sociological components about which we have far too little evidence, and almost useless for analysing any specific text–audience relationship.

Another strategy – at first glance perhaps rather an unpromising one – would be to concentrate initially on particular audiences for particular works, or at least genres, and to attempt to reintegrate these different audiences with the social totality only once we have understood something about them in the light of their involvement with their defining literary category. Dealing with specific genres actually works rather well for many non-literary genres: only rich aristocratic patrons could afford heroic landscape paintings, only religious institutions would want large religious canvases: the eighteenth-century conversation piece was a bourgeois form, and so on. In the case of literature, we may confuse ourselves a little with the perception that a particular kind of novel might suit people who like a particular kind of play – always supposing they live near enough to a theatre – but I think it best to think in terms of a particular audience for a particular genre, because the problem of the rise and fall of genres points to a theory of audience that will be most useful to us.

VI

The rise of the bourgeois realistic novel has been commemorated in Ian Watt's somewhat tendentiously entitled *The Rise of the Novel* (1957), but other genres have risen just as noticeably, and fallen. Drama rose in fifth-century BC Athens and again in sixteenth-century England and Spain; and considering how down it was practically everywhere by the mid-nineteenth century, it evidently rose for at least the third time from Ibsen onwards. The impact of *Look Back in Anger*, in England at least, suggests a tendency towards lesser up and down oscillations that may not deserve to be called death and rebirth. The *belles lettres* type of essay seems to have had it in the last fifty years, put out of business by the academic article. Poetry still seemed alive and strong up until the middle of this century; that it is a still living force today seems rather a matter of shibboleth than of self-evident fact. At any rate, really long poems, with their leisurely pace, no longer seem at all possible. Film and television may not be literature, but they involve writing, and they have very definitely risen.

This process of rise and fall obviously has a great deal to do with the nature of audiences and with structural aspects of the organisational side of communications. The relation of audience, organisational change and art can be studied, at a less than life and death level, in the history of the best documented of the older genres, drama. A quick look at the history of the London stage in the nineteenth century will show what I mean.

In the early nineteenth century, London's patent theatres, which had an official monopoly of serious drama, were in financial difficulties. Fashionable audiences were staying away; this contributed to a decline in the prestige of play-writing at a time when the income of dramatists was shrinking relative to that of novelists and poets. But the number of new non-patent theatres being opened showed that there *was* an audience of some sort, if only a lower class one. Then, after 1850, the theatre came back into fashion, and there was more money to be made from serious drama. The lower class audience could be priced out. The growth of London and the new railway networks which brought provincial playgoers within reach of the West End were factors here. The dependence on a much larger potential audience is shown by the increase in the number of performances of individual plays. In the 1800s, the repertoire changed very quickly indeed; in the 1850s, fifteen productions ran to over a hundred performances (the most was 150); in the 1860s, forty-five ran to over a hundred performances (the most 407); in the 1870s, 107 plays ran to over a hundred performances (the most 1,362).[20] The revival of the theatre's popularity made possible a great improvement in production standards, though with the possible exception of Tom Robertson in the 1860s it did not encourage the appearance of any major play-writing talent till the 1890s. Possibly the key development was the raising of ticket prices at the artistically more ambitious theatres round about mid-century, and the relegation of the poorer class audiences to the music halls. Theatre-going regained its importance as a form of conspicuous consumption, but drama failed to re- establish itself as an art form, comparable in seriousness to the novel or poetry, until changing social orientations around 1900 created an interest in shock and controversy themes, by which time the very fashion-ability of the stage conferred artistic status even on only mildly outrageous ventures.

The early nineteenth-century decline of the theatre (inevitably reflected in the poor quality of plays), the later adjustment to a potential new audience of status-conscious suburbanites rather than to the poorer but perhaps more demanding mass audience of the inner city, the emasculating effect on drama of theatre-going's rôle in fashionable society, together make up a not very heroic story: and perhaps something similar is happening today to the 'serious' novel. Although there is doubtless plenty of talent going into the novel, the market is particularly circumscribed by an opportunist coalition of publishers, academics and Arts Council experts. The low price paid for *Paradise Lost*, the return of the copyright of *Lyrical Ballads* as worth nothing, the problems of getting *Ulysses* published, are part of the mythology of our literature, frequently repeated with the implication that, 'We do things better now'. *Lord of the Flies*, I have been informed, was turned down by every other London publisher before being accepted by Faber and Faber; and even at Fabers', the reader's report described Golding's novel as 'Absurd and uninteresting fantasy . . . Rubbish and dull. Pointless', while the sales director said it was 'unpublishable'.[21] Something similar apparently happened to Richard Adams's *Watership Down*: not that I wish to hold up Adams as a latter-day Tolstoy but his initial problems show that even the potential of being a smash hit is no defence against the unimaginativeness of publishers. What gets through the net seems increasingly remote from any kind of really independent audience. The Booker Prize short lists seem at first glance a long way away from the Book Society choices of the 1930s, and if Booker Prize novels had been written fifty years ago they would possibly have been major literature: but what *contemporary* constituency do they relate to? Perhaps Booker Prize novels seem more like genuine literature than Book Society choices because they are designed for middle-class audiences that have much better formal literary educations than the middle classes of the 1930s, but even this isn't entirely true. A writer like Thornton Wilder, so much more intelligent and cultured and, at the belles-lettristic level, artistically self-conscious than Hugh Walpole, or John O'Hara, was in the end just as banal, but in his provision of what a cultured, thinking, concerned readership looked for, he went through the motions as deftly as the best of the modern generation. His modern counterparts make even those inescapable and unalterable facts of our time, genocide and the drift towards nuclear war, more acceptable, part of every sensitive, cultured person's cultivatedly uneasy consciousness.

Art involves a special level of discourse: it is this special level of discourse that makes it an art, and the specialness of the discourse has often an ideological function. At one time, for example, art benefited patrons whose political, or later purely economic, power was legitimised by their acts of patronage. Now, it seems, it is less the idea of art, than the specialness of the level of discourse which is valued. The whole Leavis movement with its shrill insistence on 'the standards by which a civilization lived' and the 'bringing of literature and the standards inherent in it to bear', its pretended monopoly of 'a necessary sense of particular kinds of excellence', and its magisterial attribution of terms like 'urgent' and 'central' and 'significant' and 'concern' and 'preoccupation' and 'disquiet' and 'rigorous' and 'alarming', had a crucial rôle in refining and defining this special level of discourse, though it has now moved on from any Leavisite pretence of reconstructing or salvaging anything. This post-post-Leavis discourse now serves to demarcate a class that is increasingly sensitive to the problems of its own identity and existence, a bourgeois intelligentsia which no longer dares call itself an élite but needs to prove itself to itself by reading the right books.[22] But the really creative and representative art of our time is probably amongst none of this literary prize literature: perhaps it is not in books at all. That's what the economics and sociology of audiences can do for art.

VII

I have argued in the previous chapter that the interest of a text, from certain historical viewpoints, relates to its literary merit, and, even if one does not accept my views on the Booker Prize, it is obvious that it is not always the case that the more socially prestigious the genre, the more elevated the literary merit. It seems that different genres have different literary importance at different times: different genres imply different audiences: this means that different literary audiences have different literary importance at different times; and since there is no relation to social prestige, this importance must be separate from the location of hegemonic power, though obviously not immune to its influence. I shall call this quality, this importance, this relation to the truly creative art of a period, *centrality*.

The way in which epic poetry was central, we might almost say natural, to pre-literate warrior societies, in both Achaean Greece and medieval Germany, the way Greek tragedy was central to the communal life of the Ionian city state, hardly need elaboration. But epic, or Attic tragedy, were essentially the culture of a dominant hegemonic grouping, though in the case of Attic tragedy at least its vitality evidently came from the participation of a wider constituency, and it was itself part of the mechanism for adjusting the tensions between competing fractions. In a larger, more ramified society, on the other hand, a central genre, though obviously incorporating social values determined by the pattern of political domination, might be of little personal interest to the dominant classes. Thus Elizabethan and Jacobean drama was essentially independent of the Court. Again, Elizabethan drama had no specific civic or religious function: its centrality as a genre lay in its relationship to the London society of its day, where the audience, though mostly literate, was only partly adjusted to the habit of solitary reading, and where the concentration of population had reached a level sufficient to create a sense of enlarged, egalitarian community but was still not yet at the level of atomisation, anonymity and anomie.

Today phenomena like electronic music and action films are central to the kind of society we live in, exploiting as they do the potentialities of contemporary technology, the spending power of those sections of society most likely to spend money on public entertainment, and the attractions of particular styles, particular social images of what is and what is not desirable in life: they indicate which is today's central audience. The young have become the shock troops of fashion: they are even further away from hegemonic power than the London mercantile and artisan community of the seventeenth century, which after all helped to overthrow the Stuarts: but today's high technology culture has its outlets in every home, and the young are mobilised at least as an audience on a larger scale than any audience has ever been mobilised before. And within that vast mobilisation there is a huge variety of diverse trends; some of them, I think, embodying a truly creative response to our Now.

There is a rather conscious sense of participation in listening even to the more recherché brands of modern music. Science fiction represents a more solitary and for the most part more cerebral response to the modern world: as the fiction of technological and sociological change it combines both the withdrawal involved in the reading habit, and an engagement with the contemporary. Science fiction films, especially those of the 1950s with their Cold War paranoia about alien invaders, on the whole short-sell a genre which may be described as *the* typical, central art form of a developing industrial society.

Part of the dynamic quality of a dynamic genre comes from the existence of an audience that has to be *held* by a constant process of innovation and exploration – as distinct from the tied, essentially inert audience for, say, romantic novelettes. Romantic novelettes, belonging to the marginal world of old ladies, bored housewives with minimal attention spans, and socially insecure shop assistants, represent the surviving power of a tradition that has long ago learnt to exploit all its possibilities. It is not simply that the readers want the same old thing: a relatively stable and predictable market encourages publishing executives to set their face against change.[23] Far from being the archetype of contemporary popular culture, as is frequently supposed, the romantic novelette is the antithesis of the main drift of popular culture, precisely because it is the genre of the psychologically marginalised members of society, as opposed to those who are involved in society's growth sectors.

In the case of rock music – pop music – modern music – whatever one calls it – since 1960 there has been the same process of developing and maturing on at least part of the audience and part of the performers as we have previously observed with Shakespeare and Dickens. It may be at a much lower level – though Dickens certainly and Shakespeare probably were also accused in their day of cheapness and triviality – but there is nothing else as original, as creative, as essentially involved with the particular features of our time. It does not seem too much to say that right through the 1970s, up to and including the assassination of John Lennon, the Beatles continued to provide images of both life and art for an entire generation. In the field of cinema and the science fiction novel, though within a different time-span, there has also been a continuing vitality. Nevertheless, when Régis Debray suggests:

> In general, the influence a given genre has over the intellectual creators of an epoch should be correlated with its index of *resonance* at that time, taking into account the size of the potential audience and the practical possibilities of entering into relations with it, given the technical level of the communications network of the epoch,[24]

it is possible he has passed a little too slickly over the problematics of subjectively perceiving the *resonance* and of gaining access to communications networks. The élitist orientation of our educational system insists on a routine undervaluation of popular culture, and it is possible that the process whereby competitive education sucks in more and more talent involves drawing it off from popular culture: at least the emphasis in our education on traditional forms hampers the recognition of the types of art constructively central to our society. At the same time, communication depends on processes of organisational complexity comparable to those of industrial production – in fact communication *is* a form of industrial production – and like other industries it is increasingly subject to monopoly control. It is not a question of one's technical ability to enter into communication with an audience, but of one's opportunity, amongst the press of all the others who are trying to communicate at the same time.

But we are drifting into polemic again, and anyway the relationship of genres to specific audiences can only be studied up to a certain point in terms of audiences. It is time to look at genre and associated categories more closely.

7

Genre and Style

He heareth sounds and seeth strange sights and commotions in the sky and the element.

I

The chief problem of studying audiences is that they aren't there any more. The theatre-goers have gone home, the booksellers' customers have left no forwarding addresses, the young men who sat up all night to discuss poetry have grown old and have died and have returned to the anonymous dust. Only the books remain. And to study books historically we need a mode of aggregating diverse examples in a useful way. Single works, as I hope I have shown in Chapter 3, raise problems that can only be solved by a context; individual *oeuvres* written perhaps over a lifetime of conflict and change pose other difficulties: one can better generalise from movements. Categories like Englishman/Frenchman or novelist/landscape painter are not useful. They are at once too narrow, and too general. The two categories I feel most useful, and most applicable to my earlier discussion of audience, are *genre* and *style*.

II

By *genre* I mean a type or category of work in which all the examples have an essential resemblance in both subject matter and treatment and, consequently, exist within some sort of conscious tradition. The novel is not in this sense a genre: the term *novel* is too inclusive and too general: the bourgeois novel of sentiment *is* a genre. It is not always easy to match a particular work to a genre. It seems stretching a point to define the Bourgeois Novel of Sentiment as being exemplified by *Pamela* and then to insist *Tom Jones* and *Tristram Shandy* belong to the same category, though both obviously have a vital relationship to it. And many works of art have features of more than one genre. Fielding, who professed to

109

be writing comic epic, introduced into *Joseph Andrews* and *Tom Jones* passages of mock-heroic, which never quite became domesticated in prose fiction, and passages in the style of the periodic essay; and much of his dialogue, especially of comic characters like Mrs Slipslop and Squire Western, seems to belong to the tradition of the stage. Indeed it may even be impossible for one genre to exclude characteristics of another: for example, the terrestrial characters in science fiction are of necessity obliged to converse in a way resembling the dialogue in other genres of fiction, and in so far as science fiction deals with the effect of material change on the human condition, it is bound to resemble other forms of social comment novel.[1] But after all the term *genre* is only an abstraction: its utility is to indicate resemblances, not to insist on differences. There is no need to allocate works exclusively to one genre or another. Jane Austen's common ground with Fanny Burney doesn't prevent *Northanger Abbey* demanding comparison with examples of the gothic novel, or of literary parody. Generic features are simply a mode of comparison between different works of art, and to articulate these generic features one needs the concept of genre.

In many cases, a genre will include some more or less definitively typical examples, but the not-so-classic examples which insist on their anomalous character and their borrowings from other genres may be equally important to a critic trying to understand a period's artistic fashions. Again, genres in different art forms often have much in common: painting has often taken its themes and conscious viewpoints from literature; but genres in different art forms must involve elements that they cannot share. The resemblances are very important, but one should never forget the differences, any more than one should forget the individuality of the artist.

Historiographically speaking the most illuminating studies of genre are those which have barely concerned themselves with the issue of quality. Sir Roy Strong's *And When Did You Last See Your Father?* (1978), for example, has shown that the popularity in the nineteenth century of historical painting was 'directly related to the papering over of vast social changes' (p. 153). 'These scenes and their heroes were selected to inspire calm, even complacency, with regard to the present. They gave expression and substance to the all-pervasive Whig interpretation of history as progress' (p. 45). Between 1820 and 1900 about 175 paintings of Charles I, Cromwell or Civil War subjects were exhibited at the Royal Academy (p. 141). These, like the also numerous paintings of Lady Jane Grey, Mary Queen of Scots and Bonnie Prince Charlie, pointed to 'the vanishing and transitory nature of monarchy' (p. 44); through them 'it was possible to meditate on the kind of disaster which was still happening on the mainland of Europe' (p. 44). It might have been superior kitsch but it is revealing as part of the vocabulary in which the Victorians articulated their ideas about themselves and their historic moment.

Historically illuminating genres which have failed to produce any acknowledged major works also provide a context for the understanding of acknowledged masterpieces. Thus, the Pre-Raphaelites began with a professed emphasis on detailed fidelity to nature; this fidelity is consistently a feature of Millais' work, though not at all that of Rossetti's, and it hardly seems the most interesting feature of the movement. But if we look further afield we find that there was something like a minor international vogue of photographic – given the technology of the time, more than photographic – detail in nature painting, often allied to interesting effects of atmosphere: characteristic practitioners include John William Inchbold, Robert Zünd and Francesco Mancini. This hyperfidelity to detail and lighting coincides, of course, with the development of photography, but also with Impressionism, which was simply a more radical exploration of the problem of how to represent light pictorially. The Impressionists may have been the great revolutionaries of painting, but that doesn't mean that nobody else was trying to keep painting up to date.

Indeed the mere fact of the existence of a particular genre, its coming into vogue at a certain moment, may point to a larger historical process that demands study. For example, the gothic novel and the antecedent genre of graveyard poetry in the 1740s seem to have grown out of a new eighteenth-century attitude to death. The whole business of hauntings, of strange things that go bump in the night, evidently relates to the area where fear of death and fear of the dark come together (as Sir Francis Bacon wrote, 'Men fear death as Children feare to goe in the darke'). The imagery of the graveyard genre is not new:

> Or hide me nightly in a charnel house,
> O'ercover'd quite with dead men's rattling bones,
> With reeky shanks and yellow chapless skulls;

> Or bid me go into a new-made grave,
> And hide me with a dead man in his shroud
> (Shakespeare, *Romeo and Juliet*, Act 4, Scene 1, lines 81–5)

But after all, what one remembers about *Romeo and Juliet* is the sunshine and sweetness, and the contemplation of mortality and decay in various authors during the following three decades usually has a religious, or at least moral element. In the 1740s, on the other hand, gloom and grisliness is piled on simply as an end in itself:

> 'Mid hollow charnel let me watch the flame
> Of taper dim, shedding a livid glare
> O'er the wan heaps; while wary voices talk
> Along the glimm'ring walls; or ghostly shape
> At distance seen, invites with beck'ning hand
> My lonesome steps, thro' the far winding vaults
>
>   Thus Eloise, whose mind
> Had languish'd to the pangs of melting love,
> More genuine transport found, as on some tomb
> Reclin'd, she watched the tapers of the dead;
> Or through the pillar'd isles, amid pale shrines
> Of imag'd saints, and intermingled graves,
> Mus'd a veil'd votaress.
> (Thomas Warton, *The Pleasures of Melancholy*, 1747)

It is a kind of pornography of death which seems to have emerged in parallel with sexual pornography. The connection between the two pornographies comes out in a notably lubricious novel of the 1790s, Matthew Gregory Lewis's *The Monk* (1796). The Monk, Ambrosio, actually a Capuchin friar, finds that he is beloved of the beautiful Matilda, who has managed to establish herself in the monastery by disguising herself as a monk. When he insists on her leaving; she asks for a rose as a parting token; 'I will hide it in my bosom, and when I am dead, the Nuns shall find it withered upon my heart.' While picking the rose Ambrosio is bitten by a snake. She saves his life by sucking the poison from the bite but sickens herself from the venom. When Ambrosio learns she has sacrificed her life to save his, his resolve weakens. 'Folded in your arms, I shall sink to sleep,' she says; 'Your hand shall close my eyes for

ever, and your lips receive my dying breath' (vol. 1, chap. 2).
Finally he makes love to the dying woman by the light of a lamp
which 'shed through the chamber a dim mysterious light'. His
appetite stirred by this experience he later drugs a young girl,
Antonia (actually his sister) so that she appears dead, and when
she wakes in her tomb he rapes her amongst 'rotting bones, and
disgusting figures, who perhaps were once as sweet and lovely'
(vol. 3, chap. 4). Her true love and officers of the Inquisition arrive
too late to save her: 'He still grasped Matilda's dagger. Without
allowing himself a moment's reflection, He raised it and plunged it
twice in the bosom of Antonia!' The same linkage of love and death
occurs in the novel's sub-plot. It seems a bit weak merely to adduce
the decline of Christianity by way of explanation. In the end we
have a very visible literary phenomenon with its causes seemingly
buried in the most arcane structures of society.

A more recent and more explicable example of the timeliness of a
particular genre is the university novel. Previously written with
nostalgia mainly by ex-Oxford undergraduates safely migrated to
London, in the last thirty years university novels have become a
serious side-line with academics in provincial Eng. Lit. departments, a change which reflects a shift in the centre of gravity of
British Higher Education. The tone of recent examples is predo-
minantly one of inadequacy and anomie, evidently reflecting
something of a crisis of confidence in academe. Malcolm Bradbury's *The History Man* (1976), a story of calculated posturing and
shrinking ideological horizons, illustrates rather deftly how the
universities, from their central rôle as part of the 1960s ethic,
converted themselves in the 1970s to a symbol of betrayal and
defeat and self-serving compromise, but there are at least half a
dozen other examples which convey the same picture.[2]

However, my point here is not to emphasise the information –
necessarily partial and misleading – derivable from genre but
simply genre's utility as a mode of aggregating texts.

III

By *style* I mean a way of doing things, a way of looking at things, a
particular emphasis and manner which distinguishes the art of one
period or movement from that of another. In recent years, the
concept of style has been under attack. In emphasising what
writers or artists of a particular period have in common, it often

obscures what is particular and unusual about them as individuals: and the orientation of the most recent literary scholarship at least is towards the individual. In many cases, there will be major difficulties in fitting a particular writer into the straitjacket of a particular style: too often he will go outside the conventional boundaries of his style for inspiration and ideas. And in any case the images and patterns distinctive of each period are created largely from materials inherited from previous periods: every war begins with the weapons and rhetoric of the previous decades.

Scholarly labels add an additional element of confusion. Some scholars propose labels where no label was previously felt necessary – Virgil Nemoianu, for example, wants there to be an English Biedermeier; some scholars propose labels which are hotly contested by others – Professors Blackmur and Hough are in dispute over Expressionism as a valid international movement; sometimes there is a problem because a movement claiming a particular label goes into eclipse at just the moment that the label establishes itself somewhere else: Modernism in Germany and Scandinavia, for example, received its obituary in Samuel Lublinski's *Der Ausgang der Moderne* in 1909, just as Anglo-French Modernism was about to make its début.[3]

Despite the definition just given of style as relating to a period, chronology is not always helpful. Thus Romanticism and Neo-classicism, if for the sake of argument these categories exist, seem to be more or less contemporary with each other. It is true that in German literature and French painting there is a neo-classical period followed by a Romantic period but if one brings in Britain and Italy, and architecture and sculpture, one will see that the two movements (defined in terms of works allegedly characteristic of them) were essentially simultaneous. And it is not just the dates which refuse to remain in hermetically sealed packages. We can give examples of Romanticism – Coleridge's *Christabel*, James Wyatt's Fonthill Abbey, Caspar David Friedrich's 'Tetschener Altar', even Adam Mickiewicz's poem *Romantyczność* – and of Neo-classicism – Louis David's 'Le Serment des Horaces', Goethe's *Iphigenie auf Tauris*, Smirke's British Museum, the sculptures of Canova – but once we go beyond the obvious examples and seek for definitions everything becomes much less simple. Let us pursue the distinction between Romanticism and Neo-classicism for a moment.

The early nineteenth century was rich in controversial statements suggestive of the irreconcilability of Romanticism and Neo-classicism, such as the controversy in England over the poetical status of Pope and the setting up in France of Ingres and Delacroix as two polar opposites in their approach to painting. Above all, it was in Germany that the Classic-Romantic dichotomy was elaborated. Goethe's remark, 'Das Klassische nenne ich das Gesunde und das Romantische das Kranke,' shows clearly enough how important the distinction between the two styles appeared.[4] This consciousness of difference is an important part of style and surely relates less to overinflated artistic egos claiming unique qualities that they objectively lack, than to the circumstance that artists, in adopting styles, are exercising choices related to cultural perceptions. The problem is that in retrospect there appears to have been a tendency to insist on differences that didn't actually exist.

To start with: Neo-classicism and Romanticism frequently admired the same models. Raphael was set up as a hero by both schools. In his discussion of the 'noble simplicity and sedate grandeur' of ancient Greek culture, Winckelmann, the pioneer neo-classicist theorist, wrote: 'Possessed of these qualities Raphael became eminently great, and he owed them to the ancients. That great soul of his, lodged in a beauteous body, was requisite for the first discovery of the true character of the ancients.' Raphael's success in returning to the antique was also a dogma with Louis David, the greatest of the neo-classical painters. But in the Romantic Wackenroder's *Herzensergiessungen eines kunstliebenden Klosterbruders* ('Outpourings from the heart of an art-loving Monk') (1797) Raphael is transformed into a proto-Romantic, and in this version inspired the Nazareners in their attempts to recapture the spirit of Quattrocento religious art. Yet in Neo-classicism's polemic against Baroque the Italian Quattrocento was as serviceable as Periclean Athens: Hancarville attacked connoisseurs and their academic formulas which had resulted in Donatello and Bramante being valued less than Bernini and his contemporaries.[5] Ossian, the medieval Celtic bard manufactured by James Macpherson, also found admirers on both sides. In many ways a precursor of Romanticism, Ossian was a favourite of Napoleon, the patron of the neo-classical David and Appiani; the paintings on Ossianic themes which he commissioned from François Gérard, Anne-Louis Girodet de Roucy Trioson and, later, Ingres were all in their different ways strikingly transitional between Romantic and Neo-classical. The Romantic implications of Ossian received their fullest expression in Mendelssohn's overture 'Fingal's Cave' (1829), while

George Harvey's rendering of Ossian in balsa-wood rhyming couplets represents Neo-classicism at its least inspired:

> Near Tura's wall, beneath the spreading trees,
> Whose verdant foliage murmur'd to the breeze,
> Cuchullan sat – his spear reclined at rest,
> Against a rock, his shield the ground possessed.

The way in which the antiquarian researches which fuelled Neo-
classicism partook of the pre-Romanticism of the type associated in
England with the poet-scholars Thomas Gray and Thomas Warton
is neatly illustrated by Hancarville's *Collection of Etruscan, Greek and
Roman Antiquities* (1766–7), where the author breaks into a prose-
poem:

> in the majestic silence of the night, in that profound solitude of
> nature, in that melancholy solemnity, [which] the absence of the
> Sun gives to all the beings which surround you, at the foot of an
> old oak, which spreds its crooked branches upon a Promontory
> washed by the briny waves, a statue of bronze is placed upon a
> Pedestal . . . [6]

The most advanced exponents of Neo-classicism frequently exhibited a subordinate strain of Romanticism. The backgrounds of
Claude-Nicolas Ledoux's megalomaniac neo-classical architectural designs are often archetypal romantic landscapes. William
Wilkins who, by the time he was 30, had established himself as the
leading intellectual of English Neo-classicism with his blandly
austere Greek-revival design for Downing College Cambridge and
his authoritative *Antiquities of Magna Graecia*, soon went on to stock
Cambridge with such banal examples of college gothic as Trinity
New Court, Corpus Chapel and the hall range at King's. Karl
Friedrich Schinkel, early nineteenth-century Prussia's version of
Renaissance Man, pioneered a distinct Romantic genre with his
paintings of fantastically structured gothic cathedrals, and his
'Felsentor' in the National Galerie at Berlin is reminiscent of Friedrich, but his most important professional work was as the architect
of neo-classical buildings such as the Berlin Schauspielhaus (1818)
and the Altes Museum (1822–3). The Romantics too showed the
inspiration of Neo-classicism. Caspar David Friedrich painted the
'Temple of Juno at Agrigento' in a light which Richard Wilson

might have admired: yet the uncompromising way the temple is presented frontally and in the foreground is typical of his eerie close-ups of outdoor objects. William Blake is generally considered as a Romantic, but just as much as the neo-classical Ingres his use of emphatic outline was influenced by the illustrations to Homer by his friend John Flaxman, the neo-classical sculptor. And there is a whole body of work in this period which simply refuses to submit itself to appropriation by either Romanticism or Neo-classicism as exclusive categories, notably the work of the Pictur-esque School in Britain, and on the Continent, the paintings of Joseph Anton Koch who, himself a disciple of the neo-classical Carstens, was an important influence on the pseudo-Quattrocento art of the Nazareners.[7]

At this stage one might not unreasonably feel that the whole question of style is a blind alley. But then if one compares, say, Schinkel's Berlin Schauspielhaus and Altes Museum with Smirke's Covent Garden Theatre and British Museum, or Dance's Newgate Prison with Heinrich Gentz's Neue Münze, or David's 'Le Serment des Horaces' with Camuccini's 'La Morte di Giulio Cesare', and asks oneself how it was that people who did not know each other's work could produce buildings and paintings so strikingly similar in ways that distinguish them from the work of earlier periods; or, if one compares the poetry of Wordsworth and Blake with the paintings of Friedrich and Runge and asks oneself how German painters could present a sensibility so reminiscent of that of English poets they had never heard of, one might after all conclude that the concept of style has some validity.

No writer ever struggled harder than Shelley to understand the relation between the writer and his society at a given historical juncture. He wrote:

It is impossible that any one who inhabits the same age with such writers as those who stand in the foremost ranks of our own age, can conscientiously assure himself that his language and tone of thought may not have been modified by the study of the productions of these extraordinary intellects. It is true, that, not the spirit of their genius, but the forms in which it has manifested itself, are due less to the peculiarities of their own minds than to the peculiarity of the moral and intellectual condi-tion of the minds among which they have been produced . . . Every man's mind is . . . modified by all the objects of nature and art; by every word and every suggestion which he ever admitted to act upon his consciousness; it is the mirror upon which all forms are reflected, and in which they compose one form. Poets, not otherwise than philosophers, painters, sculptors, and musicians, are, in one sense, the creators, and, in another, the creations, of their age. From this subjection the loftiest do not escape . . .[8]

But that still doesn't solve the problem that in Shelley's own period there appear to have been two different styles. The difficulties involved in demarcating Neo-classicism and Romanticism and of explaining their simultaneous appearance is sometimes resolved by denying 'their existence as independent categories'. Indeed since the 1920s at least there has been a scholarly tradition in Germany which insists 'on the romantic nature of Neo-classicism'; as Klaus Lankheit has put it,' Romanticism could be understood as the general movement to which Neo-classicism belonged as a special current.'[9] It seems somewhat, shall we say, *post-structuralist* to pass off one style as being part of another style representing a diametrically opposed system of values; perhaps it would be better to stick to Romanticism and Neo-classicism as labels for something distinctly different.

Of course, since we are talking about concepts that have no objective physical existence, it is not really necessary to state where one ends and the other begins. Rather than even think of exclusive categories, we might imagine the style of the period as a continuum with what we may call Neo-classicism at one end, conceptually speaking, and Romanticism at the other, and most actual works of art somewhere in between. Perhaps even better would be to think of Neo-classicism and Romanticism as simultaneous tendencies. At any rate, one has merely to remember that Wordsworth and Francis Jeffrey, Coleridge and Jane Austen were contemporaries, to be struck by the unhelpfulness of René Wellek's suggestion that period terms (like Romanticism) should be seen as 'names for systems of norms which dominate literature at a specific time'. More useful is Alastair Fowler's suggestion that 'We may allow artificial classifications so long as we recognise their purely heuristic status.'[10] Since I mean to use style simply as a means of making connections, I can go along with that. ·

After the Neo-classical–Romantic period it is generally impossible to detect a single coherent style in Western Europe. Perhaps it was that eclecticism itself became the characteristic style.[11] Indeed, we may distinguish two usages of the term *style*: one for the period before 1830 which pretends to be all-inclusive, e.g. Baroque, Rococo, and, more contentiously, our Neo-classical and Romantic, and the other for the period after 1830 which refers only to a certain tradition of work within a genre, like Neo-Flemish or Neo-Tuscan in architecture, or within a particular group of closely related genres, like *Art Nouveau* in architecture, design and sculpture, but without any suggestion of being *the* style of its period. It is quite helpful to see style terms like Baroque and Rococo as containing all the genres of their period within them. There should be no difficulty in seeing *Paradise Lost* as a baroque poem, providing one is not expecting specific lines to demonstrate a parallelism with cupolas, and though it might be a bit awkward to see *Tristram Shandy* or Gray's *Elegy* as rococo, the allocation is not without an interesting suggestiveness, bearing in mind always that the point is not hard and fast appropriations but simply the indication of similarities. And the fact that we cannot easily apply an all-embracing stylistic label for any period after 1830 should not encourage us to overlook significant groupings of shared elements in later nineteenth- and twentieth-century art.

IV

The re-establishment of an all-embracing common style is not an impossibility. We are still too immersed in our own period's culture to have an overview of its unifying features: even the nineteenth century is too close to us, so that we cannot yet clearly see if, beneath its bewildering eclecticism, there was not some distinctive common posture. Perhaps in any case nineteenth-century eclecticism consisted simply of the recycling of all the previous styles as part of a process of psychological response to the unbearable pressure of material change; perhaps the eclecticism was a symptom of an increasing ideological fragmentation as the traditional channels of authority disintegrated under the weight of these same material changes, and it was essentially the failure to establish new codes of purpose and direction which prevented a coherent common style from emerging. Such an interpretation gains a degree of plausibility from an examination of attempts to re-establish a unified and coherent order in the 1930s.

In retrospect the great art that seems distinctively of the 1930s is antagonist art, art which found its original audience in a minority that was consciously alienated from the prevailing trend of events: the paintings of Picasso, the novels of Céline, the poetry of Auden. But at the same period, in Stalin's Russia and Hitler's Germany and Mussolini's Italy, and even to some degree in Roosevelt's USA and Baldwin's Britain, there was a distinctive official art, a revived Neo-classicism tempered with Neo-realism. In retrospect one feels that its official status guaranteed that it was so second-rate as scarcely to qualify as art. But one should not forget that Hitler, Mussolini, Stalin, Roosevelt, even Stanley Baldwin, owed their positions of national leadership at least partly to the extent to which they could be identified with a prevalent mood in their countries; in the twentienth century, political régimes have come to rival art as an indicator of a society's subjective state. We can no longer suppose that official art has no widespread appeal because it is official, for it is rather the case that the factors which guarantee its official status also guarantee its appeal.

Initially all three of the great inter-war dictatorships had an involvement in modern art. This was least the case with the National Socialists in Germany, because coming to power more than a decade after the Russian Communists and the Italian Fascists they had had more time to identify intellectual *avant-gardisme* as a political enemy. Nevertheless, Hans Weidemann, the original head of the Art Section in Goebbels's Ministry of Propaganda, turned out to have modernist tastes and had to be reassigned; Goebbels himself had written an expressionist novel in his younger days and seemed to have leanings towards modern art till Hitler made clear his preferences. In Russia, the Futurists came under ideological criticism as early as 1918, though they went on to contribute some of the most characteristic images of the revolutionary period and were not finally eclipsed till the consolidation of Stalin's power and the establishment of Socialist Realism. In Italy, the ideological links between Futurism and Fascism had been originally quite strong, and though Futurism never achieved monopoly status as official art, it obviously lent itself to Fascism's commitment to projecting an image of modernity. Nevertheless, there is evidence of growing official hostility in the 1930s and by 1938 party-sponsored criticism of foreign, Bolshevist, Jewish art indicated that the opportunist, conformist, conservative element in Fascism was mobilising against the modern.[12]

Italian wartime propaganda posters seem stylistically considerably more old fashioned than their pre-war counterparts, but this is almost the only evidence of any practical change as a result of the belated reaction against *avant-gardisme* in Italy. In the Soviet Union, the tight restrictions on consumer goods and the centralised control of artists and writers enrolled in official bodies meant that Stalinist art quickly established itself. In National Socialist Germany, party orthodoxy was enforced by a great campaign of dismissal and confiscation against 'degenerate' artists; it is calculated that 15,997 works by 1,400 artists were destroyed. Yet while a much narrower range of art was permitted, in Germany and the Soviet Union at least, within that range the determining factors were what also determined best-seller art in countries without an official artistic censureship. The resemblance between Nazi art and Stalinist art has been recognised for some time.[13] But, in painting, there was a similar and very influential movement in the USA; the anti-modernist Regional movement of which Grant Wood's 'American Gothic' is the most famous example. The Regional Movement was a turning against *foreign* decadent art from a dying European culture – in effect the same pre-1933 culture rejected by Hitler, and for not dissimilar ideological reasons.[14] In literature, the emphasis on the common experience of the lower classes who constitute the backbone of society found expression in the novels of Mikhail Sholokhov, John Steinbeck and J. B. Priestley, with Mary Webb providing for the English novel a more specifically rural agragrian emphasis to the same theme: although there was no censorship in England, prime minister Stanley Baldwin dated his Preface to the collected edition of Webb's *Precious Bane* from 10 Downing St, and his well-known addresses in praise of traditional England meant that even in Britain this literary tendency was identified with the government. And in architecture Giles Gilbert Scott's Battersea Power Station and Cambridge University Library and Charles Holden's University of London Senate House are as surrealistically megalomaniac as anything built under Stalin or projected under Hitler. Indeed, the University of London Senate House (the work, rather unexpectedly, of the same man who designed those modest, elegantly modern London Transport stations in the outer suburbs) is perhaps *the* classic example of symbolically totalitarian architecture for, as the Ministry of Information in the Second World War, it provided the model for the Ministry of Truth in George Orwell's *1984*.[15]

The common features of 1930s art are its nostalgia for a world of

traditional values and its assertive optimism. The nostalgia, evident in Stanley Baldwin's addresses and Grant Wood's paintings,
was most emphasised in Nazi art, which seems largely a continuation of the traditions of Biedermeier, as exemplified by the paintings of Ferdinand Waldmüller, Moritz von Schwind and Carl
Friedrich Lessing, and seems to have had the same escapist function; with the difference that what was approved in Biedermeier
became practically compulsory under National Socialism, but with
the addition of a crude energy of emphasis in keeping with the
totalitarianism of the régime. Werner Peiner's 'Deutsche Erde',
showing a man guiding a harrow behind two horses heading
towards the endless flat vista of the German racial heartlands, is
the quintessential 1930s picture. The assertive optimism – 'They
are no longer interested in the grim uniformity of slums, urban
desolation, and dives . . . They want to be spokesmen of the
positive side of life' – did not depend on the backing of totalitarian
institutions. The sentences just quoted were by a German spokesman of Nazi art: they could have been by a British publisher of the
same period.[16]

This brief sketch should suggest some of the ideological implications of common stylistic features in art movements. But this
subject needs to be entered into in much more depth, and in order
to do so I shall return to the 1800s, the era of Neo-classicism and
Romanticism.

Part III

Part III

8

Neo-classicism and Romanticism in Historical Context

And the ancient Mariner beholdeth his native country.

I

The simultaneity of Neo-classicism and Romanticism raises issues of definition: definition of these specific style labels, and definition of the epistemological status of style labels in general. If we accept – as I think we ought to – the utility of the distinction between Neo-classicism and Romanticism, we then confront issues of even greater fundamental interest. If we were talking simply about Romanticism we could argue that perhaps English Romanticism and French Romanticism were not really the same, and that where they overlap it was because of the importation into one of elements from the other. But the simultaneity of Neo-classicism and Romanticism provides a complex antithetical pattern which shows up quite distinctively in each of the four cultures of England, France, Germany and Italy, and cannot be argued away simply as coincidence. And for the same developments to manifest themselves simultaneously in all four countries would mean either that socio-economic conditions in all four countries were essentially similar, or else that artistic developments have no fundamental connection with socio-economic conditions.

I don't believe that these artistic movements – or any other – had no fundamental connection with socio-economic conditions, but in order to trace the connection it will be necessary to enter into a much greater degree of detail than hitherto, and I shall begin with a more detailed examination of the concepts of Romanticism and Neo-classicism.

Romanticism, as the return to a more subjective, spontaneous, emotional, imaginative artistic mode, is generally understood to

125

have a fairly precise signification, and to refer to a phenomenon in European history of major importance. *Neo-classicism*, on the other hand, is frequently used to refer to different things, and in the meaning that has come into use with art historians during the past twenty years – that is, a particular late eighteenth- and early nineteenth-century style which is quite distinct from any earlier imitation of the classics and which in some respects is startlingly modern – does not seem to be current with anybody other than art historians. An article in *Journal of British Studies*, in 1969, entitled 'What *Was* Neo-classicism?' and a reply the following year 'What Indeed Was Neo-classicism?' refer to the period 1660–1800.[1] I have to confess I used the expression 'neo-classicism' in the same general sense in my last book. Judging by J. T. Shipley's *Dictionary of World Literary Terms* (London, 1970) which devotes five and a half columns to Romanticism and a mere ten lines to Neo-classicism, literary scholars simply don't find much use for the label. They would doubtless be astonished by art historian Hugh Honour's uncompromising statement, 'Neo-Classicism was the style of the late eighteenth century.' As for the proposition that the most extensive assault on the norms of mid-eighteenth-century art was represented by Neo-classicism rather than by Romanticism, this would provoke only astonishment.[2] And even if English Literature experts recognised the specific Art Historical usage of the term Neo-classical, it is doubtful if they would admit that it can refer to anything of importance in Literature. Or in English Literature at least; for in German Literature Neo-classicism (which in the restricted art historian's sense is confusingly known in German as *Klassik*) has long been acknowledged as one of the major styles.[3]

The problem with trying to wriggle out of the importance of English (or British) Neo-classicism is that even foreign books on Neo-classicism recognise the key contribution of Gavin Hamilton and Benjamin West in pioneering the style in painting, and the quality of Flaxman the sculptor and Smirke the architect as leading practitioners. Anyway, the question of *importance* invites one to ask, *important* in what sense? Something might be very important to contemporaries and not at all important to English professors two centuries later. It is the first type of importance that should establish the subject matter of history, not the second.

II

It would be a gross oversimplification to say that Neo-classicism set up ancient Greece as its model whereas Romanticism set up the Middle Ages: but it does seem that the two styles sought different things from their models. The Romantics, with their commitment to subjective emotion, admired the Middle Ages for their appearance of spontaneous vitality, their crudity, sincerity and lack of polish. The Neo-classicists found a spontaneous vitality and sincerity in the ancient Greeks, but what they particularly admired was its subordination to form. In fact both Romanticism and Neo-classicism were concerned with emotion and how to express it, but they approached the problem in different ways: perhaps we can even say that the difference between Romanticism and Neo-classicism consists in the contrasting strategies they adopted.

The Romantics, in spite of their talk about 'spontaneity' and 'negligence' and 'Shakespeare warbling his native wood-notes wild', thought rather long and hard about techniques of expression. Wordsworth's 1800 Preface, with its discussion of vocabulary and selection and the effect of metre, or Constable's water-colour sketches with their constant working away at a new painterly notation capable of expressing the effects of light and distance, are proofs of this. Yet however hard they thought about expression, what they expressed remained tantalisingly ambiguous; not merely because of a contrived ambiguity asking flirtatiously to be decoded, but because that was how the thought emerged. Blake's *The Tiger* is perhaps the most famous example of this: here is another from Wordsworth:

> A slumber did my spirit seal;
>   I had no human fears:
> She seemed a thing that could not feel
>   The touch of earthly years.
>
> No motion has she now, no force;
>   She neither hears nor sees;
> Rolled round in earth's diurnal course,
>   With rocks, and stones, and trees.

The first line may simply state that the poet slept, and perhaps dreamt; or perhaps the slumber of death – the girl's death – or the slumber of a paralysed spirit effectively put an end to his emotional growth, freezing his spirit for ever into the state it had been in at the time of her death or at some other time, exactly as if it had been closed and a seal put on it. He had no human fears, either because he believed the worst could never happen, or because it already had. She seemed a thing that could not feel the touch of earthly years, either because she seemed immortal or because, being dead, she was already beyond change. The two completely opposite meanings are not a weakness of the poem, because if the poet imagined that the living girl was immortal, it was only because he had mistaken the nature of her immortality as it is presented in the second stanza. Here she is definitely dead. She has become part of the earth. There is something chilling in that clinically precise word *diurnal*. Somehow being rolled around in earth's diurnal course doesn't seem at all wholesome and comforting and pantheistic. I have a picture of her lying there in a cold, cold grave on a rocky infertile heath with a few trees against the skyline, superimposed on a second picture of our planet spinning endlessly and for ever in a vast, empty, meaningless outer space. What picture Wordsworth wanted me to have we shall never know.

The neo-classicist strategy was to suppose that if something was worth expressing one should explore the best formal means of expressing it as clearly and as forcefully as possible, and the characteristic of all neo-classical art is an emphasis on the specific characteristics of the composition. In painting, this meant carefully structured and grouped designs with a strong emphasis on outline at the expense of subtleties of depth and colour. This resulted not simply in a vast number of dull masterpieces in which Greek-profiled heroes were assembled in static frieze-like processions across huge canvases, but also works like Louis David's 'Le Serment des Horaces' which was and is as eloquent and emphatic as any painting of the Romantic tradition. But Neo-classicism was perhaps at its most original and innovative in architecture, the formal genre *par excellence* and the area in which Romanticism, in the revival of Gothic, initially showed the worst of its tendency towards inept pastiche. Even at neo-classicist architecture's weakest, when it showed an excessive commitment to classical models, as in the Greek Revival style of Smirke and Wilkins, it rarely failed to achieve a simple and monumental dignity; at its best, in the designs of John Soane, Friedrich Gilly, Claude-Nicolas Ledoux and Étienne-Louis Boullée classical motifs were used, if at all, in a radically innovative fashion. Perhaps only in literature, in the poetry of André Chénier and Walter Savage Landor and Ugo Foscolo, did formal exploration take second place to the parading of classical references, but even here, in the criticism of Francis

Jeffrey and William Gifford, one can see the emphasis on purity of form and clarity of expression.

III

The central rôle of form in Neo-classicism helps us not merely to define Neo-classicism but to account for it. Nothing could be more wrong than to discuss an intellectual or artistic movement's origins purely in terms of an intellectual history divorced from a socio-economic context, and then seek to explain the success, the popular reception of this already matured intellectual/artistic movement as a separate process, unconnected with the genesis of the movement and involving an apparently accidental congruence with the psychological or socio-cultural needs of the day. It is true that Neo-classicism was connected with a great increase of detailed knowledge about classical antiquity owing to the rediscovery of Pompeii and Herculaneum, and the newly fashionable interest in Greece. But to say archaeology caused Neo-classicism would be to beg questions about why archaeological discoveries could be so influential at this point: moreover it would be a uselessly restrictive definition of Neo-classicism which concerned itself only with the elements demonstrably connected with mid-eighteenth-century discoveries, and in any case these discoveries were publicised so slowly that one should not exaggerate the attention they received.[4] Neo-classicism grew not out of the changing state of knowledge about classical antiquity but out of the changing needs of society: and what these needs were can be best understood by examining the formal qualities of Neo-classicism as a style, particularly as a style contrasting not with the near contemporary Romanticism but with the earlier Baroque.

Baroque was quintessentially the style of the palace and the cathedral. The palaces for the king and his noblemen, and the cathedrals for the liturgical displays of official religion, were the most important buildings seventeenth-century architects had to design, and provided the locations where most paintings could be expected to be displayed: in fact murals, the most important type of baroque painting, were inconceivable without the large walls and ceilings of palaces and cathedrals. The first revolt against Baroque involved merely a different concept of palaces: the English neo-Palladian style of the early eighteenth century was anti-Baroque, anti-Sir Christopher Wren, anti-French architectural models, because it was anti-Court; it was a suitable style for country houses that were intended to express the independence and moral elevation of wealthy aristocrats excluded from power.[5] A variety of Neo-Palladianism later established itself in the more backward areas of the Continent, in southern Italy – notably Vanvitelli's royal palace at Caserta – and in Russia – notably Quarenghi's various palaces at St Petersburg. Elsewhere the palace and the cathedral simply declined in relative importance; by the late eighteenth century architects like Jean-Nicolas-Louis Durand were placing palaces and cathedrals low down on their lists of possible public buildings: banks, bourses, prisons, barracks, the institutions of a society organised on a larger scale, were now the key structures. Francesco Milizia's enumeration of seven types of public building – for security, utility (i.e. universities and libraries), accounting (banks and tribunals), supply, health and necessities (hospitals and aqueducts), magnificence, and spectacle (i.e. theatres) – was typical of the period both in its attempt at systematisation and in its emphases.[6] And in designing buildings for new functions, architects attempted to express these functions: above all they sought to convey that these functions were *public* ones. They needed an architectural idiom that was both functional and eloquent. A pure classical style, with its essential simplicity, its suitability for the large structures required by public needs, its reminiscence of ancient glories and ancient virtues, lent itself perfectly to these requirements. The Greek Doric order, previously neglected since antiquity, came back into favour as typifying the pristine excellence of the Greek style: 'soon may we see it appropriated to all public works of a severe and dignified character', wrote one architect in 1810.[7] In prestige public buildings such as museums and theatres where a monumental element was required the Greek motifs tended to be emphasised, sometimes with dull and academic results; but where monumentality was not required, buildings were designed that sometimes seem a hundred years ahead of their day in their simple functionality.[8]

In painting, Neo-classicism manifested itself first in crowded classical subjects on large canvases by expatriate artists in Rome, in the 1760s. Though Winckelmann, the first great ideologue of Neo-classicism, admired the paintings of both Raphael Mengs and Gavin Hamilton, neither produced work that seriously threatened the foundations of baroque art. Like the costume historical paintings of Robert Edge Pine and John Hamilton Mortimer who were active at the same period, their work seems to be related to an essentially literary revival of interest in the past, characteristic perhaps of an increasing awareness of social change, but not otherwise indicative of a vital response to a new cultural mood.[9] Other painters utilised the new archaeological discoveries, but with a kind of rococo tweeness: Vien's 'La Marchande d'Amours' takes its subject and style from a painting excavated at Herculaneum, but its prettiness and mildly titillating theme are worthy of Fragonard or Boucher; Reynolds's portraits of high society personages in poses adapted from classical sculpture is similarly self-indulgent. But with Benjamin West's 'Death of Wolfe' (1771), John Singleton Copley's 'The Death of Chatham' (1779–81) and Louis David's 'Le Serment des Horaces' (1785) neo-classical painting began to establish itself as the art of public statement and public sentiment. What is essentially neo-classicist about these pictures is not, ultimately, their borrowings from classical sculpture, or Renaissance *pietàs*, or even from Poussin, the great proponent of classicism in the seventeenth century, but the way all the elements have been subordinated to a single, emphatic focus: the hero martyred at the moment of victory, the saviour of his country struck down by disease at the hour of his country's greatest need, the brothers joined together in righteous solidarity. Art has become propaganda, with an unashamedly programmatic emphasis that is in itself a kind of stylisation.

The same attempt at simple directness of communication is visible in neo-classical sculpture. The early eighteenth-century style, of which Roubillac was the great exponent, was excellent for capturing the idiosyncracies of individual subjects, and inventive in its motifs, but the new era wanted something simpler, more direct, more obvious: above all it wanted something more *idealised*. The lack of expression and animation in, for example, the work of Thorwaldsen is one result of this idealisation, but neo-classicist sculpture found its most typical successes in the depiction of public figures as mythic heroes, for funeral monuments.

In literature, apart from the *oeuvre* of perhaps minor figures like Landor, the most unambiguous manifestation of Neo-classicism was in a department of letters in which England took the lead at this period and which few defenders of Romanticism will wish to appropriate: epic poetry.

There had been a considerable amount of interest in epic poetry during the Renaissance and some attempts at the genre made during that period have established themselves as enduring classics: Camoẽs's *Os Lusiados*, Tasso's *Gerusalemme Liberata*, Spenser's *Faerie Queene*, and, as a baroque afterthought, Milton's *Paradise Lost*. Epic poetry continued to be written in the eighteenth century but only Voltaire's *La Henriade* achieved more than a temporary celebrity and except in the Netherlands there were relatively few authors willing to attempt the genre.[10] Then, about the time of the French Revolution, it came back into favour, as is testified by the 166 epic poems or large parts thereof published from 1790 to 1826 and listed below.

I have omitted the verse romances of Walter Scott, Byron and their imitators because they seemed to me to be derived from another tradition of narrative poetry, as do *Frithiofs Saga* by Esaias Tegnér and *Wladimir den Store* and *Blenda* by Erik Johann Stagnelius; the latter described his poems as *skaldedikter* though he also wrote *episka fragmenter*. I have also omitted mock epics like Evariste Parny's *La Guerre des Dieux*; on the other hand, I have included so-called *Rittergedichte* published in Germany because though earlier examples by Alxinger and Müller use an irregular eight-line stanza adapted from medieval German poetry, this gives way in later examples, by La Motte Fouqué and Schulze, to an *ottava rima* format modelled on Tasso, whose influence in the earlier examples cannot therefore be discounted. Despite the frequently Romantic-seeming subject matter, the poems listed below all seem to derive consciously from a tradition initiated by Homer though Virgil, Tasso and Milton are more frequently the actual models.[11]

Joel Barlow: *Columbiad* (1807)
Peter Bayley: *Idwal* (1817)
William Blake: *Milton* (privately printed 1804 two books only)
———*Jerusalem* (privately printed 1804)
James Bland Burges: *Richard I* (1801)
———*The Dragon Knight* (1818)
James Bland Burges and Richard Cumberland: *The Exodiad* (1807)
James Brown: *Britain Preserved* (1800)
Joseph Cottle: *Alfred* (1800)
———*The Fall of Cambria* (1808)
———*The Messiah* (1815)
Hannah Cowley: *The Siege of Acre* (1801)
Richard Cumberland: *Calvary* (1792)

Sir William Drummond: *Odin* (1817; first party only)

Alexis Eustaphieve [Evstaf'ev]: *Demetrius, the hero of the Don* (1818)

John Fitchett: *Alfred* (sections printed and circulated privately from 1808, published with final section by Robert Roscoe in six volumes 1841–2)

Elizabeth Ham: *Elgiva* (1824)

Edmund Freiherr von Harold: [*The French Revolution*][12]

W. Hildreth: *The Niliad* (1799)

Charles Hoyle: *Exodus* (1807)

John Keats: *Hyperion* (1820; two books and part of the third only)

Henry Kirke White: *The Christiad* (1807; 33 stanzas only)

Henry Gally Knight: *Iberia's Crisis* (1809; 'a fragment of an Epic Poem')

Walter Savage Landor: *Gebir* (1798)

John Lowe: 'Episode from the Epic Poem' (1803, in his volume of *Poems*)

Charles Lucas: *Joseph* (1810)

W. E. Meredith: *Llewelyn ap lorwerth* (1818)

Henry Hart Milman: *Samor* (1818)

James Montgomery: *The World Before The Flood* (1813)

Thomas Northmore: *Washington, or Liberty Restored* (1809)

James Ogden: *The Revolution* (1790)

_____*Emanuel, or Paradise Regained* (1797)

John Ogilvie: *Britannia* (1801)

Charles Peers: *The Siege of Jerusalem* (1823)

John Fitzgerald Pennie: *The Royal Minstrel* (1817)

_____*Rogvald* (1823)

Eleanor Ann Porden: *Coeur de Lion, or the Third Crusade* (1822)

Henry James Pye: *Alfred* (1801)

Samuel Rogers: *The Voyage of Columbus* (fragments only 1812)

Richard Scott: *The Battle of Maida* (1808)

Percy Bysshe Shelley: *Laon and Cythna* (1817, reissued as *The Revolt of Islam* 1818)

William Sotheby: *Saul* (1809)

Robert Southey: *Joan of Arc* (1796)

_____*Thalaba* (1801)

_____*Madoc* (1805)

_____*The Curse of Kehama* (1810)

_____*Roderick, the Last of the Goths* (1814)

John Thelwall: *The Hope of Albion* (1801: 1st Book only)

Edward, Lord Thurlow: *Hermilda* (1812: fragments only)
George Townsend: *Armageddon* (1815: first half only)
William Sidney Walker: *Gustavus Vasa* (1813)
Richard Wharton: *Roncesvalles* (1812)
George Woodley: *Portugal Delivered* (1812)
——*Redemption* (1816)

Jacque-Arsènes-Polycarpe-François Ancelot: *Marie de Brabant* (1825)
Charles-Victor-Prévot, Vicomte d'Arlincourt: *Charlemagne, ou la Caroleide* (1818)
Lucien Bonaparte: *Charlemagne, ou l'Eglise Delivreé* (1814)
François-Nicolas-Vincent Campenon: *L'Enfant Prodigue* (1811)
André Chénier: *Amérique* (fragments 1782–92 published 1819)
Jean-Baptiste-Félicité, Comte de Coëtlogon: *David* (1822)
——*Bayard Amoureux, ou les Lutins de Rambouillet* (1825)
L. Collet: *Josué, ou la conquête de la Terre promise* (1807)
Auguste-François Creuzé de Lesser: *Les Chevaliers de la Table Ronde* (1812)
——*Amadis de Gaule* (1813)
——*Roland* (1814)
——*Le Cid* (1814)
Pierre-Jacques-René Denne-Baron: *Héro et Léandre* (2nd edn 1806)
Claude-Auguste Dorion: *Le Comte de Guilfort* (1805: fragment)
——*La Bataille d'Hastings, ou l'Angleterre Conquise* (1806)
——*Palmyre Conquise* (1815)
Adolphe-Jules-César Dureau de la Malle: *Bayart ou la Conquête du Milanais* (1823)
Pierre Dusmenil: *Oreste* (1804)
——*Jeanne d'Arc, ou La France Sauveé* (1818)
Louis Marquis de Fontanes: *La Grèce Sauvée* (parts read publicly 1790 onwards: 3 cantos and some fragments published 1839)
Étienne François de Lantier: *Geoffroi Rudel, ou le Troubadour* (1825)
Népomucène-Louis Lemercier: *Homère* (1800)
——*Alexandre* (1800)
——*Moyse* (1823)
Charles-Louis Lesur: *Les Francs* (1797)
Jean-Charles-Julien Luce de Lancival: *Achille à Scyros* (1805)
J. C. Mallett: *Genève Sauvée, ou l'Escalade* (1800)
Charles-François-Philbert Masson: *Les Helvetiens* (1800)
A. P. F. Ménégault, 'Maugenet-Clemencé': *La Napoléide* (1806)
——*Le Cid, ou l'Espagne Sauvée* (1824)

Charles Hubert Millevoye: *Charlemagne* (1812 revised and reduced
from ten to six cantos as *Charlemagne à Pavie* (1814)
———*Alfred, roi d'Angleterre* (1815)
———*Clovis* (1822)
N. J. B. Montalan: *La France Pacifiée* (1823)
———*La France Constitutionelle* (1825)
Evariste-Désiré Desforges, Vicomte de Parny: *Isnel et Asléga* (c.
1800)
———*Les Rosecroix* (1807)
François-Auguste Parseval-Grandmaison: *Philippe Auguste* (1826)
J. Renaud-Blanchet: *L'École des Empires, ou la chute de la monarchie
française* (1804)
Jean-Baptiste-Gaspard Roux de Rochelle: *La Byzanciade* (1822)
Léonce de Saint-Geniès: *Balder fils d'Odin* (1824)
Alexandre Soumet: *Jeanne d'Arc* (2000 line fragment read at, and
printed in proceedings of, l'Institut de France 1826, published in
full 1845)
A. Philippe Tardieu de Saint-Marcel: *Charles Martel* (1805)
Guillaume Théveneau: *Charlemagne* (2 cantos of unfinished poem
in *Recueil des Poèsies* 1816)
Jean-Pons-Guillaume Viennet: *La Siège de Damas* (1825)
Alfred de Vigny: *Héléna* (1822)

Cesare Arici: *Gerusalemme Distrutta* (1819)
Pietro Bagnoli: *Il Cadmo* (1821)
Teresa Bandettini: *La Teseide* (1805)
Bernardo Bellini: *Il Triete Anglico* (1818)
———*La Columbiade* (1826)
Carlo Botta: *Camillo, o Vejo Conquistata* (1815)
Angelo Curti: *Pietro di Russia* (n.d. c. 1810)
———*La Vittoriade* (1821)
Tommaso Grossi: *I Lombardi alla Prima Crociata* (1826)
Vincenzo Lancetti: *L'Aereostiade, ossia il Montgolfiero* (1802)
Guiseppe Malachisio: *La Fine del Mondo* (1804)
Girolamo Ascanio Molin: *Venezia Tradita* (1803)
Vincenzo Monti: *In Morte di Ugo Bass-Ville* (1793)
———*Prometeo* (1797)
———*Il Bardo della Selva Nera* (1806: Part 1 only)
Girolamo, Conte Orti: *La Russiade* (2nd edn 1815)
Angelo Maria Ricci: *L'Italiade* (1819)
———*San Benedetto* (1824)

João Baptista da Silva Leitão de Almeida Garrett, Visconde de
Almeida Garrett: *Camoẽs* (1823)
_____*Dona Branca ou a Conquista do Algarve* (1826)
Francisco Roque de Carvalho Moreira: *Braganceida* (1815–16)
_____*Portugaida* (1816)
Agostinho de Macedo: *Gama* (1811 revised as *O Oriente* 1814)
Francisco de Paula Medina e Vasconcellos: *Zargueida, Descobrimento
da Ilha da Madeira* (1806)
_____*Georgeida* (1819)
Tomas Antonio dos Santos e Silva: *Braziliade, ou Portugal Immune e
Salvo* (1815)

Juan de Escoiquez: *Mexico Conquistada* (1798)
Juan de Plano: *El Seno de Abraham* (1803)
Felix Reinoso: *La Inocencia Perdida de los Primeros Padres* (1803)
Angel Sanchez: *La Titiada* (1793)
Eugenio de Tapia: *Sevilla Restaurada* (1821: fragments only)
Fray Ramon Valvidares y Longo: *La Iberiada* (1813)
José Vargas y Ponce: *El Peso Duro* (1813)

Willibald Alexis: *Die Treibjagd* (1820)
Johann Baptist von Alxinger: *Bliomberis* (1791)
Jens Baggesen: *Parthenäis oder die Alpenreise* (1803)
_____*Adam und Eva* (1826)
Karl Andreas von Boguslawski: *Xanthippus* (1811)
_____*Diokles* (1814)
_____*Tassilo, oder die deutschen Argonauten* (1821)
Johann Wolfgang von Goethe: *Hermann und Dorothea* (1798)
_____*Achilleis* (1799: fragment)
Daniel Jenisch: *Borussias* (1794)
Ludwig Theoboul Kosegarten: *Jucunde* (1803)
Friedrich de la Motte Fouqué: *Corona* (1814)
_____*Bertrand du Guesclin* (1821)
Friedrich August Müller: *Alfonso* (1790)
_____*Richard Löwenherz* (1790)
_____*Adelbert der Wilde* (1793)
Johann Ladislaus Pyrker, bishop of Zips: *Tunisias* (1819)
_____*Rudolph von Habsburg* (1825)
(his *Perlen der heiligen Vorzeit*, 1825, also included three mini-epics
Helias der Thesbit, 3 cantos, *Elisa*, 2 cantos, *Der Makkabäer*, 3 cantos)

Friedrich Schlegel: *Roland* (1809 in his volume of *Gedichte*)
Ernst Conrad Friedrich Schulze: *Die Bezauberte Rose* (1818)
_____*Cäcilie* (1818–19)
Franz, Freiherr von Sonnenberg: *Donatoa, oder das Weltende* (1807)
Johann Martin Usteri: *De Vikari* (1807–10, in Zürich dialect)
Johann Heinrich Voss: *Luise* (1795)

Jens Baggesen: *Thora af Havsgaard* (1814: fragments only)
Bernhard Severin Ingemann: *Waldemar den Store og hans Maend* (1824)
Adam Oehlenschläger: *Nordens Guder* (1819)

Grev Anders Fredrik Skjöldebrand: *Odin* (1816)
_____*Gustaf Erikson eller det Frelsade Sverge* (1822)
Erik Johan Stagnelius: three episka fragmenter in posthumous published works 1824–6

Willem Bilderdijk: *De Ondergang der Eerste Wareld* (1820)
Jan Frederik Helmers: *Die Hollandsche Natie* (1812)
Adriaan Loosjes: *De Laatste Zeetogt van den Admiraal de Ruiter* (1812)

One might feel that Keats's *Hyperion* is worth all the rest. Southey's five epics, Fitchett's 131,000 lines in forty-eight books totalling nearly 3,000 pages of smallish print, Baggesen's epics in two different languages, Creuzé de Lesser's four epics in three years: these are feats almost unparalleled in the history of unnecessary writing. Fitchett, as the author of the world's longest poem, has even got into the *Guinness Book of Records*. Beyond that there seems little to say. I have hunted the early nineteenth-century epic through bibliographies and literary journals, ordering up hundred weights of volumes, some handsome quartos in crumbling calf, others cheap editions with mildewed uncut pages, rare, sometimes unique survivors of the piled-up brand-new volumes which once went forth from the warehouse with the pride of the epic poet and have been long since almost all consumed by the various destructiveness and impatiences of the world; I have turned page after page insistently different yet endlessly the same, like tombstones in a forgotten war cemetery; I have searched through the obscuring medium of French, Italian, Portuguese, Spanish, German, Danish,

Swedish and Dutch for a glimmer of hitherto unacknowledged genius, a unique sensibility attempting to liberate itself from the marble blocks of verse, a voice expressing a perception of something that needed to be preserved; and sometimes I have thought that all I was achieving with my growing lists of titles was that for the first time statistical proof was being given of how many boring people there were in the early nineteenth century. But to pretend that these people, these epics, did not exist would be to present a kind of Whig history of nineteenth-century literature in which everything which does not accord with our notions of the meritorious and positive is ignored.

Like neo-classicist architects, neo-classicist epic poets tried to borrow from the ancients to make works of contemporary relevance: as André Chénier explained, 'Even when we draw modern pictures and modern characters, it is from Homer, Virgil, Plutarch, Tacitus, Sophocles, Sallust, Aeschylus that we must learn to paint.'[13] But even more – much more – than the architects the poets became bogged down in the stylistic detail of their models. David's 'Le Serment des Horaces' showed that remoteness of subject was no obstacle to topicality of reference, but most epics were stale academic exercises, sometimes virtually rehashes of previous epics, like James Ogden's *Emanuel, or Paradise Regained* or Agostinho de Macedo's *Gama*. Leaving aside the distinctive German sub-genre of *ländliches Epos*, there were relatively few attempts at contemporary subjects, and Renaud-Blanchet's *L'École des Empires* was almost certainly unique in being suppressed by the police because of its dangerous topicality. Even works with the most interesting-sounding contemporary themes, like Bellini's *Il Triete Anglico* – the title may be translated as 'England's Three Years', and the poem dealt with England's victory against Napoleon and its aftermath – or Lancetti's *L'Aerostiade, ossia il Montgolfiero* or Northmore's *Washington, or Liberty Restored*, merely underlined how anachronistic the epic format was. Yet it remained the ideal of the great poem on a theme of major public importance: thus Shelley wrote to Byron:

> I still feel impressed with the persuasion that you *ought* – and if there is prophecy in hope, that you *will* write a great and connected poem, which shall bear the same relation to this age as the 'Iliad', the 'Divina Commedia' and 'Paradise Lost' did to theirs.[14]

Essentially epic is concerned with public figures involved in public events on a public stage: it is the most public form of poetry. The fact that most – though by no means all – of these epics were commercially unsuccessful does not invalidate the proposition that their writers identified, or thought they had identified, a need and a market for poetry of this sort: a poetry about the roots of nationhood, the birth of societies, historic destiny, cataclysmic change, heroic example, ancient virtue, and the lessons of tradition. And one writer at least was quite specific about addressing himself to the political needs of the day: Shelley wrote in the Preface to *Laon and Cythna*: 'It is an experiment on the temper of the public mind, as to how far a thirst for a happier condition of moral and political society survives, amongst the enlightened and refined, the tempests which have shaken the age in which we live!'

In architecture, in painting, in sculpture and – as far as it went – in literature, Neo-classicism strove for simple, massively architectured monumental forms which were intended to convey their own message of seriousness and commitment. My contention is that this formal style grew out of – or rather grew up with – a fundamental social change in Western Europe in the second half of the eighteenth century. This social change manifested itself somewhat differently in different countries in keeping with the diversity of their pre-existing institutions, but before going on to discuss this change it may be useful to explore one feature of Neo-classicism (and Romanticism) in more detail, namely the tendency of different artists in different countries to express themselves in very similar ways without direct knowledge of one another's work.

IV

The notion that Neo-classicism and Romanticism spread by diffusion or cross-fertilisation, or some process that presupposes a common origin, is implicit in most writing on architecture and painting, because of the interest art historians characteristically show in tracing sources. The limitations of such an approach is suggested by Grigori Kozintsev's brutal remark:

It is well known that Picasso was influenced by the idols of south-eastern Polynesia. This is of course true, he was indeed influenced by them.

But what influenced Ilse Koch's collection of lampshades made
from human skin at Buchenwald?[15]

Still, literary historians, in their less controversial way, have demonstrated the influence of German literature on Britain and vice
versa.[16] One may point also to authors like Winckelmann, Mengs
and the Schlegels whose works were rapidly translated and became seminal texts in other countries. But ideas grow only in their
proper soil. It isn't true that a good idea simply has to be invented
or revived to spread by irresistible osmosis from one country to
another. If ideas or styles spread it is because they have a particular
relevance to the sphere in which they flourish: the important point
about the spread of an idea is not the idea itself but the openness to
its reception on the part of those who take it up. The truth of this is
underlined by Neo-classicism itself.

Although Neo-classicism owed much to the rediscovery of
Greek architecture and the excavations at Pompeii, most of its
inherited components – Palladio, Poussin, Virgil, and so on – were
already admired, already perfectly familiar. The individual hagi-
ography tradition of cultural history may invite us to believe that it
was Winckelmann who singlehandedly persuaded the eighteenth
century to see Greek sculpture in a new way, and indeed Winckelmann is one of those authors who seems still alive because in him
one recognises the original, classic formulation of ideas which have
subsequently become our clichés. The paintings of Gavin Hamilton, on the other hand, seem to have been always rather dead and
stuffed, and if one were to believe that it was Gavin Hamilton's
borrowings from Poussin that gave a new currency to French
seventeenth-century classicism, one would probably believe anything. The new currency of the classical past came from a shared
perception of new problems to be solved. Artists and architects in
different countries identified similar problems, proposed similar
solutions, even copied one another's expedients: but the initial
impulse was simultaneous and independent. The importance of an
artist such as John Flaxman, whose simple, emphatically outlined
drawings from Homer established one of the most clearly traceable
and widely diffused elements of the neo-classicist style, is not that
of an originator, simply that of the most authoritative and definitive exponent of a stylistic manner derived from the Greek vase
painting tradition, and already arrived at independently though

less authoritatively by, for example, Johann Heinrich Wilhelm Tischbein.[17]

A good example of how Neo-classicism was a matter not of diffusion but of congruence – what zoologists call evolutionary convergence – is provided by Vincenzo Camuccini. Born in Rome in 1771, Camuccini was the son of a coal dealer. His art studies were paid for by his elder brother. He showed an early interest in Mengs, Milizia, Winckelmann and Gavin Hamilton, and in 1793 began two vast paintings which took respectively eleven and fourteen years to complete, 'La Morte di Virginia' and 'La Morte di Giulio Cesare'. Of all the paintings executed in Louis David's lifetime these are the two which most challenge comparison with 'Le Serment des Horaces', with their dramatic but stylised grouping, emphatic outlines, sombre colours and perhaps over-obvious political import. Perhaps it is even fair to say that they have all the qualities of unconvincing melodrama and heavy-handed emotion that one might expect from a less talented artist attempting to reproduce the effect of a brilliant original. David's influence was, of course, by no means confined to France: his pupils included José Aparicio, second only to Goya as the greatest Spanish painter of his day, and Gottlieb Schick, perhaps the most important German neo-classicist of his generation. Claims that David had no followers in Italy cannot really be accepted: Pietro Benvenuti, the leading Florentine artist of his day (and a friend of Camuccini) painted his once famous 'Il Giuramento dei Sassoni' ('The Oath of the Saxons', i.e. to Napoleon after the Battle of Jena) straight after returning from a visit to Paris, where he had frequented David's studio: the outstretched hands of the defeated Saxons suggests 'les Horaces' and, even more strongly, David's unfinished painting of the oath in the Tennis Court which Benvenuti almost certainly examined in David's studio ('Il Giuramento dei Sassoni' also bears an uncanny resemblance to 'Louis XVIII Quittant les Tuileries' painted by David's favourite disciple Gros in 1817). Benvenuti's 'Le Nozze di Amore e Psiche' which is of uncertain date but which is probably subsequent to his Paris trip, also bears a strong resemblance to work of the David school. But the work of Benvenuti simply emphasises the originality of Camuccini.

The latter *may* have seen 'les Horaces' as a precocious 13-year-old art student in Rome when that painting was briefly exhibited there, but that was nearly ten years before he began his two masterpieces and twenty years and more before he finished them. It was not till he had completed these two paintings that he visited Paris, and the first print of 'les Horaces', that by Antoine Alexandre Morel, was also of a later date. A faint recollection of 'les Horaces' may have inspired Camuccini, but more probable, and more identifiable, is the influence of Caravaggio; and after all one would expect an Italian model to have the preponderant influence on an Italian working in Rome. (Camuccini's immersion in Caravaggio is most evident in his late 'La Conversione di San Paolo' of 1835 in the Basilica di S. Paolo fuori le Mura, Rome). Camuccini not original amongst neo-classicists in using an Italian school *pietà*-type group for his central focus in 'La Morte di Virginia', though he is unusually self-conscious in his quotation, for though the genders of the Virgin and her dead Son are reversed, the Magdalen and St John are exactly identifiable. And in 'La Morte di Giulio Cesare' especially one can see that, far from depending on David for his stylistic manner, he was perfectly capable of developing his own expressive vocabulary: the exaggerated massiveness of the knee and toga-wrapped fist of the assassin to Caesar's right, the dramatisation of the clothing, the sombre sameness of the colours, the disconcerting repetitiveness of the faces, which all seem to have been taken from the same very 1790-ish looking model. And whereas all David's famous pictures are of moments of poised, rhetorical immobility, in which action has been suspended, Camuccini freezes a moment of urgent movement. An effect similar to David's has been arrived at by a different route: the similarity of effect demonstrates only the similarity of intention, similarity of objective, similarity of underlying ideals, perhaps even a similarity of conscious exploitation of the public mood.[18]

The process of convergence rather than diffusion is seen also, and perhaps even more clearly, in the epic poetry of the period. Of course, certain lines of influence may be traced. Grev Anders Fredrik Skjöldebrand, author of *Gustaf Erikson eller det Frelsade Sverge* (1822) was obviously aware that his own father had published an epic on the same subject in 1768, entitled *Gustaviade*. Goethe's *Hermann und Dorothea* (1798) owed something to the pioneer *ländliche Epos*, Voss's *Luise* (1795). Landor's *Gebir* (1798) was admired by Southey, and Southey's epics were read by Shelley (Thomas Jefferson Hogg's story, that Southey insisted on reading them aloud to Shelley who meanwhile surreptitiously composed himself to sleep on the floor, should not be taken too seriously). Richard Cumberland, the author of *Calvary* (1792), not only collaborated with James Bland Burges in writing *The Exodiad* (1807) but also encouraged George Townsend in his work on *Armageddon* (1815).[19] But none of these lines of connection between living poets extended very far, and though William Sotheby, the author of *Saul*, had previously translated Wieland's *Oberon*, none of them crossed linguistic boundaries. The long dead were of much more importance than the living: Milton in England, Camoës in Portugal, Tasso in Italy, Virgil everywhere. Milton in fact went through a considerable international vogue: several new translations of *Paradise Lost* appeared in the 1790s and 1800s; but the first Dutch, French and Italian translations had appeared in the 1720s without generating any craze for epic writing, and despite the new translations into French, German and Italian, Milton's direct influence seems largely confined to Britain.[20]

The impression of an army of epic poets each busily scribbling away without any perception that he was not the only one, is rather confirmed by the fact that the period produced five epics on Charlemagne, four on King Alfred and three each on Moses and Richard the Lionheart. At any rate, we know that William Sidney Walker, author of *Gustavus Vasa* (1813), was ignorant of the Skjöldebrand family stake in his subject from the hasty way he began writing his epic at the age of 11: 'When the author began to know what poetry was, his first design was to write an epic – no matter of what sort or character, so it was an epic poem.' It probably would have made little difference if Walker had known that, some years earlier, Wordsworth had considered, amongst a variety of other subjects, an epic on

> how Gustavus found
> Help in his need in Dalecarlia's mines.

Another project of Wordworth's was to relate

> How vanquished Mithradates northward passed,
> And, hidden in the cloud of years, became
> That Odin, father of a race by whom
> Perished the Roman Empire,

but Sir William Drummond, having read the same passage about Mithradates and Odin in *The Decline and Fall of the Roman Empire*, very kindly wrote the poem for him, though possibly not as well as

Wordsworth would have done it.[21] Coleridge was equally unlucky, or equally in step with his contemporaries. 'I have since my twentieth year meditated an heroic poem on the Siege of Jerusalem by Titus – this is the Pride and Stronghold of my Hope', he wrote in 1802; perhaps not realising that Angel Sanchez had already got in first with *La Titiada* (1793).[22] Coleridge was shortly afterwards side-tracked by metaphysics and laudanum; and in 1819 Cesare Arici published *Gerusalemme Distrutta*:

> L'arme de Tito e i gravi affanni io canto
> Onde cadde a reo fin di Giuda il regno.

And Charles Peers's *The Siege of Jerusalem* came out four years after that.

There are probably numerous other instances of the same thing waiting to be unearthed: despite a great deal of hard work I am not even sure that my list of epics is complete, and I am certain that there is a large number that were written or at least begun, and never published.[23] The argument that out of so many epic poems, there were bound to be several on similar subjects, is not really convincing: Hannibal, Julius Caesar, Edward III, Oliver Cromwell and Karl XII are just five of the familiar and appealing subjects that were *not* chosen: Alexander the Great figured in one short epic of four cantos. It is obviously worth asking why some themes were more acceptable than others, but the only point I wish to make here is that there were so many people thinking independently along the same lines.

V

It seems, then, that an essentially similar artistic movement, or complex of movements, occurred more or less independently and simultaneously in most European cultures at the end of the eighteenth century. Therefore, if similar effects demonstrate similar causes, we clearly need only to identify what features were common to these societies and distinguished them from other societies (including themselves at different historical periods) in order to discover the factors which had the determining influence on art, architecture and literature. Wonderfully straightforward: except that in the features which might be thought to have the most direct influence, these societies turn out to be markedly dissimilar.[24]

France, even before the French Revolution and to a much greater extent thereafter, had a strong central government that was active in its sponsorship of the arts and, after 1792, increasingly successful as the focus of national sentiment. From 1792 onwards France was engaged in a generally victorious war. Despite major economic hardships especially in the coastal towns arising from the British blockade, the nation's commerce recovered under Napoleon from the huge upheaval of the early 1790s. Social revolution, foreign conquest and war created the psychological climate of boom. Recent research has tended to show that under Napoleon especially social mobility was by no means easy or usual, and that the richer classes were largely composed of families that had been rich before the Revolution, with a leavening of new plutocrats who had amassed fortunes during the upheavals of the 1790s. However, even if the principal social change was that the rich had become richer, the redistribution of landed property confiscated from the Church and the emigrés, the abolition of internal tariff barriers, the enormous expansion of the central institutions required for the war effort, and the supposed opportunity for *carrières ouvertes aux talents* within the army, all contributed to the creation of an aggressive, self-confident, free-spending *parvenu* society of which Napoleon, after 1801, was the fitting head.[25]

In Britain, real economic growth was actually much greater than in France. J. R. McCulloch, one of the leading economists of the day, claimed:

> The state of Great Britain, during the war, was precisely the reverse of that of France, or indeed of any other country engaged in hostilities. Her industry, far from being unnaturally depressed, was stimulated and encouraged to an extent altogether unknown in any former period of history. From being the greatest, we became the *only* commercial nation in the world.

But for many years the war was generally unsuccessful and widely unpopular and the government, unable to eliminate political opposition in the late 1790s and dependent on the support of conservative country gentlemen who resented the style and often even the policies of the ministerial élite, became increasingly weak and discredited during the crucial twelve-year period beginning in 1801. Although the war had an important effect on reheating the economy, the survival and indeed strengthening of traditional social structures meant that the psychological and social stimulus of the war was played down rather than, as in France, played up.[26]

Since Germany was not yet united under a national government, the effects of political developments were not evenly distributed nor everywhere experienced simultaneously; nevertheless, near uniformity of language, economic linkages, a growing sense of identity as Germans, and the free movement of intellectuals from one area to another justifies taking the German-speaking lands as a single community. The wars caused widespread physical disruption, and the increased commercial subordination to France (through the Continental System) and Britain (through British monopoly of overseas trade) held back economic growth except in a few areas. The wars ended with a notable upsurge of national feeling and Schinkel's and Klenze's architectural careers date from this immediate post-war period, but the broad foundations of Neo-classicism, including Friedrich Gilly's vital years as a teacher, belonged to the earlier period of economic stagnation, uncertainty and frustration.[27]

In Italy, the destruction of numerous military campaigns was compounded by outbreaks of frequently murderous class war. Under French hegemony, enlightened administration achieved only a little in the way of bettering economic conditions and Napoleon's Continental System operated generally to Italy's disadvantage. Apart from Milan, the capital of the new Kingdom of Italy, the cities declined catastrophically in population, Venice from 160,000 inhabitants in 1795 to 116,000 in 1813, Rome from 166,417 inhabitants in 1796 to 117,882 in 1812. The kind of psychological boom apparent in France was also experienced in Italy:

> The change in so many fortunes, the metamorphosis of so many individuals had generated a restlessness and a desire in everyone to leap out of his social class. Everyone wanted to improve his lot. Consequently there was not a father who, in the hope of having a judge, a magistrate or a general in the family did not procure for his sons a superior education.

But since there was no real economic expansion to back up all this, the result was an investment in unproductive office-holding and graduate unemployment. A good example of the new rich of Napoleonic Italy was Domenico Barbaja, the former café waiter who introduced roulette to Italy. By 1806 he held the roulette monopoly at Milan, Naples and twenty other cities. He shared in the management of both the La Scala Opera House in Milan and the San Carlo Opera House in Naples and later diversified into building contracting: the present San Carlo building was one of his undertakings. He became very rich as a merchant of opera and gambling. But the entrepreneurs who concentrated on the more mundane task of modernising Italian industry were frequently French, with their focus of interest not in Italy at all.[28]

The disparity between the cultural similarities and the socio-economic diversity of France, Britain, Germany and Italy at this period shows at least that social and economic conditions do not have a direct and immediate influence on culture. But this does not mean one should adopt an idealist interpretation of artistic forms as autonomous phenomena having no dependence on the actualities of different socio-economic systems. Between a mechanically socio-economic interpretation and an idealist-autonomist interpretation there are various possible intermediate modes of explanation. The diversity of socio-economic conditions in France, Britain, Germany and Italy simply indicates that the problem cannot usefully be approached from the socio-economic direction: we must start from the area of common ground, from the similarity of artistic form.

VI

The clue to the common origins underlying the common stylistic features of a period is perhaps to be found in the nature of these stylistic features. The distinctive orientation of Neo-classicism is to the *public*. Neo-classical architecture was quintessentially the architecture of government offices – Ledoux's customs posts surrounding Paris (1785–90), Gentz's Neue Münze, Berlin (1798–1800), Young's Customs House, Boston, Massachusetts (1836–47), A. D. Zakharov's Admiralty, St Petersburg (1806–15), Smirke's General Post Office, London (1824–9) – of theatres – Louis's Grand Théâtre, Bordeaux (1772–88), Smirke's Covent Garden, London (1808–9), Niccolini's San Carlo, Naples (1810–16), Schinkel's Schauspielhaus, Berlin (1818–24), Carlo Rossi's Alexandra Theatre, now the Pushkin Theatre, St Petersburg (1828–32) – of museums – Juan de Villanueva's Prado, Madrid (1787–1819), Léon Dufourny's Ginnasio, Palermo (1789–92), Schinkel's Altes Museum, Berlin (1822–8), Smirke's British Museum, London (1823–46) – of prisons

– Dance's Newgate, London (1770–84) – of barracks, such as Peter Speeth's at Würzburg (1809–10) – and of monuments. Friedrich Gilly produced an influential series of drawings for a monument to Fredrick the Great before 1800, and the archetypal neo-classicist monument is the Walhalla at Regensburg (1831–42) by his pupil Leo von Klenze. There were also numerous projects for monuments on a grand scale in Britain which were never built, probably because of lack of money: the National Monument at Edinburgh (1824–9) was left unfinished for financial reasons, and the relatively economical statue on a column was the type of large-scale monument most frequently employed – Nelson, for example, being commemorated in this way in Dublin, Glasgow, Great Yarmouth, Liverpool and eventually London's Trafalgar Square. (The numerous churches of the period, on the other hand, were mostly Gothic, and the few attempts at ecclesiastical Neo-classical were hardly distinguished.[29]) Similarly the most effective neo-classicist paintings made a calculated appeal to civic virtue, national pride, identification with the glory of the past. Again epic was the poetry of public themes, public figures working out their destinies on the public stage.

Sir William Chambers, in the Preface to his *Treatise on Civil Architecture* (1759), had claimed that the work of artists contributed greatly not merely 'to augment the Splendor of the Nation' but also 'to stamp additional Value on its Manufactures; to extend its Commerce, and increase the Profits arising therefrom'. By the turn of the century, however, people were beginning to take a much higher and large view. Louis David argued:

> The arts must therefore contribute first of all to public instruction, but by regenerating themselves: the genius of the arts must be worthy of the people it enlightens: it must always advance accompanied by a philosophy that suggests only grand and useful ideas.

As one minor English theorist pointed out:

> The arts have not only an influence on our manners, but also on our passions, and, taken in a national point of view, are highly useful. The pictures representing gallant actions, or noble achievements, rouse and stimulate to acts of heroism and public spirit.

Flaxman, the sculptor, lectured his students on learning 'to convert the beauty and grace of ancient poetry to the service of the morals and establishments of our own time and country', and in Prussia, Freiherr von Altenstein, in an official memorandum, went further still, asserting:

> It is the purpose of the State, to make Mankind share in the highest benefits, which can only happen through the fine arts and sciences. Only through them can an active and strong life and a striving towards higher things be achieved.

And even in the remotest and most backward extremities of Europe, such as Calabria, it was a matter for indignation that:

> The provinces, forever sacrificed to the capital, have never been considered under any other aspect than that of having to con-tribute to the burdens of the State. Nothing has been done for them, and consequently libraries, museums etc. are unknown words for these people.[30]

Art, evidently, was finding a new public rôle within a changing relationship between government and governed.

Part of this development was the involvement of many artists and writers in politics. To some extent this was a result of the fact that governments, more than ever before, were the principal patrons: it is not odd, therefore, that Appiani became First Painter to the King of Italy, Schinkel became Oberlandesbaudirektor in Prussia, Klenze Hofbauintendant in Bavaria; and George III's favourite, Benjamin West, was an inevitable choice as President of the Royal Academy. But careerist opportunism cannot explain why Robert Edge Pine, perhaps the most important pioneer of historical costume painting, advertised his anti-government symphathies by going to the Tower of London to paint the imprisoned demagogue John Wilkes, and later emigrated to America after the War of Independence to seek a new audience in the new republic: nor why Thomas Banks, whom Sir Joshua Reynolds considered the first English sculptor to execute works of classical beauty, should have contrived to get himself hauled in for questioning during the Pitt government's clamp-down on radicals in 1794. Another sculptor, the Italian Giuseppe Ceracchi, followed Edge Pine's example by going to the USA but left after failing to obtain a commission from Congress to execute a statue to Liberty; in 1801, he was guillotined in Paris as a principal in a Jacobin plot against Napoleon Bonaparte.[31] Jean-Baptiste Topino-Lebrun, a painter friend of Louis David, was also guillotined for involvement in this conspiracy.

Louis David is, of course, *the* politician artist of the period. He typifies the uncertain, rancorously ambitious artist trying to adjust himself to the quicksands of a political world which he has an inner compulsion to enter but which he lacks the talent to master. A protégé of Vien and of the Comte d'Angiviller, Directeur des Bâtiments, David was before 1789 a great beneficiary of the system of favouritism involved in the *Ancien Régime* and of the cliquism encouraged by the advanced development in France of painting as an established profession. It seems to have been his failure to secure appointment as Director of the French Academy in Rome, in 1787, which turned him against the *Ancien Régime*: six years later he was instrumental in suppressing the post. During the Revolution he was a member of the Committee of General Security, and for a time President of the Convention. When, during the reaction of Thermidor 1794, his friend Robespierre was shouted down in the Convention, David, who evidently had Socrates on his mind, exclaimed, 'Si tu bois la ciguë, je la boirai avec toi.' Owing to his speech impediment, this obscure remark did not have much impact on events. Four days later, Robespierre was guillotined and David, sweating great gouts of perspiration, told the Convention, 'You can't imagine how far that wretch (Robespierre) deceived me. It was with his hypocritical talk that he took advantage of me and, citizens, he couldn't have done it any other way.'[32] This very understandable cowardice perhaps helps to explain the loss of artistic direction that makes his later bloated masterpieces seem so much more rhetorical and less focused than 'les Horaces': though even in 'les Horaces' and the works which immediately followed one can perhaps detect a quality of calculation, of trying to paint for a specific audience that does not seem always very clearly perceived.

A more neo-classically heroic rôle was played by Ugo Foscolo. Before his twentieth birthday he was a veteran revolutionary soldier and secretary of the provisional municipality of Venice. As such he was sent on a mission to Bonaparte, who failed to impress him. After service against the Austrians in 1799–1800, he settled down to advocating a different Italy from the one Napoleon Bonaparte wanted. He campaigned against the abolition of Latin teaching in schools and wrote for the press in support of Italian unity. Despite his opposition to Napoleon, he decided to go into exile after Napoleon's defeat when the Austrians assumed control of northern Italy, writing to his mother and sister the day before his departure: 'as a writer I have not wanted to appear as a partisan of the Germans [i.e. Austrians] or the French, or of any other nation . . . I profess Literature, which is a most free and independent art, worth nothing when it is for sale.'[33] Shelley could not have said it better: a couple of years after Foscolo's arrival in England, the English poet emigrated to Italy.

This reorientation of art and literature was obviously part of a much larger process. Shelley believed that the new psychological and moral climate was the result of 'what may be called the master theme of the epoch in which we live – the French Revolution.'[34] But the French Revolution itself was part of a process, and one of the reasons why its effects were not confined to France was that the process was much more than simply the local business of the French; as may be shown by examining events before 1789 in other countries.

VII

Overall it was a period of modernisation of state institutions. In German-speaking lands this had begun under the Enlightened Despotisms, and was to continue with renewed vigour in the wake of the French victories over Austria in 1805 and Prussia in 1806. In France, the need to modernise the state was perceived in time to contribute to the build-up of the social pressures which were undammed in 1789. But this process was much broader than Enlightened Despotism or Revolution as it is observable in Britain as much as anywhere else. In Britain, though the parliamentary reform campaign of the 1780s was defeated, there was a constant process of purifying government from 1782 onwards; social reforms, especially in the penal field, were initiated under pressure from an increasingly organised public opinion; after 1800 there was a vast increase in the government's work of collecting and publishing statistics; and at least temporarily, the government established partial control over the national economy by its currency policies. If more was not attempted it was because of an ideological, not opportunist, commitment to the doctrines of Adam Smith: the much more developed commercial sector in Britain gave credence to theories which worked against the tendency towards more energetic central government which was exhibited everywhere on the Continent.[35]

This widespread process of modernising state institutions was itself a response to an underlying development. Previously European governments had depended on the active support of only a small proportion of their populations: the passive acquiescence of the majority – mainly peasantry – was all that was expected or required. The Seven Years' War seems to have been responsible for a fundamental change in this respect. By the time peace came in 1763 all the combatants were exhausted, none of them was satisfied, none of them had been sufficiently battered to be deterred from further military adventures. All were impressed by the size of the military effort a poor, thinly populated state like Prussia could exert if efficiently governed; all were disturbed by the discovery of Britain's growing domination of the seas and Russia's capacity to operate large armies far to the west of her borders. It was these considerations which inspired attempts at financial reform in France, the regulation of feudal burdens in various Hapsburg territories between 1767 and 1772, and the uniform land tax of 1789, the Spanish government's attempts at administrative reform in South America, the notorious Stamp Act imposed on England's American colonies in 1765, and so on.

These reforms inevitably had the effect of politicising the populations on whom they were imposed. This was most obvious in the North American colonies, but it happened even in Hapsburg central Europe.[36] Amongst conservative peasantries that were largely immune to the allure of new social and economic doctrines, innovations which coincided with worsening fiscal pressures naturally found no favour, and in the period of international upheaval following the French Revolution, as the stability of governments diminished and their economic demands increased, there was a series of peasant uprisings against what were perceived as essentially *alien* régimes: western France, 1793–6; various parts of northern Italy, 1797; Belgium and Ireland, 1798; southern Italy, 1799; Spain, 1808; the Tyrol, 1809. At the same time, the mobilisation of the middle classes can be seen not merely in the political revolutions – America, the Netherlands 1785–7, France – but more widely in the creation of new institutions to provide an organisational expression of mobilisation. Most obviously this included parliamentary bodies, in America, in France, in Sweden, where the 1809 Instrument of Government gave the Estates powers similar to those of the United Kingdom parliament at Westminster, in Norway where the national assembly at Eidsvold declared Norwegian independence in 1814, in Spain during the War of Independence against France, in Germany between 1816 and 1823: but there were also, particularly in Britain extra-parliamentary bodies, both those aiming at the reform of government, such as the Irish Volunteers of 1778–83 and the Edinburgh Convention of 1793, and those, like county meetings, aiming to put pressure on parliament on more specific issues.

All these developments can be seen in terms of the emergence of new class fractions, pressing with various success for a place within the power-bloc; but there were also less visible shifts in the balance of forces within the administrative élites of the different countries as new policies, new groupings evolved to take account of the new developments. Even before the French Revolution governments had not been totally averse to the politicisation of their subjects. Even militarily experts, such as Jacques-Antoine-Hippolyte Comte de Guibert, author of the influential *Essai Général de Tactique* (1773), perceived that new concepts of drill and of flexibility in the deployment of military formations required intelligent, committed soldiers. As it developed, the French Revolution increasingly demanded ordinary people's willing participation and even sacrifice in the public cause. As a result there was a vast increase in the attention paid to propaganda.

The most characteristic propaganda device of the period was the public festival. Vast, carefully orchestrated processions designed by Louis David were put on in Paris in the early 1790s: the Glorification of Voltaire, the Festival of Unity and Individuality, the Festival of the Supreme Being, the Victory Celebrations of 30 December 1793. Similar lavish spectacles were later organised in Milan to inaugurate the Cisalpine Republic in 1797 and the Italian Republic in 1803, and after Napoleon Bonaparte assumed the title of King of Italy his birthday, on 15 August, was regularly celebrated by vast firework displays in the presence of the court, the officers of state, ministers, and leading civil, political, judicial, military and administrative officials. In fact public ceremonies were carefully utilised by the French as a means of fostering the popularity of the puppet régimes under their control: the Festa Virgiliana at

Mantua, on 21 March 1801, and the parade of Ariosto's remains at Ferrara, on 7 June 1801, were calculated publicity stunts which successfully exploited local patriotism and, by making a military march past part of the spectacle, also advertised the new national army. Later, in the Rhineland, it is evident that local councils of commerce esteemed it an honour to be summoned to ceremonies such as the public installation of district judges.[37]

Whereas in France and French-controlled territories, the initiative for propaganda came from the government, in Germany it was groups intending to force the government's hands which attempted to mobilise popular opinion. Even before the disaster of Jena, Schleiermacher had insisted:

> sooner or later a war will break out whose object will be our convictions, our religion and education, no less than our external freedom and possessions; a war that must be fought, but that the kings with their hired armies cannot fight, only the people together with their kings.

After Prussia's catastrophic defeat at Jena in 1806, the need for radical institutional change was recognised throughout Germany. A greater degree of political participation (partly through parliamentary bodies) was seen as the best way to mobilise Germany's resources: implicit in this was the feeling that the princes must either take a lead or forfeit their authority: as Gneisenau said, 'We must win all of Germany and sweep it along with us. If the princes do not follow, the people will.'[38] Ultimately both princes *and* people were swept along in the movement, as the great national mobilisation of 1813–14 demonstrated.

In Britain, the government made some feeble efforts to compete with the French government's victory parades. There was even some attempt to indoctrinate the troops, the men whom Wellington described as 'the scum of the earth'. The rank and file were to be instructed that they were fighting 'a savage and implacable Enemy, who has the Insolence and Barbarity to aim at the Slavery of Our Persons, the extinction of Our Religion and the Destruction of Our Navy, Our Commerce and Constitution, so long the Envy and Admiration of the World'. However, very little effort needed to be expended on educating the troops with regard to war aims as they were rabidly chauvinistic already. During the retreat to Coruña in 1808, for example, the men of the 71st Foot allegedly encouraged one another by exclaiming: 'Let us all unite, whether our officers will or not, and annihilate these French cowards, and shew our country it is not our fault that we run thus; let us secure our country from disgrace, and take a sweet revenge.' The officers, of course, took pains to set a good example:

> Meanwhile a second shot had torn off the leg of a 42nd man, who screamed horribly, and rolled about so as to excite agitation and alarm with others. The general said, This is nothing my lads, keep your ranks, take that man away: my good fellow don't make such a noise, we must bear these things better. He spoke sharply, but it had a good effect; for this man's cries had made an opening in the ranks, and the men shrunk from the spot, although they had not done so when others had been hit who did not cry out. But again Moore went off, and I saw him no more! It was a little in front of this spot that he was killed. The French pointed out the place to me two months afterwards. There it was he refused to let them take off his sword when it hurt his wound! that dreadful wound! poor fellow! Yet, why poor fellow? Is death to be regretted when accompanied by victory, glory, admiration? Rather let those sigh who live and rot, doing nothing and having nothing to do, until, poor miserable drivellers, they sink under a tombstone!

But much more than in France and Germany, nationalistic fervour in Britain seems to have sprung from a broad spectrum of social classes and needed only modest encouragement from the authorities. Ultimately public funds contributed much less in Britain than elsewhere to the innumerable monuments commemorating the war.[39]

In differing countries governments were harnessing, or at least acquiescing in, a process which they anyway could not reverse. Improved communications, the increase in the availability of books and newspapers, the growth of towns, social mobility, even militarily conscription, all contributed to the wearing away of the prescriptive bonds of society. The passive obedience of a silent and subordinated majority could no longer be looked to, because it no longer seemed available. The basis of political power was changing, and while there were those within the existing power-blocs who resented and resisted these changes, there were others who recognised them as an opportunity. The importance of the French

Revolution is that it drew together, and created, an international social and political crisis out of developments which had been proceeding separately and independently in different countries. Simply as a dramatic series of events, the French Revolution inspired a vociferous pamphlet debate in other countries. In England, this developed into a carefully orchestrated, though unofficial, campaign to win over the lower classes to the side of loyalty and obedience, with a strong emphasis on the corresponding obligations of the richer and more powerful to the poor, weak and numerous. The French Revolution led, of course, to war: and first in France and later in Germany propaganda was seen as a vital means of mobilising men and money for armies. But the French Revolution did not cause the emergence of a public consciousness: it merely accelerated an existing process. In France, it was *because* the ideas of Voltaire, Rousseau and the *philosophes* were so widely disseminated before 1789 that they became so predominant thereafter. In Britain, similarly, much of the progressive thinking of the 1790s dates from the 1780s if not earlier, and the most important part of the conservative campaign was conducted by the Evangelicals who also had largely worked out their platform before 1789.[40]

VIII

The central rôle of the French Revolution in throwing into relief the increasing political consciousness of western European populations tends to disguise the fact that the socio-economic framework of this new consciousness was everywhere diverse.

In Britain, education remained largely stagnant till the 1800s, when the innovations of Lancaster and Bell at the primary level and the reform of the examination and fellowship systems at Oxford may be seen as a response to a long identified need. In the second half of the eighteenth century, the Dissenting Academies had set a brilliant example of intellectual progressiveness but had been perhaps the most important victim of the general reaction against innovation in the 1790s. In Scotland, Glasgow and, especially, Edinburgh Universities enjoyed great prestige, but Edinburgh's vivid intellectual society was composed of lawyers who were not qualified for the English bar, where they might have earned ten times as much, and professors of subjects that were not taught at Oxford or Cambridge, and the local fame of academics like Dugald Stewart simply emphasised how little was actually

going on besides scholarly talk. In England, professional intellectuals had no prestige at all – unless, like Porson, as prodigies of
drunkenness and Greek – and those like Richard Price, Henry
Beeke and Thomas Malthus who occasionally influenced government did so only on the narrowest technical matters.[41] Meanwhile,
the economy boomed.

We lack comparative economic statistics to show how much
richer Britain was than other European countries – but tax yields
seem to have been seven times higher *per capita* in Britain than in
France, and foreign visitors universally testified to the much
higher (and more equal) standard of living in Britain, or at least in
England. The notoriously pro-British Friedrich Gentz claimed.

> The economic existence of Great Britain is no less than her
> political existence, the greatest, most noble result of the activity
> of civilized man, an instructive and encouraging example to
> other people.

And even a not especially pro-British American had to admit,

> In England the various arts of Agriculture, Manufactures, and
> Commerce have been improved to a degree of perfection of
> which little idea can be formed by any thing to be seen else-
> where[42]

Political consciousness – what they called 'Public Spirit' – was the
outgrowth of the buoyancy and dynamism of propertied classes
with an established stake in society, and to a remarkable extent the
lower classes shared the same system of values. The image of John
Bull, the typical Englishman, the symbol of the English public, was
one manufactured by commercial publicists, but its success during
the 1800s argues a general willingness of large sections of society to
identify themselves with it.[43] A man who was veritably John Bull
come to life, as one can see from his *Memoirs* (1820), was the radical
leader Henry Hunt, 'Orator' Hunt, 'The man in the white hat'.
He was impetuous, prejudiced, conceited, dogmatic, illogical,
convinced of the rightness of his own opinions, mentally disor-
ganised, obsessed with his own trivial concerns, snobbish, chauvinistic, a little paranoid, horribly aggressive, and fairly rich, and as
one of the great mob-orators of English history found sympathetic
lower class audiences everywhere he went.

Psychologically at least France was more orientated towards progress. A slower rate of economic growth than Britain's was compensated for by a more articulate perception of the reactionary aspects of the *Ancien Régime* with which an enlightened and dynamic bourgeoisie was bound to come into conflict. French public consciousness focused, before 1789, on the decadence of the social system and after 1789 on its renovation, whereas in Britain throughout much of this period the dominant mood was acceptance and self-satisfaction.[44] During the eighteenth century France's thriving intellectual life had been shared between various cliques in Paris and the numerous provincial academies; the stagnating universities were abolished at the Revolution and were scarcely missed. Under Napoleon the intellectual world became more centralised in Paris as part of the *parvenu* Imperial décor; but being an intellectual was more of a lifestyle than a career, and intellectuals as such contributed much less to the tone of Napoleonic France than soldiers, administrators and government contractors.

In Germany, it was different. Economic growth was hardly a factor at all: instead the expansion of the countless princely bureaucracies provided unparalleled employment opportunities for the graduates of the most flourishing system of universities in Europe: 'it was this academic-bureaucratic predominance which distinguished German culture in the eighteenth century. Nowhere else in Europe did the literate classes have so many thousands of opportunities for state employment.'[45] Yet although there was a growth in the production of books until 1805, the German intelligentsia remained more narrowly based than its less organised and endowed English counterpart: despite the much larger population in German-speaking territories, the Germans were considerably behind the English in the establishment of authorship as a paying profession because of the smaller average circulation of individual titles.[46] But German intellectuals were less important than in England or France as the spokesmen or embellishment of burgeoning industrial and commercial classes, because they already had a more established rôle in public life. The endlessly reproduced bureaucratic hierarchies and the numerous universities which the political division of Germany involved, provided employment for a relatively large intellectual class that served rather as a substitute for a commercial bourgeoisie in providing a body of public opinion; the more so because the great commercial centres like Hamburg and Frankfurt were independent city states, cut off from the political life of the larger territorial groupings. Consequently professors like Fichte, the Schlegels, Schleiermacher, Schelling, Steffens, Hegel, often moving freely back and forth between government and academe, had an influence on public life that had no counterpart in other countries. And, much more clearly than in other countries, there is detectable the *central* audience of the period (see Chapter 6), an audience composed of the university and administrative classes: the very classes which had come to the fore in German public life after the defeat of Jena had discredited the Prussian *ancien régime*. There was nothing myopic or self-serving in the emphasis on intellectuals in Fichte's *Reden an die deutsche Nation* of 1808; an American visitor thought that from Berlin university, founded in 1810, 'a free spirit has gone forth that was wrought like a fever through all Germany'; a generation later academics were to be prominent in the liberal assemblies of 1848.[47]

Developments in Italy tended in the same direction. During the eighteenth century universities expanded and those who had been at university entered the various royal and ducal civil services in greater numbers. At Bologna, new enrolments at the university rose from less than a hundred year in the 1690s to 385 in 1802–3, though just over two hundred was the average during the following decade. New subjects were taught: Antonio Genovesi became Italy's – perhaps Europe's – first economics professor when he was appointed to the Cattedra of Commerce and Mechanics at Naples in 1754. But Italy's decaying social system could not easily accomodate this academic expansion. It was noted with disapproval in Modena, in 1799, that there were disproportionate numbers of students, even from the poorer classes, all eager to improve their social status, and that consequently there were masses of unemployed graduates: 'It was in fact university students who more than anyone gave themselves over to the Revolution in Modena and Reggio and in other cities, towns and places in the state.' Carlo Lauberg, head of the provisional government of the Parthenopean Republic in 1799, had taught at the Reale Accademia Militaria in Naples and run a private academy frequented by many future Neapolitan Jacobins; he escaped when the southern peasantry rose up against the bourgeois intellectual do-gooders and restored the monarchy, but amongst those executed in the subsequent purge were two successive presidents of the Parthenopean Republic's Legislative Commission, Mario Pagano who had been professor of

Criminal Law at Naples prior to his arrest as a subversive in 1796, and Domenico Cirillo, who had been professor first of Botany and then of Medical Pathology. And later it was Italy which inaugurated the honourable tradition of students rioting as a body against the government, when, following the arrest of a student wearing a *bonnet rouge*, Turin students battled against troops in the university building on 12 January 1821.[48]

Thus public consciousness and an intelligentsia grew, in England and France, on the back of a flourishing commercial middle-class, in Germany and Italy *as a substitute* for such a class. Different socio-economic conditions, acting through different socio-political institutions, had similar cultural results. Or at least, that would appear to hold true for the Neo-classicism side of the complex cultural movement of the late eighteenth and early nineteenth century. But how does Romanticism fit in?

IX

Romanticism is generally seen as a reaction to, even a revolt against, a phenomenon called Classicism, which may be equated with the Neo-classicism I have been talking about. The suggestion I made earlier, that Romanticism and Neo-classicism are alternate extremes of the same movement, is not really compatible with the supposition that the one was a reaction to the other. More importantly, the chronology doesn't really match up: Smirke and Schinkel began their careers, for example, well after Coleridge had stopped writing poetry and Novalis and Wackenroder had died, and if we do not adopt the textbook categories which represent so-called pre-Romanticism and *Sturm und Drang* as essentially distinct from Romanticism, then we find the latter movement under way before many important neo-classicists were even born. In any case, the notion that one cultural movement could simply be a reaction to another belongs to the idealist, autonomist view of culture which I have been arguing against. Nevertheless, my view is that Romanticism *was* a reaction: but against the same things as Neo-classicism was responding to: they were simply opposite responses to the same stimuli.

While Neo-classicism addressed men's attention to public rôles, fuelling their public consciousness with tendentious references to the public ideals of antiquity, Romanticism was an attempt to escape from the demands of the public sphere: an attempt to retreat into a private world where the individual was alone with his own individuality, or (as in German nationalism) a retreat into a corporate mysticism which served to withdraw attention from the fundamental incompatibility of conflicting ideological elements. It is perhaps because Romanticism is more concerned with the stresses and contradictions of the period that it seems often more original and insightful than Neo-classicism. This may even be an example of the possible discrepancy (hinted at in Chapter 5) between the location of hegemonic power and the location of the *central* audience of a period, Neo-classicism being the art of the dominant ideology, Romanticism of those who, psychologically marginalised by the pressure of public events and sensing longer-term perspectives, had difficulty in accommodating themselves to the neo-classical image of the community.

The retreat from the public sphere was not always voluntary. *'Il sacrificio della patria nostra è consummata . . . il mio nome è nella lista di proscrizione.'* So begins Ugo Foscolo's *Ultime Lettere di Jacopo Ortis* (1802): 'The sacrifice of our country has been consummated . . . my name is in the list of the proscribed.' The letters of which the novel consists are supposedly written from exile. Similarly Senancour, Chateaubriand, Constant, the pioneers of French Romanticism, wrote in enforced exile. Senancour's *Obermann* (1804) and, much more so, Foscolo's *Ultime Lettere di Jacopo Ortis* are reminiscent of Goethe's *Werther*, though Foscolo hotly denied any connection; leaving aside similarities of plot (unrequited love and final suicide in both Foscolo's and Goethe's novels) and concentrating on the very similar response to nature, it is interesting that while Werther withdraws from society because he has personal problems, Ortis and Obermann have been *obliged* to withdraw. Perhaps this is part of the reason why *Obermann* and *Ultime Lettere di Jacopo Ortis* are less original than *Werther*: the psychic crisis of the latter has a prophetic element, whereas Senancour and Foscolo needed to wait for events to push them into finding their subject.

In nature, the exile finds himself:

on those empty mountains, where the sky is more immense, where the air is more stable, where time is less rapid and life more permanent, there all nature eloquently expresses a higher order, a more visible harmony, an eternal connectedness: there man finds once again his changeable but indestructible nature, he breathes the natural air far from social emanations, his being belongs to himself as much as to the universe, he lives a true life in this sublime unity. (*Obermann*, letter 7)

Nature has changed as a symbol, from the pastoral ideal's nature of smiling fields and industrious swains which provided a symbol of an integrated and functioning social structure to a nature of crags and long desolate vistas, representing the dislocation and aloneness of the observer seeking his own identity in an unorganised wilderness. The Alps, even the polar regions, are characteristic Romantic settings: Mary Shelley, in *Frankenstein*, combines the two and throws in the desolate Hebrides for good measure. Even London, in Wordsworth's sonnet on Westminster Bridge –

> Ships, towers, domes, theatres, and temples lie
> Open unto the fields, and to the sky

– is seen as inert, empty of productive humanity though latent with power, like a landscape of unpopulated hills: Wordsworth could handle standing on a deserted bridge at dawn, but crowded city streets at noon were not at all to his taste.

Estranged from the contemporary, the Romantics also looked to the past. The past in this period ceased to be merely old, and because old imbued with patriarchal authority with regard to a degenerate present. The past became a mute appeal from a separate social experience, from long dead lovers of beauty who had left their memorials in quiet places, but also from men who had faced issues similar to those of a later age, though perhaps in simpler times. Obviously Romanticism's turning towards the past partook of the same antiquarian movement that provided the raw materials for Neo-classicism, but there is often a discernible difference of motive. In general, part of the attraction of the Gothic past was that it had been so long ignored and was so little comprehended that it offered itself as a kind of psychological refuge: but Major John Cartwright's interest in the Anglo-Saxon militia, and theories about the Norman Yoke were not escapist fantasies but ingredients in a political discourse of vital practical relevance.[49] Equally Greek and Roman antiquity, though studied with a much greater degree of learned expertise than the Middle Ages, could still provide opportunities for escapist self-indulgence, and this tendency was consciously resisted by some neo-classicists, for example John Flaxman who, condemning the neo-classicist interior designs of Thomas Hope's *Household Furniture* (1807), wrote:

> at such a moment as the present we confess we are not a little proud of this Roman spirit, which leaves the study of those effeminate elegancies to slaves and foreigners, and holds it beneath the dignity of a free man to be eminently skilled in the decoration of couches and the mounting of chandeliers.[50]

The picturesque movement to which Thomas Hope was such an influential contributor was essentially about protecting the wealthy patron from the harsh realities of the world, and in this sense, however dependent on classicist forms, was Romantic in spirit. The best example of literary 'picturesque' is perhaps Thomas Love Peacock. He is chiefly remembered for his satirical novels (which, be it noted, make fun of contemporary fads) but he also published a poem, *Rhodadaphne* (1818), full of classical learning and self-indulgent escapism, and asserted as a matter of doctrine that:

> Either in the scene, or in the time, or in both, it [poetry] must be remote from our ordinary perceptions . . .
> A poet in our time is a semi-barbarian in a civilised community. He lives in the days that are past.[51]

Peacock (who incidentally was by no means an unprogressive administrator at the East India Office) had a low opinion of John Keats because of the latter's blunders on classical themes; but perhaps Keats too belongs to the picturesque with his combination of neo-classical and Romantic elements. Perhaps of all major English poets – certainly of his contemporaries – he was the most preoccupied by questions of form, and the least interested in contemporary events. It would not be true to say that he lacked an intelligent understanding of politics, but for him the public was 'a thing I cannot help looking upon as an Enemy, and which I cannot address without feelings of hostility . . . I never wrote one single Line of Poetry with the least Shadow of public thought'. Later he confessed, 'Those whom I know already and who have grown as it were a part of myself I could not do without: but for the rest of Mankind, they are as much a dream to me as Milton's Hierarchies.' Thanks to his letters we see Keats more solidly, in more flesh-coloured tints than perhaps any other writer: not the wistful dreamer of the portraits but more energetic, more alert, more disputatious, an ardent youthful Napoleon of a poet; and yet, like other writers we tend to judge his *oeuvre* as a unit, rather than seeing it as perhaps we should merely as phases of a work in progress. Perhaps he did not live long enough for the real direction of his development to become evident: his attempt at epic in *Hyperion* seems as much a passing phase as his earlier tutelage to Leigh Hunt, as he himself realised:

> there were too many Miltonic inversions in it – Miltonic verse cannot be written but in an artful or rather artist's humour . . . It may be interesting to you to pick out some lines from Hyperion and put a mark X to the false beauty proceeding from art, and one ‖ to the true voice of feeling.[52]

But despite the reference to the true voice of feeling, Keats's only real subjects were himself as a poet, and his wrestlings with his own talent, and it is difficult to believe that, if he had lived, he would not have persevered in his pursuit of perfect form.

While it is Keats's preoccupation with form which associates him with Neo-classicism, with Shelley it is his preoccupation with the public. The question is not of which label we give Shelley but whom we compare him to: but it is only from the parochial Eng. Lit. point of view that he appears the archetypal Romantic. He is in fact the most unEnglish of English poets; even his verse reads as if translated. His way of looking at classical Greek culture, though apparently not derived directly from Winckelmann or Georg Forster, was fully in line with German neo-classicist views on the subject; his immersement in Greek literature and the innumerable echoes of that literature in his own work was comparable to that of André Chénier and Ugo Foscolo; his condemnation of formal imitation must be read in connection with the formal prosodic character of his later verse; even his low opinion of Michelangelo was based on typical neo-classicist criteria: 'no temperance no modesty no feeling for the just boundaries of art . . . no sense of beauty, and to want this is to want the essence of the creative power of mind'.[53] Above all his passionate political commitment, however unrealistic, was never escapist.

Shelley, of course, was one of the classic exponents of the theme of solitude and the isolated individual: the theme which appears central to Romanticism. When solitariness first came into vogue it was recommended for social reasons, as in Johann Georg Zimmermann's international bestseller *Ueber die Einsamkeit* ('On Solitude') of 1773: 'The chief design of this work was to exhibit the necessity of combining the uses of SOLITUDE, with those of SOCIETY, to shew, in the strongest light, the advantages they may mutually derive from each other; to convince mankind of the danger of running into either extreme.'[54] Romantic solitariness was precisely the type of extreme Zimmermann had deplored; but perhaps the process of retreat into solitude can be seen as a constant steady state in Shelley, who appears unchangingly poised between embracing public duties and repelling them with disgust, with the 'gloom and misanthropy' which he believed 'characteristic of the age in which we live':

> Alas, this is not what I thought life was,
> I knew that there were crimes and evil men,
> Misery and hate; nor did I hope to pass
> Untouched by suffering, through the evil glen . . .
>> (fragment, 1820)

alternates with:

> The world's great age begins anew,
> The golden years return
> (song concluding *Hellas* 1822)

Part of Shelley's problem seems to have been that his engagement with public affairs was combined with a belief that the vital moment was just past; the vital moment being the French Revolution:

> When the last hope of trampled France had failed
> Like a brief dream of unremaining glory,
> From visions of despair I rose . . .
>> (*The Revolt of Islam*, Canto 1, stanza 1)

Yet those who had lived through, and hoped great things from, the French Revolution, had had their own experience of disillusion:

> In youth by genius nurs'd,
> And big with lofty views, he to the world
> Went forth . . .
>
>   . . . The world, for so it thought,
> Owed him no service; and so his spirit turned away,
> And with the foot of pride sustained his soul
> In solitude

(Wordsworth, 'Lines left upon a Seat in a Yew Tree',
1798, lines 13–15, 18–22)

A pictorial presentation of such a retreat into isolationism actually in progress is given in many of Caspar David Friedrich's paintings: the pairs of ambiguous figures discussing weighty matters by moonlight; the man with his back to the viewer contemplating the sea of fog; perhaps most suggestive of all, the figure loitering pointlessly amongst the tombs of the *Freiheitskrieger*. Indeed Romantic solitariness seems characteristically more a movement *away* than any kind of arriving: Godwin's *Caleb Williams* is not a fictional sequel to *Political Justice* which he wrote immediately previously, it is a flight from it.[55] And who is Frankenstein if not another benefactor of humanity on the run?

X

Godwin and the Shelleys denied themselves one refuge which was vital to many of their contemporaries: religion. In England, religious revival partly took on some of the characteristics of Neoclassicism to begin with: the propaganda of Wilberforce, Hannah More and other Evangelicals had an unambiguously political motive, to reinforce the external social bonds of the public sphere and to reform public behaviour. But the main tendency of religious revival in this period was to focus on the private, individual experience of God, and to subordinate shared experience and common duties to the individual's lone relationship with Divinity. Movements like Methodism reflected a popular dissatisfaction with conventional religion and Wesley's solution was to revive and purify the practice; but another possibility was to jettison the outward forms altogether as, in Germany, Schleiermacher suggested in his *Reden über die Religion; an die Gebildeten unter ihren*

Verächtern (Discourse on Religion: to the Educated amongst its Despisers) (1794). Not simply the practice but even the symbolism of Christianity had worn itself out: Caspar David Friedrich and very different contemporaries such as Runge and Blake, even Wordsworth and Senancour, attempted to work out a new way to express and explore their experience of life in religious terms and to 'search for divinity outside the trappings of the Church'. It was not long before the Germans, the great commentators and theorists of Romanticism, produced a critical work on the use of symbolism in art to represent, even to make real, the divine: Friedrich Creuzer's *Symbolik und Mythologie der Alten* of 1810–12. More often than not it came down to what Coleridge called 'Religious meanings in the forms of Nature'. As Coleridge himself explained: 'In looking at objects of Nature while I am thinking . . . I seem rather to be seeking, as it were *asking*, a symbolical language for something within me that already and forever exists, than observing any thing new.'[56]

But the trappings of the Church had their appeal too. Perhaps even Keats's *The Eve of St Agnes* represents a flirtation with the outward show of medieval religion that goes beyond mere love of gothic scenery; at any rate the Anglo-Catholic movement in England, with its colour and pseudo-medieval paraphernalia eventually demonstrated that a retreat into the pieties and certainties of a lost past had much more emotional pull than the hell-fire-and-public-sobriety doctrines of the Evangelicals. In Germany, the depth of the religious motive in the Nazarener movement is shown by the conversion to Catholicism of three of its Protestant-raised adherents, Philipp Veit in 1810 and Friedrich Overbeck and Wilhelm Schadow in 1813–14. The two latter were actually converted in Rome; amongst native Italians, Alessandro Manzoni, in his *Inni Sacri* (1815) and *I Promessi Sposi* (1825–7) showed a strong pre-Enlightenment religious sensibility and a commitment to the devotional and pastoral side of Catholicism. Even in France Catholicism was a much more vital confessional faith after 1815 than it had been before 1789. Religious revival and Romanticism were in fact part of the same process, though sometimes the religious expression was formulated first, as with Schleiermacher, sometimes the Romanticism came first, as was partly the case in England, sometimes religion and Romanticism announced themselves together and in mutual support, as in Chateaubriand's *Le Génie du Christianisme* of 1802.

XI

The bewildering complex of attitudes in the continuum between Neo-classicism and Romanticism indicates the range of possible responses within a culture, and of possible dialectic cross-influences between them. We will scarcely find a complete *oeuvre* of any importance that is wholly either neo-classicist or romantic. It is necessary to follow the trajectory of individual careers within the vast Continent-wide melodrama of these years: not just the careers of people like Louis David and Ugo Foscolo who were in the firing line, but even, perhaps especially, of those who sought various strategies to insulate themselves from events. It should not be forgotten that Neo-classicism and Romanticism are just the name for a certain focal length of the telescope with which we examine the past: it is very very distant from us; but the people living in it saw it from far too close.

And yet if we, the observers, step back far enough certain patterns emerge, and parallels with other periods become visible. The simultaneity of Romanticism and Neo-classicism in different countries during the 1800s is comparable to the tell-tale resemblance of Nazi Art, Stalinist Art, Fascist Art and American New Deal Art which was discussed in Chapter 7: at the same time, the experience of the 1930s shows up certain aspects of the simultaneity of cultural movements more clearly than the 1800s. Except during the Jacobin period there was little systematic attempt to quarantine French ideas in the neo-classical-Romantic era, and it is the 1930s that show how cultural movements may occur simultaneously even in countries separated by barriers of political ideology: it is the 1930s which offer the clearest indication that cultural parallelism has little or nothing to do with transplanting or cross-fertilisation.

The determining factor in the congruence of artistic movements is surely the congruence of the hegemonic codings underlying them. Societies with very different economic and social structures may have very similar problems in the articulation of the hegemonic systems by which they are ruled. The political institutions of such countries may be much more widely disparate than the underlying formations, as Marx recognised when he wrote: 'Property, etc. in short, the entire content of the law and the state, is the same in North America as in Prussia, with few modifications. The *republic* there is thus a mere state *form*, as is the monarchy here.'[57]

Obviously, with different institutions, the official ideology will be very different, but official ideology is only one small part of a hegemonic coding, and in no sense can be regarded as the organising principle of the remainder. If we pursue the comparison of Hitler's Germany, Stalin's Russia, Mussolini's Italy and Roosevelt's America we will see that all four societies resembled one another in showing, for example, the coexistence of advanced industrialisation tending to organisational monopoly, and an agricultural sector retarded either completely (as in the Soviet Union) or in key areas (East Prussia and Pomerania, at least as compared to western Germany, Campania, Lucania, Calabria and Sicily, Oklahoma, Tennessee etc.). In purely economic terms it is nonsense to say that the four societies were at precisely the same stage of development – compare, for instance, industrial productivity in the USA and Italy, the size and development of the tertiary sector in Germany and the Soviet Union, etc. What *was* remarkably similar were the problems of integrating socially and geographically divided countries into a unified hegemonic system, and of legitimising hegemonic factions claiming extraordinary powers without (in three of the four cases) a genuine electoral mandate.

In the case of Romanticism-Neo-classicism it is clear that Britain differed from France, Germany and Italy, not only in its political structure but also economically, both agriculture and industry being very considerably more advanced than in Italy, and significantly more advanced than in France and Germany. Nevertheless, in all four countries there was an analogous crisis in the system of hegemony focusing on the question of the mobilising of support for the régimes, at a time when unprecedented demands were being made on the citizen's commitment to society and the legitimacy of existing governments was being questioned as never before. Marx has suggested that during particular types of crisis – what we may call crises of hegemony – there is a tendency for public rhetoric to fall into certain patterns: comparing the French second Republic to the period of the English and French Revolutions, he wrote:

just when they seemed engaged in revolutionizing themselves and things, in creating something entirely new, precisely in such epochs of revolutionary crisis they anxiously conjure up the spirits of the past to their service and borrow from them names, battle slogans and costumes in order to present the new scene of world history in this time honoured disguise and this borrowed language.[58]

Perhaps the similarity of the rhetoric even *proves* the similarity of the crises: but the rhetoric will invite much more attention than the obscure crisis underlying it, which is why the rhetoric, even in the complexly elaborated form of literature and art, might provide a good starting point for scholarly investigation.

9

Another Glance at Shakespeare

The ancient Mariner is saved in the Pilot's boat.

I

It would be simply foolish to pretend that cultural analysis can be a neat operation leaving no loose ends, like an experiment in a chemistry lab: the subject is too big and there are too many unknowns. But, as in the natural sciences, we have to take the known as our starting point: or better still, we have to take discrepancies between different known elements, because these discrepancies represent the questions we need to answer.

If we think of the English Renaissance, and the Reformation which in part preceded, in part accompanied it, as parts of a sub-epochal change which prepared England for the position of international commercial leadership which was seized in the 1700s, we will notice that one of the progressive, forward-looking features of Elizabeth's government was the way in which it sought not to enforce political uniformity but to avoid political division. It was desirable to accommodate economic and social expansion and readjustment within a framework of stability, but not to interfere with growth processes any more than was necessary to preserve continuity. In this relatively free atmosphere expansion was intellectual as well as economic, with new colleges being founded at Oxford and Cambridge – and Gresham's foundation in London – and Shakespeare's audience, and the whole generation of playwrights which included Shakespeare himself, must be seen as part of a culture of enlargening horizons. But perhaps the expansion was too rapid – perhaps one can even see in Shakespeare's overcrowded language an overcrowded culture jostling up against itself for want of psychological space in which to move – at any rate splits in the social fabric began to appear in place of those which had been patched over by the Elizabethan *Via Media*. Even the division of theatre audiences, with the establishment of private theatres, was part of a general process of social divison which prepared the way for 1642: and Shakespeare reflected this process in his plays, first with half a dozen tragedies and problem dramas exploring *angst*, uncertainty and disillusion, and then with the three final romances, fantasies of reconciliation and reassurance.

I find this interpretation rather bland and banal; this doesn't prove it isn't valid but I am more attracted by a view that emphasises not Shakespeare's participation in the intellectual currents of the day, but his aloofness. There is a theory that Shakespeare was a Catholic.[1] The theory at least is that he grew up a Catholic. The History plays, dealing with the period when all Englishmen were Catholic, might have been a kind of personal pilgrimage of reintegration into the society of his day: this complex myth of the past he constructed for a mainly Protestant audience may have been for himself a myth about essential Englishness, in which he chose Englishness rather than involvement with the secret struggles of the Counter-Reformation Catholic underground. In his only play which deals with the period of the Reformation, *Henry VIII*, he avoids entering into the religious issues even in Act 5, Scene 2 in which the attempt to disgrace Cranmer focuses on Cranmer's extreme Protestant views: there is certainly no attempt to play to a confirmed Protestant audience, though it is possible that he left the writing of this particular scene to John Fletcher anyway. If Shakespeare was a Catholic then it is perhaps no wonder he was detached from the preoccupations of his contemporaries, for he must have lived in a species of inner exile, feeling passionately – the more so in that he was intensely English – that his country and his people had gone irretrievably wrong, and lacking any means of expressing what he felt.

But one problem with these kinds of explanation is not that they may be demonstrably wrong, or fail to provide some illumination, but simply that, alongside their subject, they seem so ineffably feeble. I have been thinking this while reading Grigori Kozintsev's *King Lear: The Space of Tragedy* (1977) and remembering his film of *Lear* which I have seen four times: I have been increasingly impressed, each time, and can also testify to its spell-binding effect on rooms full of adolescents not accustomed to long films in Russian with illegible subtitles. The memory of it shows me how thin and bloodless and belittling the interpretation of *Lear* I suggested in Chapter 3 really is. What Kozintsev's *Lear* emphasises is the vileness and the horror to which the world is given over when the norms – expectations, conventions – are shoved facilely to one side. All that stuff I wrote about rôles is only the mechanism in *Lear* for the way the norms of peace and stability and growth totter and then disintegrate. All Shakespeare's tragedies – even *Romeo and Juliet* – are nightmares about the infinity of dread possibilities lurking behind the thin façades of convention amongst which we live. Perhaps this is Shakespeare's relevance to his day: his drama is the exploration of the imminent breakdown which he already saw latent in the social structures of his time.

II

Shakespeare will always constitute a warning against facile reductionism and glib answers. But difficulty in arriving at answers is no reason not to ask questions.

In literary studies as in historical studies one needs to deal with problems rather than periods: but in history most problems are immediately visible from the scale of their human effect, whereas the problems of literature have to be searched for. Great authors in isolation provide biographical and psychological problems: only in historical context do they reveal historical problems.

The search for problems means clocking into libraries day after day to examine piles of books, files of *Mss*, not to prove theories but simply to see how it was, and being willing to launch out on private voyages of discovery amongst the names which still live only in the catalogue entries of the unreadable books they wrote. Coleridge, the prototype of the intellectual whose reputation depends on knowing all about the *in* subjects he has scarcely studied, said 'there are men, who gain the reputation of a wide erudition by consuming that time in reading Books obselete & of no character, which other men employ in reading those which every Body reads'.[2] Some people may think it would be wonderful to have English departments full of youths who think they are Shelley, taught by academics who think they are Coleridge, but personally I can't help feeling that only scholars who prefer to let other people do their thinking for them will be content to follow Coleridge's advice and read only what everyone else is reading.

We must not be afraid to extend our horizons. It is worth noting how relatively brief European cultural history is, how few the paradigmatic cases one may look to. Perhaps eventually it would be useful to compare Europe with other areas where societies quite similar, subject to common influences, produced essentially independent cultures: the Indian subcontinent, for example.

And we must not be afraid of analytic complexities. My formulation of the concept of hegemonic coding leaves us still very distant from a ready technique for matching causes and effects. Ultimately I believe that an adequate understanding of a historical moment, added to an adequate biographical analysis of the individual writer in relationship to his hegemonic position, would give an adequate historical decoding of a specific text; but such analyses are not to be thought of as simple; we are talking here not of short cuts but of understanding great complexities.

We should never forget that behind the crisp hygienic scholarly editions that are so convenient to use there stand individuals whose lives were as much a myriad of detail as our own: a Shakespeare who, even if he was not a Catholic, at some stage of his life tried to figure out what religion meant to him personally; a Wordsworth who, when the postman delivered a parcel of books, seized on them with avidity and cut their pages with a knife still buttery from the breakfast table; a Marx who, before he grew his bushy Bloomsbury beard, was a poetical-looking youth with a thin face and a wispy moustache; a Wilfred Owen whose teacher thought he did not put enough commas in his school exercises. But to look only at indivduals in isolation is to squint. Reflection on my own life leads me to think how far and how completely we are each of us formed by our historical context, though also how these shared historical ingredients tend to mix and blend in unique patterns, according to unique aspects of our individual (but essentially historical) experiences acting on our individual sensibility (itself a social and therefore historical formation commencing in our infancies if not, genetically, even before). It is this quality of uniqueness, not always so very interesting in itself, which when realised effectively is what makes literature valuable as literature. The complex of processes which create the uniqueness combined with the belongingness of the individual is as exquisite and as wonderful as the uniqueness of a snowflake.

History is how all we individuals are affected together, but for our purposes it is not enough to say that literature is the result of a dialogue between the individual and his history – such a concept of 'dialogue' will only hamper our historical analysis, and the individual himself is after all part of the history. The difference between literary history and other forms of history in the end must be only one of degree: just as the individual is perceived to play a larger rôle in political history than in social or economic history, so in literary history the individual has a larger rôle than in political history – but essentially the same *kind* of rôle, historiographically speaking. To deny the historical dimension would be to deny reality: to deny the individual would be to deny much of the point and beauty of that reality.

Notes and References

1 Nations and Art Forms

1. For Conrad and James see Ford Madox Ford, *Return to Yesterday* (London, 1931) pp. 23–4. The couplet is by Hugh MacDiarmid.
2. For provincial cultural separation in France, for example, see Theodore Zeldin, *France 1848–1945: Intellect and Pride* (Oxford, paperback edn, 1980) pp. 43–85.
3. Percy Bysshe Shelley, 'Discourse on the Manners of the Ancients' *c.*1818, in R. Ingpen and W. E. Peck (eds), *The Complete Works of Percy Bysshe Shelley* 10 vols (London and New York, 1926–30) vol. 7, p. 223.
4. For an unsatisfactory comparison of Beethoven's Pastoral Symphony with Wordsworth's *Prelude* see H. G. Schenk, *The Mind of the European Romantics* (Oxford, paperback edn, 1977) pp. 166–7.
5. For Wordsworth-Constable comparisons see K. Kroeber, *Romantic Landscape Vision: Constable and Wordsworth* (Madison, Wisconsin, 1975) *passim*, and p. 9, note 9 for bibliography, and John Barrell, *The Dark Side of the Landscape* (London, 1980) chap. 4. For Constable's reading see R. B. Beckett (ed.), *John Constable's Correspondence* 8 vols (London and Ipswich, 1962–75) vol. 8, pp. 39–44. For Thomsom in the 1800s, and Bloomfield see A. D. Harvey, *English Poetry in a Changing Society, 1790–1825* (London, 1980) pp. 77–91.
6. See Michael Rosenthal, *Constable: The Painter and his Landscape* (Newhaven, 1983) espec. pp. 71–89 and 211–3.
7. The remark, 'Behold a man who has discovered the tragedy of landscape', is by the French sculptor Pierre Jean David d'Angers – see Carl Gustav Carus, *Lebenserinnerungen und Denkwurdigkeiten* 4 vols (Leipzig, 1865–6) vol. 2, p. 388. For the Friedrich quotation, see William Vaughan, *German Romantic Painting* (London, 1980) pp. 66–8. The Norwegian artist Johann Christian Dahl, who was intimate with Friedrich from 1818 onwards, left an interesting account of Friedrich's views on the relationship between nature and the artist, see Sigrid Hinz (ed.), *Caspar David Friedrich in Briefen und Bekenntnissen* (München, 1974) p. 208.
8. Ernst Jünger, *The Storm of Steel* (London, 1927; translation of *In Stahlgewittern*) p. 316.
9. The quotation is from the journal of Alex Riley, cited in Robert Rhodes James, *Gallipoli* (London, 1965) p. 199. See Paul Fussell, *The Great War and Modern Memory* (London and New York, 1975) pp. 231–69 for the Arcadian tradition, and pp. 270–309 for the homoerotic tradition in English First World War poetry. There is no comparable study for other languages but see William K. Pfeiler, *War and the German Mind:*

Testimony of Men of Fiction Who Fought At The Front (New York, 1941) and C. N. Genno, H. Wetzel (eds), *The First World War in German Narrative Prose* (Toronto, 1980); Francesco Formigari, *La Letteratura di Guerra in Italia 1915–1935* (Roma, 1935) and Mario Isnenghi, *Il Mito della Grande Guerra* (Bari, 1970); Jean Norton Cru, *Témoins: Essai d'Analyse et de Critique des Souvenirs de Combattants Edites en Français de 1915 à 1928* (Paris, 1929) and John Cruickshank, *Variations on Catastrophe: Some French Responses to the Great War* (Oxford, 1982).

10. Raymond Williams, *Culture and Society, 1780–1950* (1971, Penguin ed.) p. 248. See also Terry Eagleton, *Literary Theory* (Oxford, 1983) p. 213.
11. See Georg Freidrich Koch, *Die Kunstausstellung* (Berlin, 1967) and E. Spicknagel and B. Walbe (eds), *Museum Lernort contra Musentempel* (Giessen, 1976) and, generally, Niels von Holst, *Creators, Collectors and Connoisseurs* (London, 1976).

2 Literature, Literary History and History

1. Kenneth Clark, *The Gothic Revival* (London, 1974 edn) p. 139, cited (from earlier edition) by Raymond Williams, *Culture and Society 1780–1950* (Penguin edn 1971) p. 137.
2. Giorgio Vasari, *Lives of the Artists* (Penguin edn 1971) p. 50 originally published in 1550. The Italian is *non nella buona maniera greca ma in quella goffa moderna di quei tempi*, but I think Vasari employs the concept of style even if he does not use the word itself.
3. John Summerson, *Architecture in Britain 1530 to 1830* (London, 1969 edn) p. 245.
4. E. J. Morley (ed.), *Hurd's Letters on Chivalry and Romance* (London, 1911) p. 103 (Letter V).
5. Thomas Warton, *The History of English Poetry* 2 vols (London, 1774) pp. i–ii.
6. Louis Gabriel Ambrose de Bonald, *Oeuvres* 12 vols (Paris, 1817–19) vol. 9, pp. 378–9. Germaine de Staël, *De la Littérature, considérée dans les rapports avec les institutions sociales* (1800) also seems an obvious text to cite here: but like other of her critical works it advertises rather than illuminates its theme.
7. Thomas Love Peacock, 'An Essay on Fashionable Literature', in H. F. B. Brett-Smitt and C. E. Jones, *The Works of Thomas Love Peacock* 10 vols (London 1934) vol. 8 pp. 263–91, at p. 265.
8. G. M. Miller, *The Historical Point of View in English Literary Criticism from 1570–1770* (Heidelberg, 1913; facsimile reprint New York, 1968) p. 17.
9. Philip Henderson (ed.), *The Letters of William Morris* (London, 1950) p. 262, Morris to the editor of the *Pall Mall Gazette*, 1 Nov. 1886. Morris was referring primarily to the pulling down of old buildings but he clearly meant his criticism also in a more general sense.
10. See R. P. Bilan, *The Literary Criticism of F. R. Leavis* (Cambridge, 1979) pp. 25–8, 40–1, 133, 153–4 and Leavis's own essay, 'Arnold as Critic', *Scrutiny* vol. VII (1937–8) pp. 319–32; also F. R. Leavis *English Literature in our time and the University* (Cambridge, 1979 edn.) p. 42–4. For Eliot see C. K. Stead, 'Eliot, Arnold, and the English Poetic Tradition', in

D. Newton de Molina (ed.), *The Literary Criticism of T. S. Eliot* (London, 1977) pp. 184–206; and generally, Chris Baldick, *The Social Mission of English Criticism, 1848–1932* (Oxford, 1983).

11. E. B. Murray review of A. D. Harvey, *English Poetry in a Changing Society, 1780–1825*, in *Review of English Studies* vol. XXXV, February 1984, p. 98. For Arnold's influence in the 1940s see C. K. Stead's essay cited in the previous note, p. 185.

12. J. Bryson (ed.), *Matthew Arnold: Poetry and Prose* (London, 1954) pp. 666–7.

13. Howard F. Lowry (ed.), *Letters from Matthew Arnold to Arthur Hugh Clough* (London, 1932) p. 65, letter to Clough, Dec. 1847.

14. George W. E. Russell (ed.), *Letters of Matthew Arnold, 1848–1888* 2 vols (London, 1895) vol. 2, p. 9. Letter to his mother 5 June 1869.

15. Ibid., vol. 1, p. 96, letter to Miss Arnold 25 June 1859.

16. 'A French Eton', in Bryson (ed.) *Matthew Arnold: Poetry and Prose*, pp. 336–7.

17. See for example Edward C. Mack, *Public Schools and British Opinion* (New York, 1938); T. W. Bamford, *Rise of the Public School* (London, 1967); D. A. Winstanley, *Early Victorian Cambridge* (Cambridge, 1940); and *Late Victorian Cambridge* (Cambridge, 1947); W. R. Ward, *Victorian Oxford* (Oxford, 1965) and Sheldon Rothblatt, *Revolution of the Dons* (London, 1968).

18. 'A French Eton', in Bryson (ed.), *Matthew Arnold: Poetry and Prose*, p. 338.

19. Gordon Haight, *George Eliot* (Oxford, 1968) p. 443.

20. Bryson (ed.), *Matthew Arnold: Poetry and Prose*, p. 283.

21. 'The function of Criticism at the Present Time', Ibid., p. 354.

22. See Mary Moorman, *William Wordsworth: The Early Years, 1770–1803* (Oxford, 1957) pp. 99–102 and Ben Ross Schneider, *Wordsworth's Cambridge Education* (Cambridge, 1957) espec. pp. 263–4. See also Paul Kelly, 'Wordsworth and Lucretius' *De Rerum Natura'*, *Notes and Queries*, vol. 228 (1983) pp. 219–22.

23. T. S. Eliot, 'Poetry in the Eighteenth Century', in Boris Ford (ed.), *A Guide to English Literature*, vol. 4 *From Dryden to Johnson* (London, 1957) pp. 263–9, at pp. 263–4: this essay was originally the introduction to the Haslewood Books edition of Johnson's *London* and *Vanity of Human Wishes*, 1930, and was reprinted in Phyllis M. Jones (ed.), *English Critical Essays, Twentieth Century* (London 1933).

24. Perhaps the most influential recent tarting-up (or Freudianisation) of Eliot's theory that poetry is mainly a response to other poetry is Harold Bloom, *The Anxiety of Influence* (London, 1973).

25. F. R. Leavis, *English Literature in Our Time and the University* (Cambridge, 1979 edn) pp. 63–4.

26. Andor Gomme, 'Criticism and the reading Public', in Boris Ford (ed.), *A Guide to English Literature*, vol. 7 *The Modern Age* (London, 1973 edn) pp. 368–94, at p. 376. Actually Q. D. Leavis's documentation is far from systematic: see John Carey, 'Queenie Leavis – help or hindrance to her husband?' *The Listener*, 7 Oct. 1982, pp. 15–17, especially p. 16.

27. Leavis, *English Literature in our Time and the University*, p. 64.

28. Citations are from the London 1937 edition which is available in facsimile reprint.
29. See Perry Anderson, 'Components of the National Culture', *New Left Review*, 50 (1968) pp. 3–57, espec. pp. 7–12.
30. F. W. Bateson, 'Literary History: Non-Subject Par Excellence', *New Literary History*, vol. 2 (1970–1) pp. 115–22, at p. 116. More generous but indicating a similar conclusion is Richard Wortman's 'Epilogue: History and Literature' in Gary Saul Morson (ed.), *Literature and History: Theoretical Problems and Russian Case Studies* (Stanford, 1986) pp. 275–93; Wortman, at pp. 275–6, suggests that the interdisciplinary dream is elusive 'because each discipline works with its own set of meanings, and among the meanings it assigns are the meanings of other disciplines.'
31. See Colin Evans, 'Understanding Innovation Through Group-relations Study', *New Universities Quarterly*, vol. 36 (1982) pp. 359–74, espec. p. 372.
32. Svetlana and Paul Alpers, '*Ut Pictora Noesis?* Criticism in Literary Studies and Art History', *New Literary History*, vol. 3, pp. 437–58, at p. 444. See also pp. 559–68, Oleg Grabar, 'History of Art and History of Literature. Some Random Thoughts', and pp. 569–74, Jean Seznec, 'Art and Literature: A Plea for Humility'.
33. See the discussion in John Schellenberger, 'English and History: Yet Another Plea for Correlation', *Cambridge Quarterly*, vol. 12, pp. 174–88, at pp. 177–9.
34. Hans Robert Jauss, 'Literary History as a Challenge to Literary Theory', *New Literary History*, vol. 2 pp. 7–37, at p. 10. This is a translation of his 'Literaturgeschichte als Provokation der Literaturwissenschaft' of 1967 which has been frequently reprinted in Germany, including in *Literaturgeschichte als Provokation* (Frankfurt, 1970). See also his *Towards an Aesthetic of Literary Reception* (Brighton, 1982) and Robert C. Holub, *Reception Theory: a critical introduction* (London, 1984) pp. 53–82.
35. Roland Barthes's 'Histoire au Littérature', *Annales etc.*, 1960, no. 3; reprinted in *Sur Racine* (Paris, 1963) translated as *On Racine* (New York, 1964), p. 161 of this edition.
36. Lucien Goldmann, *Structures Mentales et Création Culturelle* (Paris, 1970) pp. 347, 410, and see John Schellenberger, 'English and History', *Cambridge Quarterly*, vol. 12, pp. 186–7.
37. Duccio Trombadori, *Colloqui con Foucault* (Salerno, 1981) p. 67. I am grateful to R. James Goldstein for bringing this text to my attention: the translation is his.
38. Augustus Henry Lane Fox Pitt-Rivers, *Excavations in Cranborne Chase, near Rushmore, on the Borders of Dorset and Wilts* 5 vols (printed for private circulation 1887–1903) vol. 1, p. xvii.
39. E. H. Carr, *What Is History?* (London, 1961) p. 18.
40. William Bowman Piper, in *The Eighteenth Century: A Current Bibliography*, n.s. 6 (1980) p. 319.
41. See *Parliamentary Papers*, 1803–4, vol. xi, pp. 1–3 and 1812–13, vol. xii, pp. 248–9.

3 Types of Information

1. Anthony Trollope, *The Prime Minister* (1875–6), chap. 7. With very rare exceptions the privy council meets (vestigially) only in the presence of the sovereign or in subcommittees. Note also how the Duchess of Omnium says 'counties' when she means 'lord lieutenancies' (chap. 6) and the Great Seal and the Lord Chancellorship become 'seals', which are the emblem of office of the Secretaries of State (chap. 8). The picture of the prime minister's work in chaps. 18 and 27 is quite unconvincing, and Sir Orlando Drought's presentation of his resignation for discussion by the assembled cabinet in chap. 38 reveals a profound ignorance of the functionings of cabinet government.

2. See John Schellenberger, 'English and History: Yet Another Plea for Correlation', *Cambridge Quarterly*, vol. 12, pp. 174–88, at pp. 180–8. A view generally similar to Schellenberger's on literature as a historical source is put forward in Kevin Sharpe, 'The Politics of Literature in Renaissance England', *History*, vol. 71 (1986) pp. 235–47. See also *passim* W. A. Speck, *Society and Literature in England 1700–1760* (Dublin, 1983).

3. See Terry Eagleton, *Criticism and Ideology* (London, 1978 edn) p. 44 foll. Eagleton's categories (or 'major constituents of a Marxist theory of literature') are: General Mode of Production, Literary Mode of Production, General Ideology, Authorial Ideology, Aesthetic Ideology, and Text. He suggests the abbreviations *GMP, LMP, GI, AuI, AI*, though he has left it to his disciples to suggest for example that

$$AuI = GMP\ (\ \frac{LMP}{GI}\ ) - AI$$

But in the end the problem with Eagleton's categories is not their psuedo-algebraic character, but their grossly simplistic terms of reference.

4. For women's sexual appetites see Nicholas Venette, *Tableau de l'amour considéré dans l'estat du mariage* (Parma, 1688) pp. 106, 158; for female virginity as a treasure or flower see Anon., *The Finish'd Rake* (London, 1733) p. 41; [R. Lewis], *The Adventures of a Rake* 2 vols (London, 1759) vol. 1, p. 91; Anon., *The History of the Human Heart* (London, 1885 edn) p. 38 (first published 1749); John Cleland, *Fanny Hill* (London, 1963 edn) pp. 55, 56 (first published 1748–9). See also A. D. Harvey, '*Clarissa* and the Puritan Tradition', *Essays in Criticism*, vol. 28 (1978) pp. 38–51 and K. V. Thomas, 'The Double Standard', *Journal of the History of Ideas*, vol. 20 (1959) pp. 195–216.

5. For a more detailed discussion of these issues see A. D. Harvey, 'The Nightmare of *Caleb Williams*', *Essays in Criticism*, vol. 26 (1976) pp. 236–49, at pp. 237–40; see also the discussion of Godwin's inaccurate treatment of English law in *The British Critic*, vol. 5 (1795) pp. 446–7.

6. Godwin's purpose, 'to comprehend, as far as the progressive nature' is quoted from his suppressed Preface to the original edition published under the title, *Things Are as They Are: Or the Adventures of Caleb*

Williams, in 1793; 'I was obviously led . . .' is from *The British Critic,* vol. 6 (1795) pp. 94–5; for Disraeli see S. M. Smith, 'Willenhall and Wodgate: Disraeli's Use of Blue Book Evidence', *Review of English Studies,* n.s. vol. 13 (1962) pp. 368–84 and Martin Fido, '"From his own Observation": Sources of Working Class Passages in Disraeli's *Sybil',* *Modern Languages Review,* vol. 72 (1977) pp. 268–84.

7. See discussion in A. D. Harvey, 'The Nightmare of Caleb Williams', *Essays in Criticism,* vol. 26 (1976) pp. 236–49, at pp. 240–3.

8. This idea has so far become folklore as to feature in a Brian Aldiss novel, *Frankenstein Unbound* (London, 1973). For Mary Shelley's use of contemporary science see Samuel Holmes Vasbinder, *Scientific Attitudes in Mary Shelley's 'Frankenstein'* (Ann Arbor, 1984) espec. pp. 65–82.

9. The question of dating the action is discussed in A. D. Harvey, '*Frankenstein* and *Caleb Williams', Keats-Shelley Journal,* 29 (1980) pp. 21–7.

10. See B. R. Pollin, 'Philosophical and Literary Sources of *Frankenstein', Comparative Literature,* vol. 17 (1965) pp. 97–108, at p. 99.

11. See A. D. Harvey, *English Poetry in a Changing Society, 1780–1825* (London, 1980) pp. 2–3 for the origins of the idea that the French Revolution caused Romanticism.

12. See A. D. Harvey, 'First Public Reactions to the Industrial Revolution', *Etudes Anglaises,* vol. 31 (1978) pp. 273–93 at p. 274–5 and 283–4.

13. Ibid. p. 282, and [G. S. Hillard, ed.], *Life, Letters, and Journals of George Tickner* 2 vols (London, 1876) vol. 1, p. 272, journal 1819.

14. *Parliamentary Papers* 1814–15, vol. X, p. 91.

15. See *Historic Manuscripts Commission, Kenyon Mss,* p. 548, Lady Kenyon to Lord Kenyon, 3 Aug. [1797]; and Lady Theresa Lewis (ed.), *Extracts from the Journals and Correspondence of Miss Berry* 3 vols (London, 1865) vol. 2, pp. 356–7, journal 22 July 1808.

16. See Hannah Cowley, *The Scottish Village, or, Pitcairne Green* (1786), National Library of Wales 1340C, pp. 10–11, M's Tour, 25 August 1801 and Robert Southey in *Quarterly Review,* vol. 8 (1812) p. 341.

17. See illustrations in Sixten Rönnow, *Pehr Hilleström* (Stockholm, 1929); pp. 179–92 gives an interesting survey of European industrial painting up to 1800. Incidentally one of the first German paintings of the period to show industrialisation is Karl Friedrich Schinkel's sketch of 1812 for a stage set showing a mine in Calabria, hardly one of the cradles of the Industrial Revolution.

18. Thomas Barnes, *Parliamentary Portraits* (London, 1815) p. 25.

19. Thomas Evans, *Christian Policy the Salvation of the Empire* 2nd edn (London, 1816) pp. 22–3.

20. Thomas, Earl of Dundonald, *Autobiography of a Seaman* 2 vols (London, 1860) vol. 2, p. 263.

21. H. W. J. Edwards (ed.), *The Radical Tory* (London, 1937) p. 169, Disraeli's hustings speech at Taunton 1835; for the 'radical' version of these views see his hustings speech at High Wycombe, 27 November 1832, printed H. W. J. Edwards, op. cit., pp. 161–8 and his pamphlet *What Is He?* (1833) printed in Edwards, op. cit., pp. 53–61. Robert Blake, *Disraeli* (London, 1966) is not very helpful on the antecedents of

Disraeli's political ideas, but he traces Disraeli's relationship with the ambiguous Tory Lord Chancellor, Lyndhurst, pp. 115–17.

22. *The Courier*, 23 June 1807: *The Daily Telegraph* of the period.
23. See Christopher Hill, *Puritanism and Revolution* (London, 1958) pp. 94–122, which discusses the Norman Yoke.
24. I.e. Isaac D'Israeli, *Vaurien* (1797); see A. D. Harvey, 'George Walker and the Anti-Revolutionary Novel', *Review of English Studies*, n.s. vol. 28 (1977) pp. 290–300.
25. For Disraeli on the novel see Robert Blake, *Disraeli* (London, 1966) p. 732 quoting memo by Montagu Corry, 15 October 1878.
26. F. R. and Q. D. Leavis, *Dickens the Novelist* (London, 1970) pp. 34–105.
27. John Carey, *The Violent Effigy* (London, 1979 edn) p. 111.
28. Raymond Williams, *Culture and Society 1780–1950* (1971 Penguin edn) p. 104; cf. S. J. Spector, 'Masters of Metonymy: *Hard Times* and Knowing the Working Class', *ELH*, vol. 51 (1984) pp. 365–84.
29. See John Schellenberger, 'English and History: Yet Another Plea for Correlation', *Cambridge Quarterly*, vol. 12 (1984) pp. 174–88, at pp. 185–6; for *Fatherless Fanny* see Louis James, *Fiction for the Working Man 1830–1860* (London, 1963) p. 109; though indeed the second part of Richardson's *Pamela* also deals with most of the implications of this theme.
30. I am strengthened in my belief that it is by no means anachronistic or forcing to suggest that *King Lear* is organised paradigmatically by the fact that a similar approach may also be seen in *Othello*, where Othello (racially and culturally) and Iago (socially) are both essentially outsiders. *Measure for Measure*, which belongs to the same period also may be read in terms of the counterpointing of characters.

4 Towards a Social Theory of Artistic Change

1. The Metaphysical Marx seems to be the alternative more in vogue at present: see John Frow, *Marxism and Literary History* (Oxford, 1986).
2. See Hannah Arendt's Introduction to Walter Benjamin, *Illuminations* (London, 1973) pp. 1–55, at pp. 11–12, 14, 47.
3. Karl Marx, Preface to *Contribution to the Critique of Political Economy* (1859) in R. C. Tucker, *The Marx–Engels Reader* 2nd edn (New York, 1978) p. 4.
4. Raymond Williams, *Marxism and Literature* (Oxford, 1977) pp. 92–4, and cf. Vladimir V. Mayakovsky, *How Are Verses Made?* (originally published 1926, trans G. M. Hyde, London, 1970) which, however, has a less materialistic emphasis than Williams; Nicos Poulantzas, *Political Power and Social Classes* (London, 1973) p. 13; Gregor McLennan, *Marxism and the Methodologies of History* (London, 1981) p. 44.
5. See Raymond Williams, *Marxism and Literature*, p. 106, in his critique of Goldmann *et al.* for the 'substitution of *epochal* etc.'; Chantal Mouffe, 'Hegemony and Ideology in Gramsci', in Tony Bennett (ed.), *Culture, Ideology and Social Process* (London, 1981) pp. 219–34, at p. 224 for 'only a fundamental class' etc. (I can't believe for a moment that this is

what Gramsci had in mind); Gregor McClennan, *Marxism and the Methodologies of History*, p. 179–83 for a critique of Poulantzas with regard to applying his theory to actual historical formations.

6. Marx, 'The Eighteenth Brumaire of Louis Napoleon', section not printed in *The Marx–Engels Reader* but see Karl Marx and Frederick Engels, *Selected Works* 3 vols (Moscow, 1969) vol. 1, p. 421 for 'an entire superstructure of distinct etc.'; letter to Anenkov, 28 Dec. 1846, *The Marx–Engels Reader*, pp. 136–7 for 'Assume particular stages . . .'

7. Marx, *Theories of Surplus-Value* 3 vols (Moscow, 1964–72) vol. 1, p. 276.

8. Williams, *Marxism and Literature*, p. 93.

9. Marx, Economic and Philosophic Manuscripts of 1844, *The Marx–Engels Reader*, pp. 88–9; 1859 Preface, Ibid., p. 5.

10. Ibid., pp. 245–6.

11. See S. S. Prawer, *Karl Marx and World Literature* (Oxford, 1978) pp. 211–31 (which deal with Marx's literary correspondence with Lassalle) and pp. 409–10; and Tony Bennett, *Formalism and Marxism* (London, 1979) pp. 153–5.

12. Williams, *Marxism and Literature*, p. 107.

13. *The Marx–Engels Reader*, p. 5; Étienne Balibar, 'Basic Concepts of Historical Materialism', in Louis Althusser and Étienne Balibar, *Reading Capital* (London, 1970) pp. 201–308 at pp. 285 and 307.

14. *The Marx–Engels Reader*, p. 291 and cf. Ibid, pp. 443–65.

15. See E. H. Carr, *What Is History?* (London, 1961) pp. 27–8 for a brief discussion of Individualism

16. 1859 Preface, *The Marx–Engels Reader*, p. 5.

17. Ibid., p. 5.

18. Poulantzas, *Political Power and Social Classes*, p. 15.

19. *The Marx–Engels Reader*, p. 595.

20. Poulantzas, *Political Power and Social Classes*, pp. 231 and 239.

21. Percy Bysshe Shelley, *A Defence of Poetry*, last paragraph.

5   Second-rateness

1. P. Orecchioni, 'Pour une histoire sociologique de la littérature', in Robert Escarpit (ed.), *La Littérature et le Social* (Paris, 1970) pp. 43–53, at p. 50.

2. See for example W. J. Keith, *The Rural Tradition* (Toronto, 1974), which is subtitled 'A Study of the Non-Fiction Prose Writers of the English Countryside' and glibly proposes (p. ix) 'to clear the ground', for a survey of the subject which includes 'significant continuities between one rural writer and another . . . the critical problems inherent in such writing . . . the cogency of thinking in terms of a possible "rural tradition"', by dealing with, for the nineteenth century, Cobbett, Mary Russell Mitford, George Borrow, Richard Jeffries and W. H. Hudson. A couple of these ought to have been omitted, according to Keith's scheme to include only 'writers whose main literary productions belong to the area of non-fiction', for we see that Thomas Hardy is left out because he is principally a novelist. Since there are hundreds

of other Victorian non-fiction writers on the countryside whom Keith doesn't mention – perhaps they are not second-rate enough to stand alongside George Borrow and W. H. Hudson – we end up with *Hamlet* minus not only the Prince but also almost the entire cast except Polonius.

3. P. Orecchioni, op. cit., p. 50.
4. F. W. Bateson, 'Literary History: Non-Subject *Par Excellence*', *New Literary History*, vol. II (1970–1) pp. 115–22, at p. 122.
5. William Wordsworth, 'Essay Supplementary to the Preface'.
6. F. W. J. Schelling, academy oration to Academy of Sciences at Munich, 12 October 1806, 'Concerning the Relation of the Plastic Arts to Nature', in Herbert Read (ed.), *The True Voice of Feeling* (New York, 1953) pp. 323–58, at pp. 331–2.
7. Orwell seems to have known the American translation of *We*, New York 1924. 'Year Nine' first appeared in *The New Statesman* in 1938 and was reprinted in Connolly's *The Condemned Playground*, 1946.
8. By Symbolism I mean the international artistic movement, not the contemporary fashion in French poetry, though this was of course connected. See the French, German and Dutch language catalogues of the International Council of Museums sponsored exhibition of Symbolist Art held in various European cities in 1975–6; the inclusion of such artists as Munch and Burne-Jones gives perhaps a misleading view of both the scope and quality of what was, however, a very diffuse movement. See also Robert Schmutzler, *Art Nouveau* (London, 1964).
9. Aleister Reid, in E. W. Tedlock (ed.), *Dylan Thomas: The Legend and the Poet* (London, 1963) p. 54.
10. P. Orecchioni, op. cit., p. 53.
11. Henry James, 'The Author of Beltraffio'. Some editions omit the bit about shams but see Scribner's New York edition of *The Novels and Tales of Henry James* (New York, 1907–9) vol. 16, p. 47.
12. Percy Bysshe Shelley *A Defence of Poetry*, last paragraph.

6 The Audience and the Artist

1. See for example Albert Asor Rosa (ed.), *Letteratura Italiana*, vol. 2 *Produzione e Consumo* (Torino, 1981) or, with a more narrow focus, R. Engelsing, *Der Burger als Leser* (Stuttgart, 1974) and Horst Albert Glaser (ed.), *Deutsche literatur, eine Sozialgeschichte*, vols 4–8 (Rembek bei Hamburg, 1980–2); for sociology of literature, the most widely circulated work is Robert Escarpit, *Sociologie de la Littérature* (Paris, 1960, 5th edn 1973); an international anthology with a useful bibliography is Alfredo Luzi (ed.), *Sociologia de la Letteratura* (Milano, 1977). In English, see two *Sociological Review* monographs: Jane Routh and Janet Wolff (eds), *The Sociology of Literature: Theoretical Approaches* (Keele, 1977) and Diana Laurenson (ed.), *The Sociology of Literature: Applied Studies* (Keele, 1978).
2. F. R. and Q. D. Leavis, *Dickens the Novelist* (London, 1973) p. 122.

3. See John Schellenberger, 'English and History: Yet Another Plea for Correlation', *Cambridge Quarterly*, vol. 12, pp. 174–88, at pp. 181–2. A very much author-bound study of this topic is Ian Jack, *The Poet and his Audience* (Cambridge, 1984).

4. As I was writing these words at Marina di Vietri, just outside Salerno, I seemed to hear a violent explosion on the other side of the bay, in the direction of Via Irno, where the Cattedra di Letteratura Italiana have their offices. Goldoni, Metastasio, Alfieri, the three greatest dramatists of the eighteenth century, after Beaumarchais; Manzoni, by far the most talented imitator of Sir Walter Scott; Leopardi, a poet who *almost* deserves comparison with Shelley; Carducci . . .

5. See the Appendix 'Numbers of Editions of Poetry in British Isles 1795–1825', in A. D. Harvey, *English Poetry in a changing Society, 1780–1825* (London, 1980) pp. 186–90 and J. D. Gutteridge's remarks in his review of this book in *British Book News* (March, 1981).

6. Information from M. Crump of the *Eighteenth Century Short Title Catalogue* (ESTC).

7. George Orwell was only an inspector in the Burma Police, and therefore not strictly speaking an officer in the military sense; but I am not sure how else one describes a member of the controlling caste in a paramilitary organisation.

8. Thomas Middleton Rayser (ed.), *Samuel Taylor Coleridge. Shakespeare Criticism* 2 vols (London, 1960) vol. 1, p. 35. Coleridge perpetuated a number of remarks that seem classics of what we now call the Victorian attitude, e.g. 'a virtuous woman will *not* consciously feel what she ought not, because she is ever on the alert to discountenance and suppress the very embryos of Thoughts not strictly justifiable, so as to prevent them remaining long enough in their transit over her mind to be even remembered'. E. L. Griggs (ed.), *The Collected Letters of Samuel Taylor Coleridge*, vol. 4, pp. 905–6, Coleridge to unknown 8 January 1819. For Coleridge and sex see Norman Fruman, *Coleridge, the Damaged Archangel* (London, 1972) pp. 370–2.

9. W. K. R. Bedford (ed.), *Letters from and to Charles Kirkpatrick Sharpe* 2 vols (1888), vol. 2, p. 37, Sharpe to Miss Pitman November 1812.

10. For *The Edinburgh Review's* remark see vol. 9 (1806–7) p. 348.

11. See A. D. Harvey *English Poetry in a Changing Society* (London 1980), pp. 166–7. Coleridge's giving up poetry for all that flood of ideas insufficiently concrete for poetry, almost insufficiently concrete for prose, was evidently related to a loss of faith in his poetic capabilities (see Fruman op. cit. pp. 328–30) but also had something to do with his increasing dependence on an exclusive image of himself as a great metaphysician (Ibid. pp. 135–6).

12. E. L. Griggs (ed.), *Collected Letters of Samuel Taylor Coleridge*, vol. 1, p. 347.

13. It used to be thought that Bunyan may have been in the Royalist army, rather than on the Parliamentary side, but see Ernest W. Bacon, *John Bunyan* (Exeter, 1983) pp. 42–3.

14. See A. D. Harvey, *Britain in the Early Nineteenth Century* (London, 1978) p. 62.

15. T. S. Grimshawe, *A Memoir of the Rev. Legh Richmond A. M.*, 5th edn (London, 1829) p. 296. *The Diaryman's Daughter* benefited from the new printing technology of the period. The figure of 500,000 often cited for *The Rights of Man* in the 1790s seems much less plausible as printing was then much slower, and to run off so many copies would have involved a major industrial enterprise of a type that the London Corresponding Society and its associates simply did not have access to: in any case the maximum total membership of lower-class reform societies was under 15,000.

16. See Louis James, *Fiction for the Working Man, 1830–1850* (London, 1963) pp. 28–44, especially p. 40 for Reynolds and pp. 36–7 for Rymer. See also V. E. Neuburg, *The Penny Histories* (London, 1968).

17. Penny Perrick, 'Why Superwoman Is Out of Style', *The Times* 13 May 1985, discusses the decline of the 24–32 age group of women as a key target for marketing: a good instance of how the competitiveness of the marketing industry causes it to be remarkably agile in throwing its weight behind trends and then abandoning them as soon as they begin to grow stale.

18. There is a surprisingly large body of scholarly work on popular literature, most of it written by scholars who assume that it lacks intellectual distinction and read it only from professional compulsion. Science fiction and comic strips are now finally being studied by people who *like* them; which, far from bringing popular literature more into line with high art represents a further methodological split.

19. The Cobden quotation is from Robert Blake, *Disraeli* (London, 1966) p. 273. For the idea that the nineteenth century was a period of bourgeois hegemony see Robert Gray, 'Bourgeois Hegemony in Victorian Britain', in Tony Bennett *et al.* (eds.), *Culture, Ideology and Social Process* (London, 1981) pp. 235–50; originally printed in J. Bloomfield, (ed.), *Class, Hegemony, Party* (London, 1977). The tax figures are an estimate based on Parliamentary Papers 1814–15, vol. X, pp. 106–7 and 1852, vol. IX, p. 462.

20. M. R. Booth, 'The Social and Literary Context', in Clifford Leech and T. W. Craik (eds), *The Revels History of Drama in English* vol. 6 (London, 1975) pp. 1–57; at pp. 8–11, 46–50, 53–4 for the decline of the legitimate stage, and p. 19 for the statistics of long runs in the 1850s, 1860s and 1870s.

21. Charles Monteith, '"Strangers from Within" into "Lord of the Flies"', *Times Literary Supplement*, 19 September 1986, p. 1030.

22. For a discussion of the kind of strategies employed in a modern intellectually respectable bestseller see Susan A. Fischer, 'Two Novels for the Price of One: John Fowles's *French Lieutenant's Woman'*, *Anglistica* (dell' Orientale, Napoli) vol. 24 (1981) pp. 45–74. See also Q. D. Leavis's classic essay, 'The Case of Miss Dorothy Sayers', *Scrutiny* vol. 6 (1937–8) pp. 334–40. Q. D. Leavis wrote of the intellectual bestseller (Ibid., p. 335) 'They have an appearance of literariness; they profess to treat profound emotions and to be concerned with values; they generally or incidentally affect to deal in large issues and general problems.'

23. The classic account of this is Q. D. Leavis, *Fiction and the Reading Public* (London, 1932) pp. 3–32. It would be difficult to think of another field

of publishing which has changed so little in its guiding principles. Incidentally, Peter H. Mann in his *The Romantic Novel: A Survey of Reading Habits* (London, 1968) and *A New Survey: The Facts About Romantic Fiction* (London, 1974) has denied that Mills and Boon find the bulk of their readers among older women: but since women over 55 years of age make up 24 per cent of his 1968 sample and only 15 per cent of his 1973 sample it is arguable that there are inconsistencies in his sampling method.

24. Régis Debray, *Teachers, Writers, Celebrities* (London, 1981) – originally *Le Pouvoir Intellectual en France* (Paris, 1979) – p. 132.

7   Genre and Style

1. For example, in H. G. Wells's *The First Men on the Moon* (1901) Bedford, with his obsessions with business opportunities, represents the same vein of social satire developed at greater length in *Tono-Bungay* (1908), I wonder, incidentally, if the tradition of lurid extraterrestrial landscape does not have its origin in the gigantic, emotionally charged, weirdly coloured exotic landscape paintings, by e.g. John Martin, Thomas Cole, Nicola Palizzi.

2. See John Schellenberger, 'After Lucky Jim: The Last Thirty Years of English University Fiction', *Higher Education Review*, vol. 15 (1983) pp. 69–76.

3. See the chapter 'Support for an English Biedermeier' in Virgil Nemoianu, *The Taming of Romanticism* (Cambridge, Mass: 1984) pp. 41–77; see Malcolm Bradbury and James McFarlane, 'The Name and Nature of Modernism', in Bradbury and McFarlane (eds), *Modernism 1890–1930* (London, 1974) pp. 19–55, at pp. 45–6 for R. P. Blackmur's proposal and Graham Hough's rejection of the term Expressionism as an international style label, and at pp. 37–40 for the decline of German Modernism on the eve of the emergence of Anglo-French Modernism. I am not sure Modernism itself is a very useful addition to our critical vocabulary. Biedermeier, of course, is the German name for the style favoured by the German bourgeoisie in the mid-nineteenth century; there is no corresponding English name as English art historians get by without discussing bourgeois taste in this period.

4. For the Pope controversy in England see Upali Amarasinghe, *Dryden and Pope in the Early Nineteenth Century* (Cambridge, 1962) and A. D. Harvey, *English Poetry in a Changing Society, 1780–1825* (London, 1980) pp. 148–65; for Delacroix and Ingres see Robert Rosenblum, *Ingres* (London, 1967) pp. 37–9; for the debate in Germany see M. L. Baeumer, 'Der Begriff, klassisch' bei Goethe und Schiller', in Reinhard Grimm and Jost Hernand (eds), *Die Klassik-Legende* (Frankfurt, 1971) pp. 17–49; for the Goethe quotation see J. P. Eckermann, *Gespräche mit Goethe* (Leipzig, 1868 ed.) p. 63 (2 April 1829).

5. For the Winckelmann quotation see David Irwin (ed.), *Winckelmann: Writings on Art* (London, 1972) p. 74; for David see Louis Hautecoeur, *Louis David* (Paris, 1954) p. 49; for Hancarville see Pierre François d'Hancarville, *Collection of Etruscan, Greek and Roman Antiquities* 2 vols (Naples, 1766–7) vol. 2, p. 32.

6. See A. Gonzalez-Palacios, *David e la Pittura Napoleanica* (Milano, 1967) pp. 22–3 and more generally P. van Tieghem, *Ossian en France* 2 vols (Paris 1917). The verses quoted are from George Harvey, *Ossian's Fingal* (London, 1814) p. 1; see also Ulrike Bolte, 'More Nineteenth-Century Epics', *Notes and Queries*, vol. 229 (1984) p. 486; the quotation from Hancarville is from *Collection of Etruscan, Greek and Roman Antiquities*, vol. 2, p. 38.

7. For Ledoux see M. Gallet, *Claude-Nicolas Ledoux* (Paris, 1980). For Blake and Flaxman see Robert Rosenblum, *The International Style of 1800* (New York, 1976) pp. 124–9 and John Buxton *The Grecian Taste* (London, 1978) pp. 87–90.

8. Percy Bysshe Shelley, Preface to *Prometheus Unbound* (1980). This is an amplification of the ideas in the Preface to *The Revolt of Islam* (1818) quoted in chap. 2 of this book.

9. See J. Mordaunt Crook, *The Greek Revival* (London, 1972) p. xi; G. Teyssot's Introduction to the French translation of Emil Kaufmann, *Three Revolutionary Architects* (*Trois Architectes Revolutionnaires* Paris 1978) p. 15 foll.; and Klaus Lankheit, *Revolution und Restauration* (Baden Baden, 1980 edn) p. 20.

10. René Wellek, *Concepts of Criticism* (New Haven, 1963) p. 129; Alistair Fowler, 'Periodization and Interart Analogies', *New Literary History*, vol. 3 (1971–2) pp. 487–509, at p. 509.

11. See John Summerson, *Architecture in Britain 1530 to 1830* (London, 1969 edn) p. 245.

12. For Germany see Albert Speer, *Inside the Third Reich* (1975 paperback edn) pp. 60–1; for Soviet Union see Christina Lodder, *Russian Constructivism* (New Haven and London, 1983) p. 50 (The term Futurist as applied to Russian art is evidently not favoured by art historians but cf. Lodder p. 48 for Russian leftist artists' own use of the term); for Italy see Enrico Crispolti, 'Appunti sui materiali riguardanti i rapporti fra Futurismo e fascismo', in E. Crispolti, B. Hinz, Z. Birolli (eds), *Arte e Fascismo in Italia e in Germania* (Milano, 1974) pp. 7–67 espec. pp. 58–61; for the lack of any uniform Fascist style see the illustrations on Umberto Silva, *Ideologia e Arte del Fascismo* (Milano, 1973).

13. The statistics for the campaign against 'degenerate' artists are from Berthold Hinz, *Art in the Third Reich* (Oxford, 1980; originally *Die Malerei im Deutschen Faschismus* Frankfurt, 1977) pp. 39–40; see Ibid pp. 30–44 and Reinhard Merker, *Der bildenden Künst im Nationalsozialismus* (Köln, 1983) pp. 125–37, 156–62 for Nazi control mechanisms generally. See also Viktor Reimann, *The Man Who Created Hitler: Joseph Goebbels* (London, 1977) pp. 166–94. An important discussion of the comparability of National Socialist art and Socialist Realism in Martin Damus, *Sozialistischer Realismus und Kunst im Nationalsozialismus* (Frankfurt, 1981). For the not very successful attempts of Nazi art theorists to establish a *völkisch* art that was distinct from classical art, see Klaus Wolbert, *Die Nachten und die Toten des 'Dritten Reiches': Folgen eine politischen Geschichte des Körpers in der Plastik des deutschen Faschismus* (Giessen, 1982) pp. 92–104.

14. In the memorial exhibition of Grant Wood's work at the Art Institute

of Chicago in 1942, after the artist's death, there was a critical on-slaught on his escapism and isolationism: the USA by then was at war with Nazism: see Wanda M. Corn, *Grant Wood and the Regionalist Vision* (New Haven, 1983) pp. 60–1. Certain features of Grant Wood's paint-ings – his odd angles of view, the stylisation of his houses and trees into children's toys, a strong element of self-mockery or spoofing – do modify his work's resemblance to what was produced under the Nazis – but then the American Mid-West in the 1930s wasn't *quite* Nazi Germany.

15. George Orwell worked for the BBC during the Second World War and the Ministry of Truth is sometimes taken to be modelled on the BBC and its headquarters at Bush House, but actually Orwell worked in an office in a requisitioned shop in Oxford Street. It is not exactly a coincidence that Europe's largest permanent display of 1930s official style painting is in England. The Imperial War Museum in South London has an impressive collection of work by officially com-missioned artists during the Second World War, in which the corpor-ative tendencies of the 1930s finally achieved classic expression under conditions of total war-mobilisation. For other examples of the Inter-national Fascist architectural style in Britain see *Architectural Review*, vol. LXXXIV, pp. 1–44, the July 1938 special number on the Glasgow exhibition. Amongst a quantity of impressive 'modern' architecture the Australian pavilion (illustrated on p. 6) and *The Times* newspaper pavilion (p. 21) both struck a totalitarian note.

16. See Hinz, *Art in the Third Reich*, p. 77 quoting F. A. Kauffmann, *Die Neue Deutsche Malerei* (Berlin, 1941) and Q. D. Leavis, *Fiction and the Reading Public* (London, 1932) pp. 24–5, 52–3, and espec. pp. 68 and 78.

8   Neo-classicism and Romanticism in Historical Context

1. J. W. Johnson, 'What *Was* Neo-Classicism?', *Journal of British Studies*, vol. 9 (1969–70) pp. 49–70 and D. Greene, 'What Indeed Was Neo-Classicism?', *Journal of British Studies*, vol. 10 (1970–1) pp. 69–79; the latter finds the term unhelpful.

2. Hugh Honour, *Neo-Classicism* (London, 1968) pp. 13, 17–21, 29; David Irwin, *English Neoclassical Art* (London, 1966) pp. 116–19.

3. Gerhard Fricke, *Geschichte der Deutschen Literatur* (1949 – a quarter of a million copies printed by 1970) has chapters 'Entstehung und Vollen-dung der Klassik' and 'Zwischen Klassik und Romantik'. Leo Krell's 1950 revision of Josef Rackl and Eduard Ebner, *Deutsche Literatur-geschichte* 14th edn (1971) has 'Die Klassik: Goethe und Schiller' and 'Zwischen Klassik und Romantik'. These are school textbooks. At a more scholarly level *Geschichte der Deutschen Literatur* published by Philipp Reclam has as its vol. 2 Werner Kohlschmidt, *Vom Barock bis zur Klassik* (Stuttgart, 1965); pp. 668–893 deal with Klassik. See also the anthology ed. by H. E. Hass, *Sturm und Drang – Klassik–Romantik* 2 vols (München, 1966). Probably the best survey of German literature in this

period is in Italian: Ladislas Mittner, *Storia della Letteratura Tedesca dal Pietismo al Romanticismo* (Torino, 1964); pp. 375–616 deal with 'classicismo'.

4. See Francis Haskell and Nicholas Penny, *Taste and the Antique* (New Haven, 1982) pp. 74–6. The volumes of the official *Le Antichità di Ercolano* which began to appear from 1757 were originally only presentation copies and were not available on sale till 1773: the volume on marbles never even appeared. Haskell and Penny suggest (op. cit. pp. 64–5) that statues excavated at Hadrian's Villa at Tivoli in the 1730s and 1740s made a greater impact: but then we have a time-lag to account for since it was in the 1760s that Hamilton and Mengs established their neo-classicist style.

5. See John Summerson, *Architecture in Britain 1530 to 1830* (London, 1969 edn) p. 189 and Frederick Antal, *Hogarth* (London, 1962) p. 246, note 74.

6. Jean-Nicholas-Louis Durand, *Précis des Leçons d'Architecture donneés à l'École Polytechnique* 2 vols (Paris, 1802–9) vol. 1 p. 1; Francesco Milizia *Principj di Architettura* 3 vols (Finale, 1781) part 2, cap. IV 'della varie specie degli edifici', vol. 2 pp. 39–304 of the Bassano 1813 edition which I have consulted.

7. Edmund Aikin, *An Essay on the Doric Order of Architecture* (London, 1810) p. 23; cf. David Watkin, *Thomas Hope, 1769–1831 and the Neoclassical Idea* (London, 1968) pp. 85–7 and pp. 245–9.

8. Two good examples are Schinkel's Kaserne der Lehr-Eskadron, Berlin 1817 (see M. Kuhn (ed.), *Karl Friedrich Schinkel: Lebenswerk* pt. 3 *Berlin* by P. O. Rave (Berlin, 1981) pp. 181–3) and Carl Ludwig Engel's grain magazine at Tampere, Finland, 1838 (illustrated in R. Zeitler, *Die Kunst des 19 Jahrhunderts* (Berlin, 1966) plate 368b). Both Schinkel and Engel were, of course, masters of the academic, monumental Greek Revival style. A simple functionality enriched by the perspectives of an academic tradition came rather late to Britain, cf. Alexander Dick Gough and Robert Louis Roumieu's Milner Square London 1841 (for which see A. D. Harvey, 'Pioneering Classical Barbarism', *Transactions of the London & Middlesex Archaeological Society*, vol. 34 (1983) pp. 271–4) and Lewis Cubitt's King's Cross Station, London, 1851–2. Large industrial buildings in Britain in the late eighteenth century, designed by country builders without educated pretensions, were invariably old fashioned in stylistic detail, e.g. the seven Venetian windows in the central range of Masson Mill, Cromford, Derbs. 1783, and the small open bell cupolas, apparently adapted from seventeenth-century stable buildings or almshouses, decorating e.g. Etruria, New Lanark, and many other large factories of the period. But a little later John Rennie's use of classical motifs in his bridge designs 'reveals an awareness of their vital national importance' (L.T.C. Rolt, in Brian Bracegirdle *et al.*, *Archaeology of the Insdustrial Revolution* (London, 1973) p. 18).

9. The most notable amongst the expatriate artists pioneering Neoclassicism in Rome were Raphael Mengs and Gavin Hamilton; see D. Honisch, *Anton Raphael Mengs und die Bildform des Frühklassizismus* (Rechlinghausen, 1965) and David and Francina Irwin, *Scottish Painters*

at Home and Abroad, 1700–1900 (London, 1975) pp. 101–5. For relation to Baroque see Joseph Burke, *English Art, 1714–1800* (Oxford 1976) p. 241. Hamilton may have been anticipated by a couple of years by John Parker: see *Historic Manuscripts Commission Charlemont MSS*, vol. 1, p. 251, Parker to Lord Charlemont 4 October 1758, where he writes of having completed a number of paintings on what later became standard neo-classical themes; none of Parker's history paintings survive, cf. Ellis Waterhouse, *The Dictionary of British 18th Century Painters in Oils and Crayons* (London, 1981) p. 266. For Pine and Mortimer see Roy Strong, *And When Did You Last See Your Father?* (London, 1978) pp. 17–20: the development of a literary consciousness of history in this period is discussed in A. D. Harvey, *English Poetry in a Changing Society 1780–1825* (London, 1980) pp. 36–9.

10. In England, Richard Glover's *Leonidas* (1737, French translation 1739, German 1766) was something of a success, more so than his *Athenaid* (1789). Other British epics between 1737 and 1790 were George Cockings, *War* (1760); James Ogden, *The British Lion Rous'd* (1762); William Wilkie, *The Epigoniad* (1769); John Harvey, *The Bruciad* (1769, extended version of his *The Life of Robert Bruce king of Scots 1729)*; William Hayward Roberts, *Judah Restored* (1774), and George Cockings, *The American War (1781)*. The Netherlands, with a considerably smaller population produced Arnold Hogvliet, *Abraham de Aartsvader (1728)*; Willem van Haren, *Gewallen von Friso* (1741); Otto Zwier van Haren, *Aan het Vaderland* (1769, reissued as *De Geusen* 1772) Lucretia Wilhelmina van Merken, *David* (1767) and *Germanicus* (1779); and Johannes Nomsz, *Willem de Eerste* (1779).

11. For a more detailed discussion see A. D. Harvey 'The English Epic in the Romantic Period', *Philological Quarterly*, vol. 55 (1976) pp. 241–59 and Ibid., 'The Epic in Western Europe 1790–1826', *Pubblicazioni dell' Università degli Studi di Salerno, studi di letteratura e di linguistica*, no. 3 (1984) pp. 125–34. See also Roger Simpson, 'Epics in the Romantic Period', *Notes and Queries*, vol. 231 (1986) pp. 160–1. *no. 7*. For the origin of the verse romance format as used by Scott see A. D. Harvey, *English Poetry in a Changing Society, 1780–1825*, pp. 98–9.

12. This is the only one of these epics of which I have been unable to trace a copy; the only contemporary reference, which does not give the title, is printed in *Historic Manuscripts Commission* 8th Report, Appendix Pt. 2 (1881) p. 196 foll.; and see John Schellenberger, 'More Early Nineteenth-Century Epics', *Notes and Queries*, vol. 228 (1983) pp. 213–14.

13. G. Walter (ed.), *André Chénier: Oeuvres Complètes* (Paris, 1958) p. 440, notes for 'Amérique'.

14. F. L. Jones (ed.), *The Letters of Percy Bysshe Shelley* 2 vols (Oxford, 1964) vol. 2, p. 309, Shelley to Byron 16 July 1821.

15. Grigori Kozintsev, *King Lear: The Space of Tragedy* (London, 1977) p. 21.

16. E.g. F. W. Stokoe, *German Influence in the English Romantic Period 1788–1818* (Cambridge, 1926); V. Stockley, *German Literature in England 1750–1830* (London, 1929); Frederic Ewen, *The Prestige of Schiller in England, 1788–1859* (New York, 1932); H. Oppel, *Der Einfluss der*

Englischen Literatur auf die Deutsche (Berlin, 1954); see also Peter Vassallo, *Byron: The Italian Literary Influence* (London, 1984).
17. See David Irwin, *John Flaxman, 1755–1826* (New York, 1979) pp. 81–3. Flaxman probably developed the outline technique while working for Josiah Wedgwood the potter. Louis Hautecoeur, *Louis David* (Paris, 1954) p. 44 suggests that the French sculptor Jacques Lamarie was developing a similar technique in the late 1770s, while Flaxman was still working for Wedgwood. Another possible independent developer, and almost certainly the first to apply the technique to something other than drawing, was Felice Giani, whose Flaxman-like frescos in the Palazzo Laderchi (now Palazzo Zacchia), Faenza, date from 1794. See also George Cumberland, *Thoughts on Outline* (1796).
18. Camuccini's two pictures are in the Museo e Gallerie Nazionali di Capodimonte, Napoli. Carlo Falconieri, *Vita di Vincenzo Camuccini* (Roma, 1875) pp. 337–41 denies David's influence in Italy, and mentions Benvenuti by name – p. 341 – as amongst those *not* influenced. But the influence was obvious enough even to contemporaries, cf. Francesco Hayez, *Le Mie Memorie* (Milano, 1890) pp. 11–12. A recent account of Camuccini is Ulrich Hiesinger, 'The Paintings of Vincenzo Camuccini, 1771–1744', *The Art Bulletin* (1978) pp. 297–320. Hiesinger, following C. A. Böttiger, *Sitten und Kulturgemälde von Rom* (Gotha, 1802) p. 253 foll., says that 'La Morte di Giulio Cesare' was completed in 1799 but, because of adverse criticism, destroyed, a revised version being begun in 1804 and virtually completed by 1806, while 'La Morte di Virginia', commissioned, like 'La Morte di Giulio Cesare', in 1793 was begun in 1799.
19. F. L. Jones (ed.), *The Letters of Percy Bysshe Shelley*, vol. 2, p. 485 (Appendix VIII, Shelley's Reading) lists eleven references in Shelley's journals and correspondence to Southey's *The Curse of Kehama*, and four to *Thalaba*; cf. Thomas Jefferson Hogg, *The Life of Percy Bysshe Shelley* ed. Edward Dowden (London, 1906) p. 294. For Townsend and Cumberland see George Townsend, *Armageddon* (London, 1815) pp. vi–viii.
20. *Paradise Lost* was originally translated by J. van Zanten, *Paradys Verlooren* (Haarlem, 1728), N. F. Dupré de Saint-Maur, *Le Paradis Perdu* 3 vols (Paris, 1729), and R. Rolli, *Il Paradiso Perduto* (part only London, 1729, complete poem Verona 1730). Stylistically it would be difficult to distinguish the influence of Milton from that of Virgil in poems written in other languages, but it will be noted that epics in religious subjects were much commoner in English than in other countries; Bodmer, the most successful translator of *Paradise Lost* into German, went on to publish a number of long religious poems in the 1750s and 1760s, and Gessner and Klopstock achieved a short-lived international fame in the same genre; but their influence is not apparent after 1790.
21. William Sidney Walker, *Gustavus Vasa* (London, 1813) p.x; William Wordsworth *The Prelude*, 1805 version, Bk 1, lines 211–2 and 185–9; cf. Edward Gibbon, *The Decline and Fall of the Roman Empire* vol. 1 (London, 1776) p. 246 and note 12 p. xxxvi. See also G. Walter (ed.), *André Chénier: Oeuvres Complètes* (Paris, 1958) p. 424. The hero of Drum-

mond's poem is not actually Mithradates himself, but his son Pharnaces: but the general theme is the same.

22. Earl Leslie Griggs, *Collected Letters of Samuel Taylor Coleridge* 4 vols (Oxford, 1956–9) vol. 2, p. 877, Coleridge to Thomas Wedgwood 20 October 1802.

23. For example, there is an unpublished epic on the Battle of Marengo by John Blackner, author of *The History of Nottingham* (1815), in Nottingham County Record Office.

24. I should mention at this point an East German study, Günther Klotz, Winfried Schröder, Peter Weber, *Literatur im Epochenumbruch* (Berlin and Weimar, 1977) which examines eighteenth- and early nineteenth-century literature in terms of the transition from feudalism to capitalism, complete with anti-feudal struggles, rise of the bourgeoisie and emancipation of the peasantry. The authors are aware of the problem of equating social change all over the Continent; they begin with 'Zur territorialen und regionalen Ungleichmässigkeit des Übergangs vom Feudalismus zum Kapitalismus'; but their whole thesis depends on being able to force the whole of Europe into a uniform mould in which revolutionary legislation counts for more than grass-roots reality.

25. See Louis Bergeron, 'Problèmes Economiques de la France napoléonienne', *Révue d'Histoire Moderne et Contemporaine*, vol. 17 (1970) pp. 469–505; on the social mobility question see D. M. G. Sutherland, *France, 1879–1815: Revolution and Counter-revolution* (London, 1985) pp. 385–6 (with bibliography pp. 468–9) and Jean Tulard, *Napoleon: The Myth of the Saviour* (London, 1984) pp. 185–6, 192–5.

26. J. R. McCulloch is quoted from *Edinburgh Review*, vol. 32 (1819) p. 50. His opinion of Britain's spectacular growth was shared by Thomas Malthus, see *Quarterly Review*, vol. 29 (1823) p. 229, and by numerous other experts. See also A. D. Harvey, *Britain in the Early Nineteenth Century* (London, 1978) pp. 323–39 and A. D. Harvey (ed.), *English Literature and the Great War with France* (London, 1981) pp. 1–19. I am currently working on this problem and my provisional conclusion is that growth in the home market was much greater than in overseas trade, so that the moderate growth in foreign trade shown by customs returns represents a smaller proportion of GNP. I hope to publish my conclusions by 1990.

27. See Hans Mottek, 'Zur Vorbereitungsperiode der Industriellen Revolution in Deutschland', in Hans Mottek (ed.), *Studien zur Geschichte der Industriellen Revolution in Deutschland* (Berlin, 1960) pp. 18–26 at p. 20–4; F. G. Dreyfus, 'Bilan économique des Allemagnes in 1815', *Révue d'Histoire Économique et Sociale*, vol. 43 (1965) pp. 433–64; Roger Dufraisse, 'Franzözische Zollpolitik, Kontinentalsperre und Kontinentalsystem im Deutschland der napoleonischen Zeit', in Helmut Berding and Hans Peter Ullman (eds) *Deutschland zwischen Revolution und Restauration* (Königstein, 1981) pp. 328–52.

28. See E. V. Tarle, *Kontinjental'nia Blokada* (Moscow, 1913; translations Paris 1928 and Torino 1950); Mario Romani, 'Economia Milanese nell'età Napoleonica', in G. Treccani degli Alfieri (ed.), *Storia di Milano*, vol. 13 (Milano, 1959) pp. 353–97; Renzo de Felice *Aspetti e*

momento della vita economica di Roma e del Lazio nei secoli XVIII e XIX (Roma, 1965); Carlo Capra *Etá Rivoluzionaria e Napoleonica in Italia 1796–1815* (Torino, 1978). Figures for decline of Italian cities are from Carlo Capra pp. 191–2. The quotations beginning 'The change in so many fortunes . . .' is from Giuseppe Pecchio, *Saggio Storico sull' amministrazione finanziera dell ex-Regno d'Italia* (Livorno s.d.) [London 1830] p. 163 (Pecchio was a former official in the finance Ministry of the Kingdom of Italy). For Barbaja see John Rosselli, *The Opera Industry in Italy from Cimarosa to Verdi* (Cambridge, 1984) pp. 30–1.

29. Kenneth Clark, *The Gothic Revival* (1974 edn) pp. 95–6 states that of 214 churches built in England under the Church Building Act of 1818, 174 were Gothic; as M. H. Port, *Six Hundred New Churches* (London, 1961) p. 125, n.3 indicates, Clark's figures refer merely to the *first* 214 churches built under the Commissioners for Building New Churches, in the period 1818–29. Clark argues (p. 96) that Gothic was preferred because it was cheaper to build in brick (though surely Gothic was not the only alternative to Greek Revival and stone) but anyway Port's figures, p. 132 foll. do not bear out Clark's suggestion as to the cost benefit of Gothic. Neo-classical was preferred in the large cities, especially London, because fashionable neo-classicist architects were willing to tender designs for city churches; elsewhere provincial, traditionalist, architects monopolised the work. Of the London neo-classicist churches, John Nash's All Souls, Langham Place is interesting for its handling of the site, but, on the whole, these so-called Waterloo churches are extraordinarily uninspired in their application of stylistic ideas compared to the London churches designed by Nicholas Hawksmoor, Thomas Archer and James Gibbs a hundred years previously.

30. Louis Hautecoeur, *Louis David* (Paris, 1954) p. 139, quoting from David's report to the Convention of 25 brumaire an II (1793); E. W. Brayley (ed.), *The Works of Edward Dayes* (London, 1805) p. 252; John Flaxman *Lectures on Sculpture* (1838 edn.) p. 232; Karl Freiherr von Stein zum Altenstein, Riga Memorandum 11 Septemter 1807, in Georg Winter (ed.), *Die Reorganisation des Preussisches Staates unter Stein und Hardenberg* 2 vols (Leipzig, 1931–8) vol. 1, pp. 364–566 at p. 454; verbale 1809 from consiglio provinciale della Calabria Citra, quoted Umberto Caldora, *Calabria Napoleonica 1806–1815* (Napoli, 1960) p. 388.

31. For Ceracchi see Renzo de Felice, *Italia Giacobina* (Napoli, 1965) pp. 59–130.

32. Louis Hautecoeur, *Louis David* (Paris, 1954) pp. 143–4.

33. Ugo Foscolo, *Opere*, ed. Mario Puppo (Milano, 1967) p. 1110, Foscolo to family 31 March 1815.

34. F. L. Jones (ed.), *The Letters of Percy Bysshe Shelley*, vol. 1, p. 504, Shelley to Byron 8 September 1816.

35. For the influence of Adam Smith on British Government economic policy see A. D. Harvey, *Britain in the Early Nineteenth Century*, pp. 311–14.

36. See Ernst Wangermann, *From Joseph II to the Jacobin Trials* (Oxford,

1959) pp. 5–35 for the effect of Joseph II's policies in educating the Fourth Estate in Austria.

37. For the Paris festivals see D. L. Dowd, *Pageant Master of the Republic* (Lincoln, Nebraska, 1948) and Mona Ozouf, *La Fête Révolutionnaires à Paris* (Paris, 1979); for Italy see Alfredo Comandini (ed.), *L'Italia nei Cento Anni del Secolo XIX (1801–1900)*, vol. for 1801–25 (Milano 1900–1901) *passim* and pp. 9, 18, 245 and 649. For the Rhineland see J. M. Diefendorf, *Businessmen and Politics in the Rhineland 1789–1834* (Princeton, 1980) pp. 193–4.

38. Schleiermacher quoted in Friedrich Meinecke, *The Age of German Liberation* ed. P. Paret (Berkeley, 1977) p. 34; Gneisenau in W. M. Simon, 'Variations in Nationalism During the Great Reform Period in Prussia', *American Historical Review*, vol. 59 (1953–4) pp. 305–21, at p. 309.

39. For English victory parades see Linda Colley, 'The Apotheosis of George III: Royalty and the British Nation 1769–1820', *Past and Present*, no. 102 (February 1984) pp. 94–129, at pp. 109–10; for indoctrination of troops see War Department circular 1801, a copy of which is preserved in Devon Records Office 152M/C1801 OM 14; for chauvinism of the troops see Anon., *A Journal of a Soldier of the 71st, or Glasgow Regiment* 2nd edn (1819); for General Sir John Moore setting a good example to the troops see William Napier, *The Life and Opinions of General Sir Charles Napier* 4 vols (1857) vol. 1, p. 96; see also in this context John Keegan, *The Face of Battle* (London, 1976) pp. 178, 188–91; for monuments see *Gentleman's Magazine*, vol. 77, p. 128; vol. 78 p. 1032; vol. 80 pt. 2 p. 414; vol. 81 pt. 1 p. 390; vol. 87 pt. 2 p. 579. Parliament granted nearly £100,000 for commemorative statues to senior officers who died in action (*Parliamentary Papers*, 1841, vol. VI, p. 534) but these were mainly in St Paul's and could not have had the same effect as major monuments in city parks and squares.

40. See A. D. Harvey, *Britain in the Early Nineteenth Century*, pp. 112–14; Hannah More's, *Thoughts on the Importance of the Manners of the Great in General Society*, one of the most influential texts during the 1790s, was actually published in 1788.

41. William Pitt was influenced by Richard Price with regard to the sinking fund, and later by Thomas Malthus on the Poor Law. Henry Beeke, Regius Professor of Modern History at Oxford and later Dean of Bristol, seems to have advised the Addington ministry on the income tax. For Richard Porson see W. Maltby's, *Porsoniana* printed with [Alexander Dyce, ed.] *Recollections of the Table Talk of Samuel Rogers* (London, 1856).

42. Friedrich Gentz, *Essai sur l'État Actuel de l'Administration des Finances et de la Richesse Nationale de la Grande Bretagne* (London, 1800) p. 246; Joseph Sansom *Letters from Europe, During a Tour Through Switzerland and Italy, in the Years 1801 and 1802* 2 vols (Philadelphia, 1805) vol. 2, pp. 371–2; see also A. G. Goede, *The Stranger in England* 3 vols (London, 1807); and E. J. Geijer, *Impressions of England 1809–10* ed. A. Blanck (London, 1932). For tax revenues see *Parliamentary Papers*

1806 vol. ix, p. 3 and Marcel Marion, *Histoire Financière de la France depuis 1715* 6 vols (Paris 1927–31) vol. 4, p. 334. J. G. Boetticher, *A Geographical, Historical, and Political Description of the Empire of Germany . . . to which are added Statistical Tables exhibiting a view of all the States of Europe* (London, 1800) contains somewhat unreliable revenue and population statistics for all the states of Europe in the 1790s. With regard to the best term by which to refer to the country of which London was the capital, it may be noted that revenue statistics for Ireland for this period are almost non-existent and for Scotland fewer than for England. Wales, having substantially the same administrative system as England, is equally well covered with regard to statistics; but they show that Wales was much poorer than England itself.

43. According to F. G. Stephens and M. D. George, *Catalogue of Political and Personal Satires Preserved in the Department of Prints and Drawings in the British Museum* 11 vols (1870–1954), there were, not including foreign prints and repeats of the same design, 15 prints utilising the John Bull motif in the 1780s, 101 in the 1790s, 280 in the 1800s and 146 in the 1810s.

44. The prefaces to each volume of the *Gentleman's Magazine* in the 1800s provide a good example of English self-satisfaction.

45. T. C. W. Blanning, *Reform and Revolution in Mainz 1743–1803* (Cambridge, 1974) p. 14. For German officials see H. Gerth, *Burgerliche Intelligenz um 1800* (Göttingen, 1976) pp. 72–9; for universities see Ibid., pp. 34–45, Blanning, op.cit., pp. 11–14; and Friedrich Paulsen, *The German Universities* (New York, 1895) pp. 57–65; for the new rôle of *Bildung* see Hans Rosenberg, *Bureaucracy, Aristocracy and Autocracy: The Prussian Experience, 1660–1815* (Cambridge, Mass., 1958) pp. 182–7. New enrolments in German universities fell from 4,400 in 1720 to 2,920 in 1800. This was partly due to the emergence of rival non-university institutions and to the decline of philosophy faculties, though in fact certain universities such as Freiburg, Ingolstadt, Heidelberg and Königsberg kept up their numbers quite well and Göttingen's enrolment peaked only in the 1770s; Rostock, on the other hand, declined from 153 new registrations in 1700 to 14 in 1780 and 29 in 1800 (Franz Eulenburg, *Die Frequenz der Deutschen Universitäten von ihrer Gründung bis zur Gegenwart* (vol. 53/1 of *Abhandlungen der Königl. Sächsischen Gesellschaft der Wissenschaften* – vol 24 no. II of *Abhandlungen der philologisch-historischen Klasse*; Leipzig, 1904) pp. 285–99, Anhang 1, cf. pp. 130–45). By the end of the century there was much criticism of universities as outmoded in their courses and organisation. (R. Steven Turner, 'University Reformers and Professorial Scholarship in Germany 1760–1806' in Lawrence Stone (ed.) *The University in Society*, 2 vols (Princeton, 1975) pp. 495–531, at pp. 500–2. W. H. Bruford, *Germany in the Eighteenth Century* (Cambridge, 1965) pp. 237–46 suggests that despite the new foundations at Göttingen and Halle, German universities were passing through a phase of decadence before 1800, but though this may be true in comparison with the nineteenth century it is clear that in eighteenth-century Germany there was an

intellectual culture centred on the universities to a much greater extent than in any other country except Scotland.

46. For book production see H. Gerth, *Burgerliche Intelligenz um 1800*, p. 66; for authorship see W. H. Bruford, *Germany in the Eighteenth Century* pp. 276–84, cf. R. Engelsing, *Der Burger als Leser* (Stuttgart 1974) and Alberto Martino and Marlies Stützel-Prüsener, 'Publikumsschichten, Lesegesellschaften und Leihbibliotheken', in H. A. Glaser (ed.), *Deutsche Literatur, eine Sozialgeschichte*, vol. 5 (Rembek bei Hamburg, 1980) pp. 44–57, and Henri Brunschwig, *Enlightenment and Romanticism in Eighteenth-Century Prussia* (Chicago, 1974) pp. 140–6.

47. [G. S. Hillard ed.] *Life, Letters, and Journals of George Ticknor* 2 vols. (London, 1876) vol. 1, p. 103, George Ticknor to Elisha Ticknor 6 July 1816.

48. See Marina Ruggero, 'Professori e studenti nelle università tra crisi e riforme', in Corrado Vivanti (ed.), *Storia d'Italia: Annali 4: Intellecttuali e Potere* (Torino, 1981) pp. 1039–81, at pp. 1077–81; for Bologna statistics see Luigi Simeoni, *Storia della Università di Bologna* 2 vols (Bologna, 1947) vol. 2, p. 89, 172; for the report from Modena in 1799, see O. Rombaldi, *Gli estensi al governo di Reggio dal 1523 al 1859* (Reggio Emilia, 1959) p. 120. Simon Schama, *Patriots and Liberators* (London, 1977) pp. 24–58 shows how in the Netherlands in this period economic stagnation tended to encourage a transfer amongst the middle bourgeoisie from the sphere of profit-making to that of politics and public opinion: Italy may be a longer drawn out example of the same process.

49. For Cartwright see his, *England's Aegis* (London, 1804) pp. 73–83; for the Norman Yoke see Christopher Hill, *Puritanism and Revolution* (London, 1958) pp. 94–122.

50. *Edinburgh Review*, vol. 10 (1807) pp. 478–9.

51. Thomas Love Peacock, 'The Four Ages of Poetry', *Ollier's Literary Miscellany* 1820, reprinted in H. F. B. Brett-Smith and C. E. Jones (eds), *The Works of Thomas Love Peacock*, vol. 8, pp. 3–25, at pp. 19–20. For *Rhodadaphne* see Douglas Bush, *Mythology and the Romantic Tradition in English Poetry* (Cambridge, Mass., 1969) pp. 180–6.

52. Hyder Edward Rollins (ed.), *The Letters of John Keats, 1814–1821* 2 vols (Cambridge, 1958) vol. 2, pp. 192–5, Keats to George and Georgiana Keats September 1819 for his knowledge of politics; vol. 1, pp. 266–7 Keats to J. H. Reynolds 9 April 1818 on his attitude to the public; vol. 2, p. 146 to Reynolds 25 August 1819 on the 'rest of Mankind'; and vol. 2, p. 167 to Reynolds 21 September 1819 on *Hyperion*. For Peacock's low opinion of Keats see Brett-Smith and Jones, *The Works of Thomas Love Peacock*, vol. 1, p. lxxxii.

53. For Shelley and the Greeks see his 'A Discourse on the Manners of the Ancient Greeks', in R. Ingpen and W. E. Peck (eds), *The Complete Works of Percy Bysshe Shelley* 10 vols (London and New York, 1926–30) vol. 7, espec. p. 223; and F. L. Jones (ed.), *The Letters of Percy Bysshe Shelley*, vol. 2, p. 74 Shelley to Peacock 23–24 January 1819. For Shelley's reading see Ibid., vol. 2, pp. 467–88, Appendix VIII; he appears to have read Winckelmann a little later and Forster not at all; for Chénier see Stephen Rogers, *Classical Greece and the Poetry of*

Chénier, Shelley and Leopardi (Notre Dame, 1974) pp. 13–51; for Foscolo see *Dei Sepolcri* (Brescia, 1807); for Shelley and prosodic form see E. L. Jones (ed.), *Letters of Percy Bysshe Shelley*, vol. 2, p. 221 Shelley to Keats 27 July 1820; vol. 2, p. 309 Shelley to Byron 16 July 1821; vol. 2, p. 364 Shelley to Gisborne 22 October 1821: in the latter he describes his *Hellas* as 'a sort of imitation of the Persae of Aeschylus', but John Buxton, *The Grecian Taste* (London, 1978) p. 167 finds it, despite quotation from Aeschylus, more in the style of Sophocles; for Shelley and Michelangelo see E. L. Jones (ed.), *Letters of Percy Bysshe Shelley*, vol. 2, p. 80 Shelley to Peacock 25 February 1819 and also vol. 2, p. 112 Shelley to Hunt [20 August 1819].

54. Johann Georg Zimmermann, *On Solitude* 2 vols (London, 1799) vol. 2, p. 308. Originally published as *Von der Einsamkeit* (Leipzig, 1773), title changed to *Ueber die Einsamkeit* in Leipzig 1784 edn. French translation 1788, English translation 1791, of which 8th edn 1799 is edition quoted.

55. See A. D. Harvey, 'The Nightmare of *Caleb Williams*', *Essays in Criticism*, vol. 26 (1976) pp. 236–49, espec. pp. 240–43 on the relationship between Godwin's doctrine of Necessity in *Political Justice* (London, 1793) book 4, chap. 5 and 6 and the plot of *Caleb Williams*.

56. The 'trappings of the Church' phrase is from Robert Rosenblum, *Modern Painting and the Northern Romantic Tradition* (London, 1975) p. 15; 'Religious meanings in the forms of Nature' is from Coleridge's 'Fears in Solitude' (April 1798) and the longer quotation is from his *Notebooks* ed. Kathleen Coburn, 2 vols (New York, 1957–61) no. 2546.

57. Karl Marx, Preface to *Contribution to the Critique of Political Economy* (1859), in R. C. Tucker, *The Marx–Engels Reader* 2nd edn (New York, 1978) pp. 21–2.

58. Karl Marx, 'The Eighteenth Bruimaire of Louis Napoleon', in *The Marx-Engels Reader*, p. 595.

9 Another Glance at Shakespeare

1. See E. A. J. Honigman, *Shakespeare: The Lost Years* (Manchester, 1985).

2. Earl Leslie Griggs, *Collected Letters of Samuel Taylor Coleridge* 4 vols (Oxford, 1956–9) vol. 2, p. 679, Coleridge to Thomas Wedgwood 18 February 1801.

Index of Personal Names

Names appearing only in the list of poems on pp. 132–7 or only in the notes, and names repeated in the notes merely by way of citation of sources, have been omitted.